THEATRE STREET

THEATRE STREET

The Reminiscences of

TAMARA KARSAVINA

A DANCE HORIZONS REPUBLICATION

One of a series of republications by Dance Horizons
1801 East 26th Street, Brooklyn, New York 11229

This is an unabridged republication of the revised and
enlarged edition published in 1950 by
E. P. Dutton & Co., Inc.

Standard Book Number 87127-043-9
Library of Congress Catalog Card Number 73-77506
Printed in the United States of America

FOREWORD

TO THE REVISED EDITION

I *FINISHED writing this book on August 20, 1929, the day I heard of Diaghileff's death. I did not change then what I had written about him : I left him still alive as I had known him. In this revised edition I have done the same. But I have added a chapter in an attempt to bring some unity into the features of Diaghileff's personality, some of which features are scattered about the book, and some of which are newly told.*

This chapter does not aim at being a condensed biography, nor yet a psychological analysis ; it is just a portrait in the mirror of my affection.

T. K.

OCTOBER 20, 1947

v

CONTENTS

PART ONE—THE PUPIL

CHAPTER I   PAGE 3

My Earliest Memories—" Fat Nannie "—My Mother—St. Petersburg—" Douniasha "

CHAPTER II   PAGE 10

My Father—Marius Petipa—Our Life—A Harmless Lunatic—" Amelia "—A Terrifying Dream

CHAPTER III   PAGE 18

Lessons—Early Love of Theatricals—A Narrow Escape—Father's Farewell to the Stage—Thoughts about my Future

CHAPTER IV   PAGE 27

My First Dancing Lessons—Xmas—Grandmother's Tales—Fortune-Telling

CHAPTER V   PAGE 36

Lessons with Father—Religious Fears—Examinations—The Imperial School

CHAPTER VI   PAGE 44

Black Marias—My First Year at School—A Death in the Theatre—Kyasht—School Traditions—Andrey—A Premature Burial—Death of the Emperor

CHAPTER VII   PAGE 52

I Become a Boarder—Etiquette—" Lunatic Ann "—School Discipline—First Contact with the Theatre—A Forgotten Speech

CHAPTER VIII   PAGE 64

Moscow—Money Difficulties—Legnani—Classes—Pavlova—Infatuations—A Worldly Priest—The Haunted Music-room—The Tzar

CHAPTER IX   PAGE 78

The Confiscated Wine—Make-up—The Grand Duke Vladimir—Command Performance for the Kaiser—Holiday Escapades with Lydia—Drama or Ballet

vii

CHAPTER X   PAGE 91

Cartwheels — Prince Volkonsky — Methods of Rehearsal,
Guerdt—Progress—" Little Lopokova "—Kosloff—Johannsen
—My First " Love Affair "

CHAPTER XI   PAGE 107

Teliakovsky—Lydia's Diphtheria—The School Performance—
Chinese Theatre at Tsarskoe Selo—Final Examinations—My
First Trousseau—My Début—Farewell to School

PART TWO—THE MARINSKY THEATRE

CHAPTER XII   PAGE 123

The Marinsky Theatre—A Benefit Night—Increasing Popularity of Ballet—The *Balletomanes*—The Brothers Legat—
Johannsen—Social Life

CHAPTER XIII   PAGE 135

My First Leading Rôle—A Criticism—Additions to my Repertoire and Promotion—First Appearance of Bakst—Kshessinskaya—Volkonsky's Resignation

CHAPTER XIV   PAGE 143

Illness—Visit to Italy—Beretta Nicolini—Performance at the
Court Theatre—Chaliapin—Progress—Nijinsky's Début—
" The Eighth Wonder of the World "—An Unfortunate
Incident

CHAPTER XV   PAGE 153

The Russo-Japanese War—Preobrajenskaya—A Provincial
Tour—Strange Reception in Warsaw

CHAPTER XVI   PAGE 158

A " Ballet " Revolt—Pavlova, Fokine and Myself as " Revolutionaries "—Tragic Death of Sergei Legat—Lovat Fraser

CHAPTER XVII   PAGE 166

The Rhythm of Theatre Life—Petipa—The Beginning of
Fokine's Régime—Isadora Duncan—Fokine's Creative Efforts
—*Cleopatra*—Prague

CHAPTER XVIII   PAGE 179

Sokolova—*The Swan Lake* and *Corsair*—Svetloff

PART THREE—EUROPE

CHAPTER XIX   PAGE 189

Ballet in Paris—Oneguin—Diaghileff—First Performance of the Diaghileff Ballet—A Galaxy of Talent—" La Karsavina "—An Open-air Performance—Marinelli

CHAPTER XX   PAGE 204

My First Visit to London—First Impressions—The Coliseum—Adeline Genée—A Bribe—First English Friends

CHAPTER XXI   PAGE 210

Diaghileff—Beginning of our Long Association—Thamar—Stravinsky—Changes—The Ballet To-day

CHAPTER XXII   PAGE 218

Two Engagements at Once—Lopokova in Paris—*Giselle*—Differences with Nijinský—I am made " Prima Ballerina "—Chaliapin—Complications and Tears—Nijinsky and the Empress—His Dismissal

CHAPTER XXIII   PAGE 227

Lady Ripon, the Good Fairy—Sargent—South America—Nijinsky's Wedding—" Maestro "

CHAPTER XXIV   PAGE 236

L'après midi d'un Faune—Dawn of Modernism—Rehearsals with Nijinsky—Debussy—Cocteau—J. L. Vaudoyer—*Spectre de la Rose*—Strange Beginning to a Friendship—Dethomas—Nijinsky's Tragedy—Our Last Meeting—Strauss—Massine—Felix—Da Falla—Picasso

PART FOUR—WAR AND REVOLUTION

CHAPTER XXV   PAGE 251

The Journey Home — The Theatre in War Time — The " Wandering Dog "—Diaghileff in War Time—Rasputin—Paléologue—Hugh Walpole—Learning English

CHAPTER XXVI   PAGE 260

Episodes of War and Revolution—Kshessinskaya's Palace—A President in Tarlatans—Douniasha's Tragic Death—The Chancery Servant—I am Suspect—Lev and the Commissar

ix

CHAPTER XXVII   PAGE 269
     The Dangerous Journey

                PART FIVE—DIAGHILEFF

CHAPTER XXVIII   PAGE 279
     Diaghileff's sway over the Minds of his Collaborators—His
     Exhibition of Historic Portraits in the Taurida Palace—Seen
     through the Eyes of a Common Friend—His Meekness over
     my First " Scene "—A Ripple on the Surface of our Friendship
     —His Indifference to Box Office Success—His Mind and
     Background

ILLUSTRATIONS

ENTRANCE TO THE IMPERIAL BALLET SCHOOL, THEATRE
STREET

GRADUATES OF THE IMPERIAL BALLET SCHOOL, 1902

MYSELF IN RUSSIAN DRESS BY GONTCHAROVA

MOZART (DANCE FOR SALZBURG, 1921). COSTUME
DESIGNED BY KONSTANTIN SOMOFF

NIJINSKY IN "LE SPECTRE DE LA ROSE," 1910

THE LION BRIDGE, PETERSBURG

MYSELF IN "PAVILLON D'ARMIDE." PARIS SEASON, 1909

MYSELF IN "SCHEHERAZADE"

MYSELF IN "GISELLE." PARIS, 1910

MYSELF IN "FIRE BIRD." PARIS, 1910

MINIATURE, 1920

COSTUME OF THE YOUNG GIRL IN "LE SPECTRE DE
LA ROSE"

MYSELF IN "THE THREE-CORNERED HAT," 1919

MYSELF AT HOME. PETERSBURG, 1913

MYSELF IN A "REVUE INTELLECTUELLE." PARIS, 1927

MYSELF IN "SLAVE GIRL." MUSIC BY ARNOLD BAX

DIAGHILEFF

*The costume for "Le Spectre de la Rose", is from a drawing by
Leon Bakst; and the Lion Bridge, Petersburg, is reproduced from a
drawing by M. V. Doboujinsky.*

ENTRANCE TO THE IMPERIAL BALLET SCHOOL,

THEATRE STREET

LYDIA KYASHT   MYSELF

GRADUATES OF THE IMPERIAL BALLET SCHOOL, 1902

MYSELF IN RUSSIAN DRESS BY GONTCHAROVA

MOZART (DANCE FOR SALZBURG, 1921). COSTUME DESIGNED BY
KONSTANTIN SOMOFF

NIJINSKY IN "LE SPECTRE DE LA ROSE," 1910

THE LION BRIDGE, PETERSBURG

MYSELF IN "PAVILLON D'ARMIDE." PARIS SEASON, 1909

MYSELF IN "SCHEHERAZADE"

MYSELF IN "GISELLE." PARIS, 1910

MYSELF IN "FIRE BIRD." PARIS, 1910

MINIATURE, 1920

COSTUME OF THE YOUNG GIRL IN "LE SPECTRE DE LA ROSE"

MYSELF IN "THE THREE-CORNERED HAT," 1919

MYSELF AT HOME. PETERSBURG, 1913

MYSELF IN A "REVUE INTELLECTUELLE." PARIS, 1927

MYSELF IN "SLAVE GIRL." MUSIC BY ARNOLD BAX

DIAGHILEFF

PART I

THE PUPIL

CHAPTER I

My Earliest Memories—" Fat Nannie "—My Mother—St. Petersburg—" Douniasha "

IT is partly from my Father's tales, told to me in later years, and partly from my own early recollections that I can piece together a fairly consecutive story of my childhood, a story made up of a series of little pictures like those in a child's alphabet.

My Father loved to talk to me of the time when I was quite small. When, in his spare hours, he sat by the window with his album and water-colours, I used to stand or sit by him watching him work. I can see even now the little pictures he used to make of different national costumes—Spanish, Hungarian, Ukrainian, Polish—each man with his lady on the opposite sheet. All their dresses were minutely done, but the faces all looked to me to have rather large noses, and the ladies' complexions seemed too tawny.

He never took his eyes off his work as he mimicked some incident of my babyhood. He would only pause now and then to wash his brush and suck it. The pictures were meant to help such of his pupils as wanted to learn national dances.

My first clear recollection is how my nurse put me down on the path outside some house. Holding me under the arms, she first steadied me and then left me on my own. I started off toddling, at first fairly straight. Then my feet carried me faster and faster till I could not follow them. Father caught me up just in time.

Next comes to my mind a summer at Ligovo, near Petersburg. The house we occupied stood in the park of Count Posen's estate. We came down in early spring. I was recovering from inflammation of the lungs, and the doctor said I must drink

3

birch sap. Just at the back of the house there was a plot of grass encircled by young birch-trees not yet in leaf. I often watched with interest the sap being drawn from a hole drilled in the tree. It spurted out in a strong jet and we gathered it, usually in the morning, in an earthenware jug. The juice had a sweet astringent taste.

Of the preceding illness I remember very little, only lying on a big ottoman converted into a bed, in my hands a small mirror with which I darted " sun rabbits " across the ceiling and on the striped wall-paper. I dreaded the appearance of Mother with a cold compress which she changed on me several times a day. She told me afterwards that she dreaded it too, as I used to cry ever so pitifully and feebly. My memories of this time are somewhat blurred. A few things, however, were impressed so deeply on my mind that even now they stand out clear and have not lost all their magic. The house we then had at Ligovo seemed vast and beautiful to me ; and very likely my child's impression of it was not far wrong. What I remember of a large round room with a domed ceiling and niches seems to me now as if it could only have belonged to a fairly big country house of the late eighteenth century.

Though so very different from the small flat in which we lived in town, the place had a strange familiarity to me. In some inexplicable way, faint detached images of a life I had never seen and never could have heard of took hold of me. They had no beginning and no conclusion ; just very vivid episodes, like sudden flashes, that I could not fit in anywhere. One especially insistent image, amounting in its vividness almost to a memory, puzzled me greatly. I could describe a pond, still and regular. I, a child, and a woman that seemed to be my Mother, stepped out of a carriage. She held my hand and we walked round the pond towards a large house with a somewhat flat façade and many windows.

I moved with some difficulty ; the path was gravel, and my high heels made me unsteady. My dress was voluminous, heavy and stiff, not my everyday one. I felt timid, as I always did when taken on a visit. There the image stopped abruptly, and it teased me so not to know whom we thus went to see that I put endless questions about it to my Mother. She seemed amused by my story, but neither then nor afterwards tried to find a matter-of-fact explanation of it.

How big the grounds were of our Ligovo house I could not realise. The place then must have been in its decline. I do not remember any flower-beds. The park was shady and over-grown; and there was in it, at some distance from the house, a pavilion with minarets, called a Turkish bath, one of the ingenious devices of a Russian *maison de plaisance* of this time. Father told me that we spent a summer in it once, but never went back, as it was damp. An artificial pond in front of it had a circle of very green starlike weeds round its edges. The pavilion stood empty, and my brother and I were allowed to go into it to play. Our great delight was to look through the small pane of the tall Moorish windows. The panes were all of different colours; and, seen on a sunny day, the world outside appeared luminous—red, green, yellow—always unreal and attractive.

On hot days the nurse often took my brother to bathe. He was two years older than I. We had to walk some way down to a shallow, rapid stream, to a place where it formed a small, clear pool. I was not allowed to go into the water, so Nannie used to carry me on her shoulder to a big stone in the middle. There she would sit me down while they bathed. She held my brother by both hands, and they plunged down and bobbed up repeatedly like in a frog dance. She sang " Ladoushki, Ladoushki, we went to Baboushka," one of the nursery-rhymes she knew so many of, with no particular sense in it.

Nannie, " Fat Nannie," as we called her, was forbidden to frighten us. But she was a simple peasant woman, full of superstition, and it was asking too much of her. Out of a multitude of horned, hoofed, taily creatures, inherent in the belief of Russian peasants, she brought out one " Buka," whom she used when her own authority with us failed. Buka took away disobedient children. He was always at hand waiting for his opportunity when children would not go to sleep. It was not quite clear who he was, perhaps a mild devil suited to nursery purposes. I asked Father about him. He did not deny the existence of Buka. From his description, though, Buka appeared quite unalarming, impish perhaps, but homely and easily appeased. He was woolly, it seemed, and had a tail. My Father's description made me think of Buka as a kind of dog.

At this time I was rather afraid of Mother. It appears that, when I was quite small, I used to have terrible fits of screaming. I choked and went blue in the face. It usually happened in the morning at dressing time. When my screams reached Mother's ears, she summoned me ; and Nannie reluctantly took me to her room. Mother dipped a big sponge in cold water and squeezed it on my naked body. The sudden shock cut my screams at once. Mother used to describe afterwards how I stopped with a gasp in the middle of a word.

Mother often said her love for her children was " rational." I remember her stern at times and never foolish and tender. She had a way of checking my effusions, and these checks made me doubly timid, and were at the bottom of my occasional outbursts of childish revolt against her. In time, however, I realised that she would stop before no sacrifice for our sakes. Deep in my heart there was a great admiration and pride for her. I liked watching her dress to go out. She had a very small waist and tiny feet, of which she was proud. I had ambitious schemes for her. " When I grow big I will build a grand house for Mother," I often used to say. When offended, I hid under a bed or a table and snapped out repeatedly : "I won't build you a house." Mother's quiet answer, " And who, if you please, wants your house ? " sobered me at once. It was like another cold douche to me.

Our punishments were mild. " Nose in the corner " was

a more humiliating degree of simply being put in a corner, face to the room. Lev, my brother, usually shortened his penance by gently asking pardon. This, nothing would induce me to do on the spot; I only felt contrite when Father spoke to me kindly. He often took me by the hand and brought me to Mother to ask her pardon. Rebukes, even when deserved, wounded me deeply. Unchild-like, I never gave way to tears in front of anybody. At times, when I thought I could yet tip the scales of justice in my favour, I gave warning in a small trembling voice, "I will cry." If the answer from Mother came, "Cry, if you like," I ran fast to the furthest room and there cried under the bed or behind the petticoats of Mother's dressing-table. In after days I laughed when Father used to act the scene for me, but then I felt it a tragedy.

*   *   *   *   *

In St. Petersburg we lived on the top floor of a five-storied house belonging to a wealthy merchant widow. All business dealings with the landlady were of a patriarchal character. There were no such things as house agents. Once a year Mother went to see her, and always came back with the glad news that the lease was renewed for another year and the rent not raised. £4 a month seems an incredibly low figure, but in those days it was the normal price of a good-sized apartment of five or six living-rooms. When, at a later time, our means became straitened, the landlady accommodated us with a cheaper flat in another wing, in all respects very like the one we had, only without a porter in livery at the front door.

The house stood on the canal, where it curves round to join the River Fontanka. Along our quiet stretch of street hardly any traffic passed. Our front windows looked on a canal, busy in summer with barges carrying wood; in winter it froze, and we used it as a short cut to the other side. To us children the main attraction of this flat was to look out of the window at the watch-tower of the fire station opposite. There was always a sentinel walking round the parapet. It was a beautiful sight to watch the firemen in all their array, brass helmets, bugle blowing, issue forth at the alarm and tear down the streets, four horses at full gallop. It took our breath away, that show of reckless speed.

To a Russian the fascination of a fire is irresistible. Running to look at a fire was quite a feature of Russian life. Not only the simple people, but even ministerial clerks would rush off, leaving their work, electrified by the word " fire."

Firemen were the heroes of all children and the best young men of all cooks. A usual condition put by a cook applying for a situation was for her " Kum pojarny " to be allowed to visit her. Very often the employer broached the subject first, asking how often the fireman would be in the kitchen.

I was about five years old when " Fat Nannie " was dismissed and Douniasha recalled. Douniasha was originally my foster-mother. For some reason she had been dismissed; but, after her return, she never left us. She eventually became a maid and then the only servant, following the fortunes of the family. During the period of her disgrace she often came to see me, sometimes at the house, but more often to meet me on our walks. She always brought me some sweets or little toys, and parted from me sobbing. Her tears flowed easily, and Mother sometimes said she was a humbug. But I could not take it that way. She had an unrestrained pity for all creatures in trouble, and taught me many a lesson in it.

She was tall and gaunt; and at the time when there were two nurses in the house, she and my brother's, everybody called her " Long Nannie." The name remained with her for ever. Her indisputable beauty was her hair, unusually long and thick. She put quantities of kerosene mixed with lamp oil on it, and said it was what made it so thick. Douniasha worried that my hair would not grow long, and she started using kerosene on me. It smelt revolting, and Mother put a stop to the practice.

"Nonsense," said she when I asked her to let me use kerosene in the hope that I would have hair like Douniasha's, "have a good head on your shoulders, the hair will take care of itself."

All Douniasha's possessions were neatly piled in a large wooden chest. It had on the outside a pattern of nails and narrow bands of thin, white, hammered iron that looked like moiré silk. I always watched the chance of her opening her chest. Inside the lid there were little pictures cut out from illustrated comic papers. She let me gaze at these, but she did not like my touching and fumbling amongst her things.

CHAPTER II

*My Father—Marius Petipa—Our Life—A Harmless Lunatic—
"Amelia"—A Terrifying Dream*

MY Father at this time held the post of first dancer and
mime at the Imperial Ballet. According to rule, he had
to retire on a full pension after twenty years' service. Service was
counted from the age of sixteen, even though still at school.
He was then about to terminate his twenty years, and there was
much talk and speculation between him and Mother as to his
being kept for a second term of service. I gathered that he
was still in his prime and a very fine dancer, but that there was
some intrigue against him. The name of the then all-powerful
Marius Petipa was often mentioned.

Petipa was the great ballet-master. He was French, and
never learnt to speak Russian, though he came to St. Petersburg
very young and remained in the service of the theatre till his
death. Perhaps my Father was not quite impartial; but, from
what he told, Petipa was more feared than liked by the artists.
His influence with the Director Vsevolojsky was unbounded,
and he made "*la pluie et le beau temps*" at the theatre. In my
time everyone had access to the director, who usually held
audience twice a week. Every artist could come and could
pour out his grievances. But Vsevolojsky never or seldom
received artists. Only Petipa had his ear.

My Father had been Petipa's pupil, and at one time his great
favourite. What spoiled their relations I do not know. My
Father had a great talent for imitation. He always admitted
that Petipa was a gifted and imaginative producer and also
a marvellous teacher, though not a great dancer; and it was
this and his acting that Father so often ridiculed. Trembling

knees, roving eye, gnashing of teeth, stamping feet—all the arsenal of false pathos—such was the imitation. We children constantly asked for a scene from Faust in Petipa's acting, but Mother used to say : " I wish, Platon, you would be more guarded with your tongue ; all your boon companions and dear friends are only too glad to report all this ridiculing."

Father usually left the house early in the morning. We all had tea with buns or rusks by way of breakfast, but he never ate anything—only drank three or four tumblers of tea. Lunch never exists in the ballet world ; rehearsals usually follow classes, so it was natural that Father would come home after rehearsal ravenously hungry. Sometimes he came at three, sometimes at four in the afternoon, expecting the soup-tureen to be on the table. It was difficult to fit the meal to the varying hour of his return, but any delay with dinner used to ruffle his otherwise imperturbable good nature. He never listened to reason, but grumbled impatiently, " The kitchen full of wenches, and a hungry man can't get his dinner."

Drinking tea was a real passion with him. He never was without his glass of tea by his side, and drank it the whole day long. As soon as he finished one glass he called out, " Wenches, tea." Mother used a little handbell sometimes, but as a rule we either called or went to the kitchen to fetch the servant when anything was wanted. In time Father modernised and bought himself a small primus lamp to keep his tea hot. He carried it from room to room with him. It kept him going in tea when the samovars were not in action.

After tea we were sent out for a walk. Dressing took a long time, and I often grew impatient, especially when, if dressed first, I had to wait for Lev to be got ready. In winter I had to wear, for going out, a red flannel petticoat and knickers under my dress, and felt boots. Over a bonnet padded with cotton-wool, a knitted shawl was tied and tucked inside my coat ; on very cold days it would be drawn over my mouth. The shawl made my collar so tight that I could not move my head, and often protested, " Nannie, you're strangling me." If protesting too loud, Mother's voice came from the other room : " Tata, stop your caprices." A muff was hung over my head on a ribbon, and woollen gloves joined by some silken string also hung on my neck to save losing them. On very cold days my face, which had once been frost-bitten, was greased. I was strangled, choked and weighted ; but, once out, was none too warm.

As we went down Mother stood on the landing giving parting instructions—not to go on the ice, not to play with stray dogs, not to talk when out, and to breathe through the nose. There was time for all that and more while we descended five flights. Lev liked to slide down the banisters, but I in my garb could only move down sideways, the same foot always forward. The felt boots prevented my bending the knees.

Before the canal froze, going alongside it was perhaps the most interesting walk. A quantity of logs, dropped off the barges, drifted down the canal, and street boys had a very clever way of picking them up. At the end of a long rope they had a heavy stump of wood with a long nail driven through it. This they threw at the logs, and seldom missed their mark. The weight of the stump drove the nail into the floating log, which could be easily pulled out. Some of the boys had bob-sleighs to take home their spoil. It was a regular way of poor people to get wood, and the police never interfered with it. The price of wood, as of everything else, was often discussed at home. Mother said it was getting dear. A square sagene (7 English feet) of best birch logs went up in winter to 4 or 5 roubles (8 or 10 shillings). Pine wood was much cheaper, but did not give the same heat.

There were few passers-by on our side of the canal, and every unusual figure attracted our attention. One day a man, dressed very neatly and wearing an odd cap, passed us. As he did so, he took his cap off and bowed to us gravely. He passed on, and we saw him giving the same salute to a small crowd of

street urchins.   Further down there was a place with steps down
to the water and a landing-place for barges.   Several workmen
were unloading a barge.   The man stopped and took off his
cap several times, nodding to all sides.   The workmen all had
their backs to him, and the whole proceeding looked so absurd
that we could not help laughing.   Soon we saw him crossing
the street and coming back by the other side.   We ran across,
too, to meet him and make a mock bow.   We came home that
day full of imitations of the funny man.   Father knew him.
He was a madman, very gentle and inoffensive, and fancied
himself an exalted personage.   On learning this, I felt deeply
ashamed of having tried to tease the poor man.   Father never
moralised; his was a kind and humorous way of talking about
people; and, without being able to give a name to the ever-
present pathos of life, he made it very evident and clear to us.

Our harmless lunatic was looked after by his two sisters, old
maids that lived in the next house but one.   It was a one-storied
wooden house, painted pink.   The small windows, low from
the ground, were full of pots with geraniums and balsams.
Later on, our nurse got to know the sisters, and several times
she took me there.   Both women were dressed in black and
had on their heads black kerchiefs not unlike nuns' veils.   Their
room impressed me very much.   A great number of ikons were
in a corner cupboard, image lamps before them.   On the walls
were pinned cheap coloured prints of Mount Athos and of the
Solovietsky Monastery.   For all that, the room looked not a bit
austere, but gay and liveable, breathing placid content and
comfort.   Hand-made runners with knots of bright-coloured
rags drawn through lay across the floor.   A big press by the
window was covered by the same kind of carpet.   The sisters
were gay and talkative in a sedate way and extremely hospitable.   They never let us go without entertainment.   A samovar
was put on the table for us and several kinds of jam and a plate
of cracknels were brought in.   We never saw the brother on
our visits.   For a long time we met him out walking.   Some

years afterwards, when I came on holiday from school, I asked after him, and was told he had died.

That unvarying background of my childhood is what I like looking back upon. The rare treats were events anticipated, fully enjoyed and remembered. For lack of outside excitement, all the trivial everyday things became of interest and full meaning.

Except for early bed-time, there was no special nursery régime for us—no ingenious devices for our education and entertainments, no social treats. We had our meals with the parents, and, hearing them talk, we shared their interests. Father was usually very patient in answering our numerous questions, and only when our curiosity became tiresome, a mild " Who knows too much, grows old too soon " put a stop to them.

Even at that time of comparatively easy existence, Mother often talked about the difficulty of making both ends meet. She had absolute authority in the house and complete control over the money. Father gave her all his salary, only keeping some small change for his daily expenses. She took all responsibility as well, and when in difficulties found her own way out. She often pawned things, sometimes even borrowed money, and at times had to see the landlady about arrears. Only necessary things were bought for us, and that after some deliberation. Practically all our clothes were made at home by her. When she started on something ambitious, like cutting out of her green plush pelisse, of a shape called " rotonda," a winter coat for me, she would send for Aunt Katya, Father's sister, who lived a long way off beyond the Narva Gate.

Mother often called me to be fitted, and made me stand a long time while she pinned some pleats on me or lopped off bits of stuff. I found these fittings very trying. They probably were so to her too, as she said she was " off her feet " with all she had to do, and my fidgeting irritated her. Once—it was a particularly long fitting—a pleat would not stay in its right place, and I pulled it up—to help. " Don't paw the material with your dirty hands ; stand still," she cried impatiently. But, seeing my mouth twitching, she softened and explained that she was trying to make me smart. She devised one very pretty dress for me; it was two printed kerchiefs joined together, and did not require much fitting.

In these circumstances there was no room for even small luxuries. But we always had a Christmas tree, and that was the time when we were given some toys. We had few toys, but I had a lot of treasures, mostly of my own finding—amongst them some fungus growth from birch-trees. It became hard when taken off and dried and had a flat semi-round top. I thought it might be pretty fixed on the wall as a bracket with something on top of it. Big plane leaves, dried in a book and beaten with a hair-brush till they became quite transparent and as made of lace, were also treasures. I had a handsome set of doll's drawing-room furniture, a round table, sofa and arm-chairs covered in red plush. The doll that owned it never was my favourite; almost entirely bled of her sawdust, she looked sickly and insipid. I much preferred to her the tiny creatures I cut out of paper and arranged in a row in the deep window-sill in our nursery. Amelia, my favourite, was my masterpiece. She had a long slim waist, and I drew her face in pencil. She lived a turbulent life owing to her beauty. For some reason not clear to me she had to elope from her house. Often the pursuit overtook her because of a broken wheel in her carriage. Once or twice she was led home and had to elope again. Sometimes she was kidnapped by gipsies. At other times she hid in a convent. But she was always in trouble, and only eventually she married and kept house with her sisters in the red drawing-room set. Soon I had to stop cutting out more dolls, as Mother said it blunted her scissors.

The name Amelia belonged to a friend of my Mother's. She was half German, married to a Russian. As children, she and my Mother had been at the same preparatory pension. Mother spoke of her with slight contempt, calling her " Sparrow-brain." We sometimes went to play with her children.

I looked forward to our visits. The small flat, extremely neat with lots of knick-knacks on countless little shelves, looked so different from our flat where there were no adornments at all. I felt that only our drawing-room, with its furniture of blue damask and a bronze clock on the console, could stand some comparison. As to the nurseries, ours had for a divan a wooden chest covered with a rug; and here there were some white-painted low chairs and white-enamelled beds with muslin curtains for the children. Zina, the small girl, had a pink bow to her bed.

Amelia Antonovna usually kept us to supper, and it was a great treat because of the sweet course. She usually played with us herself and enjoyed it just as much as we. It was a good house to play hide-and-seek in; the rooms had much furniture, sofas, screens, and a round table covered with a long cloth with motives *appliqués* on it. There was also a wall cupboard in the ante-room and one darkish room up a few steps from the nursery. But more often we played sedate games. One of the two boys had an injured spine, and had to lie in bed with a stiff corset on. We sat round his bed and played lotto. For scoring we were given some acid drops, and piled them at our side. The invalid was cunning, and used to lick his acid drops in the hope that we would refuse them as payment.

I was very fond of Amelia Antonovna, and thought her very pretty. I asked Mother if she was really pretty when young, and Mother said: " Yes, she was lovely, but just a flaxen-haired German doll; as for her intelligence, she could hardly finish the prep., and could not even teach her children to speak properly." It was true that the children often mixed German words with Russian: " Bobby wants essen," or " I do not want to go schlafen."

* * * * *

It is strange, and not justified by circumstances, that in the even and happy tenour of my life should come a sense of lurking

16

terror, of some dormant but ever-present menace. At this time I was haunted by an oft-recurring-dream. The setting of it varied, but always the same somebody with pallid face and red hair falling in curls wanted to lead me off. The apparition had nothing horrible or distorted ; its fascination and muteness were uncanny and filled me with exquisite anguish. It must have been the beauty of a destroying angel. Sometimes in this dream I had to traverse a long enfilade of dark rooms. I moved warily, hid and waited. But something forced me to go on till I came to the last room, to find there the pale mute stranger. A grim and stealthy hide-and-seek began. I hid, crept out and dodged in the chaotic disorder of the room. The horror of absolute silence, as if the world had suddenly ceased, was on me. At times I was in a room full of people. All of a sudden the silence fell. I asked anxious questions, but all eyes looked at me and no word came. I knew the pale man had come for me.

CHAPTER III

Lessons—Early Love of Theatricals—A Narrow Escape—Father's Farewell to the Stage—Thoughts about my Future

MY brother was now seven years old, and Mother had for some time been teaching him to read and write. He was very quick at learning. There was no fixed time for these lessons. Mother came into the nursery whenever she had time to spare, bringing her work with her. I was allowed to play quietly by, or to look at a picture-book. But I had an ambition to learn; and, partly from listening to the lesson, partly by asking what this or that letter was, I soon picked up a lot. I was not fully aware then that I could read: nor was anybody else. It came as a revelation. I was looking at some pictures in the newspaper. The most comfortable way for me to do this was to sit on the floor, Turkish fashion, and place the sheet on the table hanging down so that it was on a level with my eyes. The family was gathered round the table. I read out a heading. Mother was surprised, but thought I must have learnt it by heart. She bade me read out a few sentences, which I did with a slight hesitation. Then she called to my father: "Listen, Platon, Tata has learnt to read all by herself." To me she said: "But newspapers are not reading for children." I pleaded with her to let me read a serial. "And what is this serial?" she asked. The answer must have sounded very odd, especially as I still lisped. "'The Victim of Passion.' A criminal novel." Mother was startled, but Father laughed to tears, and said: "Let her read 'The Victim of Passion.' It won't do her any harm."

Reading soon became of absorbing interest to me. Lev was also passionately fond of books. Amongst the few books in the cabinet in Father's room was a complete edition of Poushkin and of Lermontoff, with pictures. No control was exercised over our reading; and, when other children would have been given some feebly moralising stories about Good Petia or Disobedient Misha for their intellectual food, we drank of the Castalian spring. Such is the divine simplicity of Poushkin's verse, and such the limpidity of his prose that even to me, a child of six, it set no riddles; and, though unable to analyse the beauty of his writing, I felt it by instinct. His magic spell has never since loosened its grasp on me.

Later in the country I played sometimes with Nadejda, the daughter of our peasant landlord, a child of twelve, and I took it into my head to read Poushkin to her. I doubt now whether she derived any pleasure from it, but she was very submissive, and sat patiently while the reading went on. One day Father came across our party. I sat on the steps of the house reading out loud. Nadejda, squatting on her heels, was fanning me with a green branch to keep off mosquitoes. Children were playing round us. "The Queen of Shamacha and her court," laughed Father.

As I see it now, my reciting and reading out loud must have been prompted by an instinctive love of performing. Father's joke made me self-conscious, and I never read Poushkin again to my rustic audience, but my histrionic leaning found its outlet in a more definite form. Now, in the country, all the fantastic and heroic element of my reading suddenly came to life, took shape and fitted into my new surroundings. I began by acting in the garden; a shed became the tent of the wizard Chernomor. I had a hat on that was to make me invisible, and so allow me to avoid his persecution. The ikon of St. Michael Archistratig in shining armour, which I had seen in Church, furnished me with heroic episodes for my plays. I led a fierce battle against the high nettles by the stream.

I learnt Poushkin's poems by heart, and liked reciting them. This greatly amused my Father, especially as I still had a fault in speech and said " l " for " r." He often stood me in front of him and made me recite the prologue of Russlan. In his album he drew for me Chernomor carrying off Ludmilla, and the learned cat that walked on a golden chain round the green oak. As the cat went to the right he told fairy-tales ; as he went to the left he sang songs.

Everybody teased me about my speech, and that annoyed me. I strove hard to say " r," and when I got it I rolled it, to the still greater merriment of my audience.

Father gave us sometimes a little money, usually a copper or two. We saved our coppers till a sum of 10 kopeks (twopence) was reached. It would buy us a small book each. Our walks, hitherto only constitutional, had now a purpose—either to get a book or to gaze in the bookshop window to decide what book we should buy when next we came into money. The only books accessible to us were those of the cheap edition devised for the people by the Ministry of Education. They were so small and so thin that we called them diminutively " Knijonki " (little books). The print was small and bad, but the contents mostly good. By means of the " knijonki " we read all the epic stories of the Kieff Knights, folk fairy-tales, some short stories from the classics, and sometimes translations. " Parasha la Sibérienne," by Xavier de Maistre, we bought after some discussion. We usually discussed our prospective purchases at length, so as not to risk wasting our pennies. Lev was for getting it, but I did not like the name " Parasha " ; it did not sound attractive to me. We got it, however, and I liked it very much. It was a touching story of a Siberian girl who walked on foot all the way to Petersburg to plead for her father, wrongly accused. How she found her way into the precincts of the Palace and to the very feet of the Empress was of thrilling interest to us.

* * * * *

About this time an event happened that nearly led to the expulsion of Douniasha. One evening Mother came home

from a party, and, before she took her things off in the ante-
room, she realised that the air was heavy with charcoal fumes,
an ever-present danger of Russian stoves. She ran into the
nursery and opened the door of the stove. The stove had been
shut before the wood had burnt itself out. Charcoal fumes
often mean death. Douniasha was found in the kitchen where
there was a party for some reason or other. Mother left all the
explanation till after. The immediate thing was to pull us out
of bed, dress us, in spite of reluctance and tears, wrap us in
woollens and shawls and take us out of doors, where Douniasha
walked us till the small hours of the morning. In the meantime Mother threw all the windows open and ordered a fire to
be lit to ventilate the room completely. Next day Douniasha
stood sobbing before Mother in wrath. "That is what you
care for the children. . . . Vassily is in your mind. . . . Off
with you." Douniasha crying in her apron, heaping terrible
imprecations on her own head, calling all the saints to witness :
"Elia the Prophet strike me with thunder. May my eyes burst
if I do not love the Barishnya." Mother was unappeased.
Douniasha went through the whole calendar of saints and
martyrs. Lev and I cried, too, not to turn Douniasha out.
Mother gave in, and Douniasha remained.

The Vassily alluded to in Mother's imprecation had a great
part in Douniasha's life. He often sat in the kitchen, often
gave a hand in the house or was sent on errands. He was
comely and neatly turned out in a Russian blouse and high
boots. Douniasha spent much time in sewing these blouses
for him and embroidering the cuffs in cross-stitch. Vassily
worked in a factory. He came often in the evening and always
on Sundays. When in my Mother's presence, he spoke in
a hoarse, deferential voice. He was fully accepted in the house,
and we children never had any curiosity as to what he was to
Douniasha. Somehow we knew that he was not her husband.

Douniasha's protestations of her love for me were not mere
words. To understand her feeling one must know that she

had lost her own children, and that her whole tenderness was centred in me. When I was scolded she used to creep into the room and cry silently, casting reproachful glances at Mother. She grumbled secretly at Mother if she put me in the corner. " Mamasha think worlds of their Levoushka. They never have a word of praise for my child." I felt her devotion, and my mind refused to accept Mother's criticism of her. I heard Mother telling once how she first engaged Douniasha. There were several women Mother had to choose from for my foster-mother. Her thin and gaunt appearance were against Douniasha, and some other candidate seemed more fit for the post. " But when," said Mother, " I told her she wouldn't do she gave me an odd look, and I felt suddenly sorry for her. It was as if she had bewitched me, and I cannot account for having chosen her against my better judgment. She must have learnt some tricks from her Finns ; they are all uncanny." Douniasha had been a foundling, and from a foundling home she was given into the care of a peasant and his wife in a Finnish settlement near Petersburg. She often said they were like real parents to her, and more so as they put her before their own children on the plea that she was an orphan. The old peasants sometimes came to see her, always bringing us presents of butter and eggs. Finns are supposed to practise witchcraft, but I thought these two did not look at all like wizard and witch. They were dear old people. Her father especially was nice and jocular ; and under his uncouth appearance, there was a true delicacy of feeling. Whenever, on a visit in our kitchen, he sat crouching before the stove and pulling at his short pipe, he took care to send the puffs of smoke up the chimney, not to offend.

It is true Douniasha had an extraordinary odd look at times ; her eyes seemed to roll inwardly, and her mouth muttered. But it surprises me now that Mother, with her intelligence and education, should have sincerely believed in witchcraft.

*   *   *   *   *

THE PUPIL

This year's Carnival brought an event of some importance
to us. Father was to have his farewell benefit night, and he
chose the last Sunday before Lent. All the theatres were usually
crowded during Maslenitza. In those days the observance of
Lent was in full rigour. All entertainments ceased till Easter,
and everybody wanted to have a full share of gaieties while they
lasted.

A very charming story was told us by Father about a carnival
week some years before. The Imperial Family was present at
the afternoon performance. The Emperor, Alexander III,
expressed a wish to eat pancakes with the artists. All flew into
commotion. "As at a pike's bidding," as the Russian fairy-tale
has it, tables were spread on trestles all along the stage, and
everything provided. At the end of the performance Their
Majesties came on the stage. Marie Feodorovna sat at the
head of the table, and everyone came up with his plate while
she filled it out of a big dish of pancakes placed in front of her.
She put on a little apron for the occasion. The Emperor
alternately sat or walked amongst his guests and had a gracious
word for everybody.

Father's farewell night came, and Lev and I were unusually
carefully dressed and taken to the theatre. It was the first time
I had ever been there. We sat in a box. The lights and
warmth made me think of Paradise, and I kept gazing at the
huge crystal chandelier in the cupola. I was in such a state of
exhilaration that at moments my heart rose throbbing to my
throat. I felt awed by the magnificence of the place, and
dreaded lest I should be asked how I liked it. There were no
adequate words in my mind. Mother was too agitated and
nervous herself to ask questions. She said several times, " So
ends his career before his time. All this is like a funeral pomp
to me."

The ballet was *Pharaoh's Daughter*. When the curtain went
up, Lev and I looked for Father and kept asking " Which is
Father ? " at every new appearance. But he did not come on

till the second act. He appeared in a *pas d'action*, consisting of two other male dancers and a ballerina with four solo dancers. So different he looked from his usual homely self that I could not identify him and kept losing him, especially as now they would dance together, now by twos and threes, and then a solo each. After Father's solo there was an ovation, and we clapped, too. In after-times Father explained to me that his solo was considered a most difficult bit of dancing, and was a touch-stone for a male dancer. He had to do double pirouettes in the air landing on one foot, moving diagonally, and finish with a triple pirouette. I know now that it was what Nijinsky did afterwards in *Pavillon d'Armide*. Father had to encore his dance, and Mother said he should not have done it, and that she always had to look the other way when he encored, as it made her very nervous.

In the interval the curtain was raised and the whole company came on the stage. Father was led in and stood in the middle, and there were presents and wreaths brought on, and speeches made by different deputations. When it was over, Father stepped forward and the audience began clapping. He bowed first to the Imperial box, then to the director's, and then to the audience in the approved fashion, hand on heart.

At home there was a supper prepared, to which came many of Father's colleagues. Lev and I were allowed to stay for a while and eat a little supper. Mother soon sent us to bed, saying : " Run along to bed. You can't keep your eyes open." The party broke up late. We heard merry voices and speeches as we were getting ready for sleep, but we knew that both Mother and Father were sad in heart.

For days afterwards we spoke of nothing else at home but the farewell night. The proceeds of the benefit were good ; and, besides some presents of silver from the public, Father received an emerald signet ring and an ornamental bronze clock from the Tzar, as well as a thousand roubles (£100) " from His Majesty's own casket." The ring soon disappeared, leaving a token of its short stay in the form of a pawnbroker's ticket, added to a considerable pile of other such mementoes. But the clock remained with us for many years, and became a delight of my childhood. The drawing-room was little used; I loved to idle there in lonely contemplation of the celestial globe and the pensive Urania. The gilded bronze had the light opaque glow of a pale buttercup, and the chiselled emblem of the Muse—stars and compasses—round the pedestal were in the low relief which, in after years, I learned to associate with Empire workmanship.

As I have mentioned before, our parents talked things over in front of us. Their worries were no secret to us children. I could gather that now, with Father leaving the stage, there would be a considerable straitening of means, just, too, at the time when we both were to receive education. Father now had only his pension and the salary of teacher at the Theatre School. He also gave lessons to amateurs and took ballroom dancing.

Mother always had a high courage. Nothing ever daunted her, and now she hoped that, with more time on his hands, Father would be able to get more lessons, and that things would be all right. But I think the blow to their pride meant more than financial considerations to them. After all, we always lived from hand to mouth, never looking ahead, spending more when there was something to spend, fitting in somehow when there wasn't. Father had reason to expect his being kept for the second service, like other artists of his standing. He was sore at heart parting with the stage. In after years he often spoke of it.

The question of our future often came up in conversation. Mother always said that the ballet was not a career for a man, and that even the best of them have but a secondary importance there. They both agreed that my brother must have a superior education. As for me, Mother's dream was to make a dancer of me. "It is a beautiful career for a woman," she would say, "and I think the child must have a leaning for the stage; she is fond of dressing up, and always at the mirror. And supposing even she does not become a great dancer, the salary of the *corps de ballet* is more than an educated girl can expect to earn elsewhere. And that alone will make her independent."

But my Father was of a different mind. He had never approved of this scheme ; and now, with his premature retirement rankling in his heart, he was more than ever against it. "You don't know what you're talking about, Matoushka," he always answered. "I do not want my child to live amongst all the intrigues of the stage. Moreover, she will be like me, too meek to stand up for herself."

Whether it was my Mother's words that definitely formulated in my head the idea of the stage, I could not tell ; but somehow it lived with me long before I was taken to the theatre for the first time. Being extremely fond of Father, I always looked forward to his coming home, and simply beset him with questions about the theatre. His narrative was very vivid. He usually acted as he told about different happenings, and it made me see another world, a world which seemed as luminous as that which I had looked at through the coloured glass of the Turkish pavilion. Even the intrigues and anxiety of it looked to me as only another side of its glamour, and did not convey any sordidness.

CHAPTER IV

My First Dancing Lessons—Xmas—Grandmother's Tales—Fortune-Telling

IN the winter of 1893 Mother took the first steps towards her scheme to make a dancer of me. She arranged with Madame Joukova, a retired dancer, to give me lessons. Aunt Vera, as we called her, was a friend of the family, and there was no question of a fee. To show her gratitude, Mother used to make her presents at Christmas and on her name day. A little ceremony accompanied the offering. In good time before the occasion I had to learn some verses chosen by Mother on account of some appropriate feeling in them. She usually introduced the name of Aunt Vera whether the rhyme permitted it or not, and made me recite it daily to her, correcting my phrasing. On the day of the presentation, dressed in my best and slightly embarrassed, I appeared before Aunt Vera. I waited self-consciously for the right moment to step back and begin my recitation, and once it was over I felt great relief.

I went to my lessons accompanied by Douniasha. One end of the dining-room was cleared of furniture and a small bar fixed on hinges across the door : the bar was removable. Aunt Vera put on carpet slippers and had a small stick to beat time. For the first two months she kept me to bar practice ; and only when my feet were turned out properly did she begin to give me some exercises in the centre. This is the orthodox way in Russia. Gradual and systematic practice is spread over seven or eight years. Before the end of that period no dancer is considered fit for the stage. The dryness of the lessons was at first tedious to me. I had had visions of my dancing straight away, of high leaps and pirouettes as I had seen in the ballet. To my first lesson I came with a great thrill and expectation of wonders to be done by me. When Aunt Vera said " Now turn round " I promptly left the bar and tried to spin. Before I could realise it I lost my balance and was on the floor, looking foolish and contrite. My teacher laughed and explained that she only wanted me to turn round slowly and do the same exercises with the other foot.

Douniasha's attitude was disapproving. She disliked the very idea of my dancing. Not infrequently on the way home she sighed and grumbled, " Mamasha took it into their heads to have the child tormented." I argued with her that it didn't hurt a bit, but she obstinately repeated, " I know what I am saying, Miloushka. I knew an acrobat, every bone in his body broken. They did it to make him soft." In her obstinacy she would not be persuaded that an acrobat and a dancer were not the same. That incident and many others of its kind recurred to me when, years later, I found her once looking at my photograph where I am on my points and sobbing bitterly over it. On the occasion of my début Mother took her to the theatre. Her grief became so intense on seeing me and her sobbing so loud that an angry " Hush " hissed round, and Mother had to send her home, where, on our return, we found her still sobbing and talking piteously about broken bones.

Gradually I grew more and more keen on my lessons. The physical effort required even for the simple exercises became an achievement and an interest in itself. When I learned a few simple steps, my mistress set them in a little dance for me.

In my pride I could not help exhibiting my skill before Lev in the nursery. He declared he could do much better, and began taking me off. I could not help laughing, so ludicrous he was, skipping and prancing with affected primness. But I was annoyed with him and with myself for laughing, and often grew peevish. The result of his teasing was usually a loud quarrel, when Mother would appear and lead us to different rooms. My

Mother, who was fond of coining little doggerel sayings, used to characterise our relations in some words like this :—

> Lev likes to quarrel and you can't forgive;
> Together you squabble, but apart you can't live.

My lessons were kept secret from Father. Very wisely, Mother wanted to see first if I had any pronounced capacity for dancing before she set about overcoming his objections. It was part of her plan to keep my enthusiasm alive, and with that view she took me to several ballet matinées. Her belief in my keenness for the stage was now fully confirmed on seeing with what absolute rapture I followed the performance. One day we went to see *La Sylphide*, with Nikitina in the principal part. Unearthly, fragile, she seemed to be of the same substance as the moonlight which flooded the stage. This ballet had been created by Taglioni and was full of the devices of the romantic school. The use of the wire was one of them. I was not aware of any mechanism helping the performance, and my illusion was complete ; but were I to see it again, with full experience of stage tricks, I doubt if my knowledge could destroy any of the fascination then felt. Even now, I only have to shut my eyes to recall the moment of supreme beauty. Her lover's arms encircle, but cannot detain, the pale immaterial Sylphide. A last sad look of earthly longing, and the slender form floats swiftly through the air and vanishes. We sat in the stalls and I had to dodge my head to see the whole of the stage. To Mother's horror, I suddenly sprang on the seat and sat myself on the back of my stall. She pulled me down by my feet, and it brought me back to earth and the realisation of my offence. Later on, she used this instance in the argument with Father as a proof of my artistic temperament.

At this time, our stock of books grew richer. Father started collecting what he proudly called a " library " for Lev. He sometimes bought cheap editions of classics and bound them himself; the supplements of a weekly magazine added to our stock. Somebody gave us *Round the World* for past years. It contained stories of adventure, translations of Jules Verne, Fenimore Cooper and other masters of that type. I also read the whole of Hoffman's *Serapion's Brothers*. Not all of his meaning was clear to me, but his quality of blending the fantastic with everyday reality appealed strongly to me. It added a new colour to my life. Nothing was commonplace any more; it only seemed so. From now on, I lived in expectation of marvels, looking for latent mysteries all round me. Being very reserved and undemonstrative, I never showed any signs of that secret exultation. Mother thought me odd at times. She could not understand my complete loss of interest in toys. When a rare visitor came, I liked staying in the room; their talk interested me, but Mother called it loafing, and frequently sent me away to play or to occupy myself in some way. " Odd the children now are," I heard her saying to a friend, " she is bored to play with her doll. When children, we never knew what boredom meant." But I never felt bored ; my interest had merely shifted from dolls to people.

Though we were never made to believe in Santa Claus, the approach of Christmas and its celebrations brought home to me that feeling of wonder about to happen, great expectations and something still more wonderful, a mystic benevolence all round. Around churches, on boulevards and even in the middle of the streets, Christmas markets appeared in great number and forests of fir trees on their stands. Our curiosity was all agog at home. Mother came with parcels and took them straight into her room. We knew it meant presents. We crept into her room one evening, but she discovered the attempt and kept her door locked till Christmas.

Grandmother, Maria Semenovna, came over for Christmas from Mother's sister, with whom she lived at this time. I always looked forward to Grandmother's visits. Humorous in the extreme, she also had an unparalleled equanimity of temper and a capacity for enjoyment that even her penniless existence could not subdue. Once a beauty, she still retained the remarkably large dark eyes and the smooth skin which might have belonged to a young woman, but for its pale waxen quality. She referred to her aquiline nose as " Roman." Her rather unusual appearance was due to some Greek blood in her. Her maiden name had been Paléologue. That, as well as her history, she often told us children. There was nothing she would not tell as long as she had a listener. It didn't matter to her who it was—children, servants, family, outsiders; she was equally communicative with everybody. How often in the middle of some gay narrative of the time of her youth Mother tried to stop her. " Mama, you forget you are talking to children." As for us, we eagerly urged her to talk. Written down, her tales would not be unlike the *Arabian Nights* in that she hardly ever could come to the end of her story for its ramifications. I always tried to get her back to her narrative when she digressed too far.

With what gusto she would tell us children under ten about the masked balls at the Salle de la Noblesse at Petersburg, where she had an intrigue with the Emperor Nicholas Pavlovitch, and about her husband's infidelity, and how he often confessed his peccadilloes and said, " Mary, my angel, you will understand and forgive me." Grandfather died early, having squandered his patrimony, and left her a young widow with three children. Her poverty at this time had been extreme, but she referred to it without any bitterness and even quite humorously. A meagre pension was all she had then. Often she had no other meal but a salt herring and a slice of bread, and she used to depend on what she could pick up from the barges for her fuel. The care of the children was taken off her. " A single soul is never poor," was Baboushka's motto. The boy was placed in the Naval School, and the two girls went to the institute for orphans. Their home became that of their guardian, Prince Mychetzky. Now she lived mostly with my aunt, and at times

with us. This time Baboushka brought our cousin Nina
with her.

* * * * *

It was Christmas Eve and we planned to have some fortune
telling in the evening, as was the custom. The Christmas tree
had been bought the day before, Lev and I having gone with
Father to choose it. Father was very fond of the custom and
was particular in choosing a nice shapely tree. We brought it
home on a bob-sleigh. Next day we started decorating it.
Father brought the kitchen table in, put a chair on it and got
up to fix the big star of red gelatine on the very top. We handed
him different ornaments and candles to be put high up and busied
ourselves with the lower branches. Decorating the tree was a
joy hardly inferior to that of seeing it lit up. I felt fascinated
handling the tinsel ornaments and gingerbreads, some shaped as
lambs, some as soldiers ; the tiny little wax angels with golden
wings suspended on elastic thread by the middle of their backs.
They swayed gently in their stationary flight, and I took care
not to put them near the candles. We put a quantity of gilded
walnuts and small red Crimean apples, no bigger than apricots,
called Paradise apples. When all the candles were fixed we
scattered handfuls of cotton wool here and there to look like
snow, and hung tinsel thread all round, and the whole tree
shimmered like a spider's web of gold and silver.

Mother was busy giving directions in the kitchen for the proper
baking of a ham and only occasionally came into the room, but
Baboushka sat with us. She was reading the newspaper and
commenting on it. She constantly called to Father, whom she
liked very much. " Listen, Platosha." Political news did not
interest her, but she ran through all the casualties. In some way
it now led her to talk about Nina's skating. Baboushka anticipated no end of disasters from this recreation. " She is a
tomboy," Baboushka was saying, " she does not mind tumbling

down, but what if she has a nasty fall. God forbid that she should have her face stitched and the ' family pride ' on one side ! " Nina's nose, which slightly resembled that of her own, Baboushka called the " family pride." She was quite a tease and designated the same feature in me as " button." Lev, she considered, had a fairly handsome nose. " I do love boys," she often added, " girls are given to sloppiness " ; but that judgment did not prevent her being fond of me, and she liked my reading to her and all my ways. She was on equal terms with us, and we both, Nina mostly, teased her often with questions. The favourite one was, " Why is your hair white, Baboushka, and your chignon black, and why do you wear a fillet over it like a fish in the net ? " She explained at length that this one was only her everyday chignon ; the other one she kept for great occasions, and it was better matched. She also led us to try her snuff, saying it cleared the eyes. Our violent fits of sneezing, first real and then feigned, amused her highly.

Nina was older than me by two years. She was a reckless scapegrace, adored Lev and preferred a round of fisticuffs with him to any other pleasure. She was a most entertaining, imaginative and disinterested liar. She grew into a frank, open girl of an astonishing sincerity, but even when a child she never lied with a view to any profit. But she would tell amazing stories, of which she was always the heroine, about her riding a wild horse in a steppe or running alongside a train keeping pace with it.

We had our round of fortune telling in the evening. We melted some wax and poured it into cold water. When it hardened we held it against the lamp and looked at the shadow it cast on the wall. The same bit turned differently presented different shapes. Most often it was unlike anything ; but our imagination helped to see a definite prophecy in it. My bit looked like a rabbit with long ears, and now it looked like a hermit in his hood.

After supper we children were sent to bed, but we agreed to

keep awake till midnight. We knew that Mother was going to look into a mirror and had seen the preparations for it. Soon after the lamp had been put out and Douniasha left the room, we crept out of bed and tip-toed down the passage to Mother's door, Nina being the leader. There in turn we tried to peep through the keyhole. We held our breath, but in pushing each other from the hole couldn't help making a noise. Mother called to us to go to bed that very minute.

So highly strung was my imagination this evening that I fully believed a ritual of witchcraft went on beyond the locked door, when, in my turn at the keyhole, I saw first the faint light of the candles and then a big shadow leaped across, as Mother got up to come to the door. Her voice rang different to me and the ugly idea of a changeling filled me with a sickly horror I could not reason. I lay awake far into the night, tormented by distorted visions. I do think even now that there is something uncanny in the custom of mirror gazing. One mirror is placed on the table in front, another at the back of the seer. Two candles are lit, and their reflection perpetuates in an enfilade of lights. The gazing has to be begun before midnight, at which moment a vision is believed to arise in the mirror. I have heard from Mother how a friend of hers on one Christmas Eve sat gazing at the mirror. She was heard to scream and found lying on the floor in a swoon. When brought to herself she said she had seen a funeral procession, a coffin borne and the face in it her own. What Mother saw this Christmas was a cheerful vision; it sounded like a pageant from her description.

Mother made us recite Christmas prayers that she had told us to learn. I looked forward greatly to the evening when the tree was to be lit up and the presents put under it, and also to other children coming. I was even slightly nervous before the party, as it was unusual in our house, and also secretly flattered by Mother saying that Lev and I were to be hosts and see that our guests were happy. On no account were we to quarrel and squabble over the toys when we were allowed to get some from the tree ; we must let them choose first. Two noisy schoolboys, Lev's friends, came to the party, and at first slightly intimidated me, but at the end they admitted me to their game. It was to load a small gun with peas and fire at a cardboard fortress.

CHAPTER V

Lessons with Father — Religious Fears — Examinations — The Imperial School

WITH the beginning of the new year Mother took the matter of my future well in hand. Father's opposition (if his mild protests could be called such) gave way to her arguments and to Aunt Vera's testimony about my capacity for dancing. " Let it be, then," he said, " she will be the third generation to go on the stage." His father had been a provincial actor and playwright.

From now on, Father taught me himself. Usually he took me in the evenings. Most of his day was spent abroad giving lessons. Father was a most exacting teacher, and when he sat there, his ever-present glass of tea by his side, he even assumed some sternness of manner. To the tune of his fiddle I exerted myself to the utmost. He never considered I had done my best unless sweat trickled down my face. He told me that when he worked for his début he literally sweated blood. He played a great variety of tunes for my exercises, bits of ballet music, bits of *Faust* and *Lucia of Lammermoor*, occasionally singing the words. His favourite was a Jewish polka. The one for which I often asked was the *Marseillaise*. The *grand battement* was not half so exhausting when done to its brave tune. Sharp, pithy remarks, " Do not hold your arms like candelabras ; knees bent like an old horse," urged me on. The occasional swish with the fiddle-stick I half resented. Father belonged to the old school of masters who believed that, unless a rigorous discipline is established, the pupil will let himself go. He taught me to put the utmost effort into every task. He got up occasionally to show me some steps. Once, feeling hot and thirsty, I took a

36

gulp of tea behind his back. He checked me severely. "You will ruin your respiration if you do that," he said to me. Nor did he allow me to sit down directly after my lesson, explaining that a sudden relaxation of muscles after a great strain weakens the knees. Once changed, I had to walk up and down for some time like a racehorse before I might either sit or drink. I often led Father on to talking about his stage experiences and famous dancers he had seen. With Dellera and Adele Grantzova he danced on their appearance in Petersburg. He spoke with great enthusiasm of Marie Sergueevna, the first wife of Marius Petipa, who died early, at the height of her fame and beauty. Crowds of admirers usually waited outside the stage door to see her step into her carriage. Her husband always accompanied her : he was said to be inordinately jealous. Once, on her coming out, it was a rainy night ; students threw down their coats under her feet. " Ramassez donc vos pelisses, Messieurs," she said, and passed on. The word *pelisse* as applied to the threadbare coat of the Russian student was rather out of proportion.

Lev shared my interest in everything concerning the theatre, and it was his idea to ask Father to make us a toy theatre. Very dexterously Father made us one out of an inverted cardboard box. He painted twisted columns and crimson draperies on the frontal of it. Our theatre had no curtain. We introduced the characters through slits at the top. They were little painted figures pasted on cardboard, and we held them on a wire. The first play produced was *Rousslan and Ludmila*. Father painted the miniature back cloth and the wings. We recited in turn as we slid down our actors. The wizard Chernomore flew across the stage on his wire and would have been very impressive had not Father exercised his wit in making him so grotesque that the audience, that is us, burst with laughter every time, thus spoiling a dramatic moment.

Though the initial knowledge required for entering the theatre school was quite slender, Mother made her occasional lessons with me more regular, meaning me to be well prepared. She praised my spelling ; though I had not sufficient knowledge of grammar I visualised the words as they should be, the result of much reading. To the first rules of arithmetic and the Old and New Testament was now added French. My uncommonly good memory made learning easy to me. On the other hand, it encouraged a lazy habit of mind ; and in after times I often shrank from a task that presented any difficulty. I lacked concentration, and my attention often wandered from the subject of my lesson to follow Mother's work. She either knitted as she dictated to me or curled old ostrich feathers with the aid of scissors. The distant, though always certain, prospect of the stage now became a thing of the near future ; but the joy of expectancy was undermined by the state of my mind, then deeply troubled with religious fears.

" Whosoever is angry with his brother without cause shall be in danger of the Judgment . . . but whosoever shall say ' Thou fool ' shall be in danger of hell fire." Childish logic, incapable of compromise, brought me to the conclusion that the occasional quarrels and bitter words of my parents, as well as my own frequent angry outbursts with Lev, put a stigma of irredeemable sin on me and on all those I loved. After the Epistles I came to the reading of the Revelation. Its symbolic meaning I could not grasp. The flamboyant vision of the Last Judgment filled me with an agony of awe. I had seen before, under the arcades of the old Nikolsky Market, the frescoes of the Last Judgment. I was even then drawn by their terrible fascination, but the whole of their meaning was now revealed to me. The last trump of the Archangel, the sea and earth giving up their dead, in the gaudy imagery of an obscure master, entered into my vision, there to grow and torment with ever-increasing terror. I would not admit before Douniasha that I was afraid of going through the market. Whenever we passed through I tried in vain to avert my eyes. At every angle of the arcades there were dark old ikons of Byzantine type, their severe eyes fixed on me.

There was no escape from their gaze. I must have become very hysterical, and was unable to control my tears. Once, during my lesson with Father, the thought came to me of how vain was all we were trying to do in life when in suspense of utter damnation. I burst into sobs. Father interrupted the lesson; he thought I was ill, and went to speak to Mother about it. She found me in the nursery still crying. " Ungrateful child," she called me, " not appreciating the care of your parents. Do you think Father would not have preferred to read his paper instead of teaching you when he comes home tired out ? But you must upset him with your caprices." She mistook the cause of my crying : a sharp, bitter pity for them both was at the bottom of my tears. So puzzled was my Mother at my incomprehensible behaviour that she even threatened me with a beating. Worst of all was my misery at night. I waited till I heard Douniasha's soft snore and then crept out of bed and knelt before the image. Fatigue sent me to sleep. Eventually I took a decision. I made up my mind to run away from home to a convent, and there, by constant praying, to redeem us all. In a roundabout way I tried to find out if Douniasha also thought that we all lived in sin. She comforted me as she could, and admitted with a sigh that we were all sinners, but the Lord had a long patience and mercy for all. It brought me no consolation, and one day I told her my plan, entreating her not to tell Mother anything, but to come with me. I started preparing a small bundle of things I wanted to take ; inconsistently perhaps my favourite treasures were among them. How and where I should find a convent never entered my head. Douniasha naturally told Mother everything, and Mother came one day and sat long with me and made me talk. I have never seen her so gentle. She took me on her lap and let me cry while she stroked my head and held me close to her, talking all the while. She said it was a mistake to have read things I was not able to understand. She explained to me that all sins could be forgiven to those who believed and repented ; and gave me the instance of Barabbas on the cross. She said

I was now old enough to go to confession, and that whatever my sins might be they would be forgiven. Her talk was healing to me.

As soon as Lev's school closed for the summer holidays we went down to Log, a village near Pskov. Lev took the next form without exams; his marks were so good. Father hoped that much would be done with me in the summer. According to him, the body was more supple on hot days, and he put me through stricter training. To my disappointment, my favourite amusement, running on stilts, he forbade on the same principle as skating in winter; both were bad for a dancer and stiffened the muscles. Thus began a long series of small privations that a dancer is subject to. I watched Lev wistfully as he ran and hopped on stilts. There were still some games which I could share with him. We often played *lapta*, a cricket of sorts, with peasant boys, and also leap-frog. In climbing trees I was almost as good as Lev and fearless, but Mother did not like it as I ruined all the flimsy little frocks she had made for me. Once she got quite cross with me and said I was careless of my things and a ruinous child and she could hardly afford making new frocks for me. " I will have you dressed in devil's skin; you are worse than a tomboy." I wept at that accusation. The thought of my ruining my parents was bitter to me; and the devil's skin, coarse leathery material, was distasteful, as I did care for prettiness and my dainty frocks. Father may have thought Mother was too hard on me, and besides my tears always moved him to pity. He went to the shed, fetched his spade and said, " Come to the wood : I will get something nice for you." There he dug out a beautiful feathery fern and planted it for me in the shady bit of the garden by the brook. This done, he said, " Now run to Mother and kiss her." In token of peace Mother made me some coffee and we had it with little buns fresh from the oven.

* * * * *

Early in August we came back to town. A petition was to be sent first to the school; only a matter of form. All the candidates had to go through a thorough examination, and comparatively few were accepted. The first year at school was a test of pupils' capacity, and at the end of the year the weak ones were weeded out. Those who did not show sufficient progress were dismissed, the best of the remaining numbers taken as boarders, tolerably good ones being given the chance of a second year as day pupils. On the morning of the examination, August 26th, 1894, I was beside myself with fear that I might yet be refused. My hair had been put in papers overnight. I could not drink my tea in the morning, neither could I eat anything. Even the new white frock and bronze shoes I had on for the occasion could not take my mind off the ordeal.

On the way to school Mother took me to a hairdresser. While he was arranging my hair, at that time cut in a fringe and in loose curls at the back, I grew more and more impatient. I kept asking Mother whether it was not yet time to go. When we arrived at the school, the sight of the beadle's livery with the Imperial eagles on it, made me feel very small. We left our coats and wrappings in the vast hall and went upstairs. On the way, Mother gave a final touch to my dress and hair, and said the white set off my sunburn very prettily. In the big room on the first floor there were already many small girls waiting. We waited for some time, and I took the opportunity of going round looking at the portraits of the Imperial family on the walls before a stern-looking lady in black sailed in with six other ladies in cashmere dresses of light blue. They were the directress, Varvara Ivanovna, and governesses. The lady in black went round, saying a few affable words to parents here and there. Mother had told me before that she was a distant relation, and I expected to be petted; but Varvara Ivanovna only looked at me with her cold grey eyes and exchanged greetings with Mother. The governesses arranged us in twos and marched us off to the next room, where benches were set on both sides and a row of tables and seats by the mirrored wall for the examiners. The doors were shut on the waiting parents. I saw Father sitting with other masters, but he did not give me any sign that he noticed me. A few names were read out at a time, and those called came into the middle of the room and stood there while the masters went round looking at them. We first stood still, then we were told to walk, then to run. That was to judge our looks and whether graceful or awkward children. Then we stood with heels together for our knees to be looked at. These preliminary tests took some time, as there were over thirty children. After the first test many were dismissed as unsuitable. Again we were arranged in twos and this time led through a long enfilade of classrooms to the infirmary to be examined by a doctor. We had to undress completely and were given some linen dressing-gowns in which to wait for our turn. The examination was very thorough. Some children were dismissed on account of weak hearts; others had a slight deviation of the spine. Sight and hearing were tested too. When the doctor's examination was over, we were taken to the so-called " round room " and given some tea and sandwiches. During this interval for lunch Father looked in, and I ran to him, asking whether I was accepted. He put me off with his usual " Who knows much . . ."

After lunch the music mistress made us sing a scale to judge our ear for music. Examination in reading, writing and arithmetic followed. The final choice was yet to be made, as the number of pupils had to be limited. So we again were led to the big room where the dancing masters sat. Only ten were taken, and I was amongst them. By the time we came home it was six o'clock. All that had happened had to be lived through again in happy conversation. Mother wanted to find out from Father if the examiners were impressed by my looks. She maintained I was the best-dressed child of the whole lot. I also had to tell Lev and Douniasha how all went on and what was said to me and what the other children were like.

The classes were to begin on September 1st, and in the few

remaining days my school outfit was to be ready. It consisted of a brown cashmere for classes and a dancing frock of a special pattern in grey holland. Father took me out to buy a school box. Particular joys to me were a satchel which I chose in imitation of tiger skin and all the small requisites like the pen, pen case and its fittings. I had a delightful feeling of property in handling all these. Up till then I had never had a pencil I could call my own.

We lived a good way off from the school, and to get there in time I had to leave the house with Father before eight. In those days we had no tramways, only street cars, pulled along the rails by a couple of horses.

* * * * *

On arriving at the school the day pupils changed into dancing frocks on the entresol, under the auspices of a tiny, grey-haired, mousy-looking, kindly old woman and went straight upstairs to curtsy to the governess and then in to the smaller practice-room. The dancing classes were held in the morning. We then changed and had lunch in the round room. Tea was provided by the school, but we had to bring our own sandwiches. Sometimes, in the way of a treat, Father would buy me some hot jam pies from the arcade of the Gostinoy Dvor close by. Gourian, the beadle, handed me the little parcels " from Papa." The pies were of rich pastry, delicious, highly indigestible.

CHAPTER VI

*Black Marias—My First Year at School—A Death in the Theatre
—Kyasht—School Traditions—Andrey—A Premature Burial—
Death of the Emperor*

MY first year at the school was not distinguished by any
marked progress in dancing. I had to be in the beginners' class, though I was sufficiently prepared for harder work.
The personality of our dancing master was uninspiring. He was
Father's contemporary on the stage, and now indulged in the
luxury of an elaborate moustache, pomaded and curled at the
ends. His black hair was dressed *à la Capoul*, but for all that
he looked an elderly cherub and spoke with a languishing drawl.
If then I had known Mr. Mantalini, I would have nicknamed my
master after him.

The ballet performances were given on Wednesdays and
Sundays. In accordance with tradition, the last act of the ballet
was constructed on the lines of a *divertissement*; and very often
a dance for pupils was introduced, thus giving them a stage
training along with the learning of steps. The beginners, like
myself, only appeared in the crowd. I longed for this opportunity to be actually on the stage, which was to me what Mecca
is to a good Mussulman. However, for quite a long time the
choice never fell on me. From other pupils in my class who were
often sent down to the theatre I heard wonderful tales. I saw
them imitating the ballerina, and it was all I could do to hide
my mortification and not to cry. I confided in Father, and it
came out that he had asked them to spare me, as it meant late
hours. But realising my disappointment he promised to say
" a word." As a result of the " word " I was chosen to be one
of the crowd in *Coppelia*. It is no exaggeration to say that I

had a feeling akin to stage-fright on my first appearance.
Brought to the theatre by Mother hours before the last act, in
which we had to walk up and down the stage, I was handed to
Mlle. Virshault, the stern French governess.   When the dresser
brought in our costumes, I pounced on the one I thought the
prettiest.   Mlle. Virshault said it was not for me to choose, and
I must be pleased with what costume was given to me.   I
smarted under the rebuke, but was pleased right away with the
bright velvet bodice and the little muslin apron given to me ;
and I gazed in the mirror at my new self till I was called to be
made up.   We came in turn before the governess and she slightly
rouged our cheeks with the aid of a hare's foot.   When arranged
in twos, we began descending the flight of stairs.   I had a feeling
that all were looking at me and admiring my costume.   I stepped
lightly with a springy step I did not know myself to possess.
On the stage at first all was bewildering ; the audience looked
like a black gap beyond the haze of the footlights.   The lights
and the space made me somewhat giddy.   I was not conscious
of any consternation around me, but when Mother brought me
home I learned what had happened in the theatre on that night.
She spoke to Father in a hushed voice as we sat down to supper.
" Yes, as he was, in costume and grotesque make-up.   Heart-
failure."   I picked out from this and other sentences not really
meant for my ears that the old actor Stoukolkin, who played
Dr. Coppelius, had died suddenly in his dressing-room.   It
happened just before the last act, and the interval was prolonged
to give the understudy time to dress.

It did not matter to me how insignificant my part so long as
I was in this fascinating stage-world.   To be in the crowd was
quite a sufficient thrill to me.   Soon, however, the scope of my
activities grew larger.   I became one of the six pages of Lilac
Fairy, in the *Sleeping Beauty* ; and in *Corsair* I had to come on
the stage all by myself and kneel before Medora, offering her a
rose on a damask cushion.   These small parts could not have
been done without rehearsing.   Not to interfere with dancing

classes, our rehearsals were held in the afternoon. The appearance of a governess in the midst of an afternoon lesson to call out pupils wanted for rehearsing was always a welcome sight, especially when it happened during arithmetic. We rehearsed mostly at school, but whenever it was required, went to the theatre. The capacious fourwheelers, nicknamed "antediluvians," drew up at the side door, from there to convey us to the theatre. They accommodated six. When more than one carriage was needed we had two governesses with us, a maid and a beadle outside. Long ancient vehicles, with one window at the end, holding fifteen people, were used for great occasions. These equipages resembled Black Marias. The theatre owned its own stables. The carriages went to fetch the artists and brought them to their respective homes after the performance. The ballerinas had a carriage exclusively to themselves.

The boy pupils we hardly ever saw. Their quarters were on the floor above, and we only met at ballroom lessons and at rehearsals. Talking with the boys was strictly prohibited. Sedately we went through all the figures of quadrilles, lancers and the minuet without as much as raising our eyes to our partners. If any breach of the rule was espied by the governess, the offender was reproved and sometimes punished. In spite of these precautions, mild flirting had its roots deep in the school life. Lydia Kyasht ran to me excitedly before the ballroom lesson one day. "I told my brother to become your admirer," she informed me, "he will be your partner to-day." I knew enough by this time to realise that an admirer was necessary to my good standing, and, though I knew from Father, in whose class he was, that the boy was a little ruffian, I meekly accepted the situation.

Our school was full of little affectations, and I soon assumed the *bon ton* required by tradition. My new manner did not at all please Mother. She disliked "gentilities" as she called it. As to Lev, he ridiculed me wittily and pitilessly.

"Whom do you adore?" the older girls often asked me.

We all had to adore somebody. The two principal ballerinas, Matilda Kshessinskaya and Olga Preobrajenskaya, were the idols of the school, and divided it into two camps. Masters were sometimes considered worthy of adoration. Unfortunately, there were only two youngish and handsome masters, one of them the fencing master. The rest seemed to have been chosen from a panopticon. My choice fell on Pavel Guerdt. Though over forty, he ever remained the "first lover" on the stage, and his looks did not betray him. I could fix my worship on him in good faith, as I always admired his appearance and manner. It did not occur to me till then, though, that I adored him. He was my godfather, and from time to time came to see us at home, always bringing a large box of chocolates for me. At this stage of his career he did not dance much owing to recurring trouble in his knee, but he supported the ballerina and acted principal parts. Fair and handsome, he was almost boyish on the stage, a first-rate actor. He taught pantomime at the school, but only advanced pupils attended his class.

When I knelt with my rose in *Corsair*, I could not foresee that years later I would be Medora and he my Conrad. I looked forward to his visits ; he always said something encouraging to me. What I specially liked in him was that he never patted me on the head or otherwise treated me as a child. He addressed me with the same gallant bow, bringing his heels together, as he did to Mother. One day as he came to us I hurried to meet him.

"Well done, god-daughter," he said to me. "Very good expression, excellent carriage, very artistic the way you walk on the stage." Whether there could have been any special merit in walking on the stage I doubt now, but then I felt immensely proud.

On this visit I was sent out of the room, to my great disappointment. Godfather wanted to talk on some confidential matter. On going away he thanked my Mother repeatedly. The mysterious purpose of his visit I soon learned. His brother,

Andrey, was then about to be released from a mental home. Poor Andrey had temporary fits of insanity and had been in a mental home several times. Now the doctors pronounced him sane, but still to be watched. He wrote pathetic letters to his brother begging to be taken out, promising implicit obedience. Pavel was in great difficulty, as his wife positively refused to take the responsibility. He came to my father begging him, for the sake of old friendship, to take Andrey under his care. Father was not a man to refuse this request, and my mother always had been generous in the extreme, and it was decided that Andrey should live with us.

The addition of a new member to our small household meant some rearranging of accommodation. Father gave up his room to the newcomer, and from now slept in the study on a big ottoman. Both my parents took great care of Andrey, and were genuinely fond of him. In his dress he was tidy and even fastidious, and he was docile and dependent as a child. He regarded Mother as his guardian ; he used to give her his pension money for keeping, and consulted her whenever he wanted to buy anything. On Saturdays he trotted off happily with Father and Lev to a steam bath. His entire day was spent in following our occupations, but now and then he retired to his room to write his memoirs. He read bits of them to Mother. The ghastly memory of his incarceration haunted him still. In one of his fits he had been thought dead. He had come to himself after a coma that lasted about three days to find he was lying in a coffin, candelabras lit at the head and foot. For a time he listened to a monotonous voice reading Psalms, before his consciousness returned completely, and he screamed and struggled out.

Orthodox law requires the dead for three days and nights to be laid out in a chapel, psalm-readers relieving each other in uninterrupted prayer over the body previous to the funeral service and to the closing of the coffin. His was indeed a narrow escape.

A period of sanity followed, and he was taken out of the hospital. On one occasion, when he became troublesome, his brother, referring to the incident, said cruel words to him, no doubt without meaning it. " Next time I will take great care they nail your coffin before you can walk out of it." The perpetual dread of being buried alive preyed on him; and even when telling of it he would be in a pitiful state of nerves.

" That is all right, Andreich," Mother comforted him, " it will never happen again. You will never go to the hospital if I can prevent it." He made my Mother promise that, whatever happened, she would not let him be incarcerated again. God knows she struggled hard to save him. There was a soft spot in Mother's heart for all mentally afflicted. Her own father had had spells of temporary insanity and it left an indelible impression on her mind.

For a time all went well. Peaceful home-life was as paradise regained to poor Andreich, and to all appearances he was quite normal, but for an occasional sudden and senseless remark. Evening tea was the time when we all sat long and sociably round the table. The samovar would be removed and brought again singing and steaming by Douniasha. She often tarried in the room, standing by the door in her favourite attitude, her cheek leaning on one of her hands and the other folded for support, smiling beatifically and at times venturing some remark.

Towards spring Andreich grew restless, and had fits of melancholy followed by sleeplessness. In the night he often got up and roamed about the house. Once he walked into the nursery. I woke up and called to him, slightly frightened. He turned round without a word and walked off. Another night he came to Father and apparently stood there talking for some time before Father, a sound sleeper, awoke. " Look here, Platon," Andreich went on. " You must prevent the children from hearing the explosion." " What are you talking about ? " asked Father. " Why, don't you know ? I am about to burst and the noise will be tremendous." Father succeeded in quietening and leading him off, and Mother came and gave him some valerian drops. To Mother he was as obedient as a lamb. Next day she called a doctor, who said the poor man was not safe to keep in the house. Personal discomfort Mother did not mind, but she was alarmed for our sakes. In spite of that, she refused to send him away. From now on he rapidly grew worse. Silent and gloomy, he wandered about, and it was evident he suffered from hallucinations. His eyes would become fixed and he would suddenly rush forward clapping his hands, as if killing flies. " One less," he would say in grim satisfaction. He chased small devils, as he explained. One night a terrible commotion arose in the house. In a frenzy Andreich tried to tear his tongue out. Father could hardly hold him. There was no choice left. Mother rushed out in the night to fetch assistance from St. Nicholas Hospital for mental trouble. When the doctor and two men arrived he said it was delirium tremens, and the patient must be removed. The poor wretch defended himself desperately, and the men could hardly handle him. Mother had the painful duty of inducing him to follow the doctor. At her word he dressed obediently, but insisted that my Mother should go with him. She went, heartbroken. She told afterwards how he became quiet and lucid on the way, big tears running down his cheeks. His resistance was broken. He never left the hospital, and died in a short time. Mother could never think or speak of it without tears.

* * * * *

One morning Douniasha came as usual at seven o'clock to call me. She shook me gently in my sleep and as she leant over me, said, " The Tzar passed away in the small hours. His soul be in peace."

Later, impressed by the black draperies that decorated the houses and the funeral arches erected on the way of the procession, I started composing a funeral ode in seven metre verse, but it didn't go further than two stanzas.

I had been writing verses for some time. All my writings on odd bits of paper I used to sign with my full name, roll up and hide behind the stove in our room.

As the result of a dancing examination in the spring, I was made a board pupil. The idea of separation did not enter my head. It was not to be till next autumn, and I had the whole summer at Log to look forward to. In the meantime the idea of a pretty blue dress was an attraction to me.

CHAPTER VII

I Become a Boarder—Etiquette—" Lunatic Ann "—School Discipline—First Contact with the Theatre—A Forgotten Speech

I PUT away my treasures and went through my favourite books with something like melancholy before leaving home for school, where this time I was to remain. But uppermost in my thoughts was the anticipation of a new life and a feeling amounting to the exhilaration of a votary. The prolonged farewells stirred my emotion, and I shed some tears at parting. Mother comforted me by saying she would come to see me on the reception day. But the one sorely afflicted was poor Douniasha. She took me to school on the last Sunday evening in August. In the omnibus she never broke silence, but surreptitiously wiped off her tears and blew her nose loudly. It made me rather self-conscious, though nobody paid great attention to us. She kissed me good-bye on the landing. Wetting my cheeks with her tears, she crossed me three times, repeating odds and ends of prayers and invocations to the Holy Virgin and St. Nicholas. I turned back once more before I entered the door leading to the classes and saw her still making signs of the Cross underneath her shawl. One of the school maids told me afterwards that when I disappeared from her sight Douniasha broke down completely. The maid gave her some water and tried to comfort her. Once inside, I felt a sharp pang of remorse. I wished I had had more to say to Douniasha.

Many girls were already gathered in the big room. The governess stood there checking the names. With her stood Varvara Ivanovna, in whose presence I always felt shy and timid. I went up to curtsy. " Goodness," she said, " why all these frills ? You are not coming to a party." She turned to the governess, " Olga Andreevna, will you see that this fringe of hers is brushed back ; your Mother may like dressing you up, my dear, but we do not want these fanciful coiffures." My blue hat tied up under the chin was not unlike that of a smart doll ; it had been my particular pride. Mother paid quite a lot for it as she could not resist it, she said.

Varvara Ivanovna retired to her apartment, and we were taken to change our dresses. During the year I had been a day-girl I had seen nothing of the living quarters, only the class-rooms and dancing-rooms. The room where the small pupils dressed was called the washing room, from a large copper tub raised on a platform in the centre, like a gigantic saucer with a cauldron in the middle. Every morning and evening we had to stand round it under a cold tap.

From the wardrobe mistress I received a blue serge dress. It was cut on old-fashioned lines, tight bodice cut low and a full gathered skirt coming down to the instep. The white plain fichu of starched lawn had to be pinned at the back and crossed in front ; black alpaca apron, white stockings and black pumps completed the costume. On Sundays we wore a white apron with tucks. I soon learnt a doggerel rhyme which we all said, fingering the tucks like a rosary :

> Shall I be a titled lady ?
> Or as poor as well can be ?
> Shall I wed a simple sailor ?
> Will a general marry me ?

A long enumeration of possible alliances finished with

> Or a spinster always be ?

That first evening I committed a great offence from not knowing the customs of the school. When ready, I wandered aimlessly from one room to another. Our floor was divided into two parts, the schoolrooms and living-rooms, generally called the " other side " ; the dancing-rooms belonged to the other side. That division was purely fictitious, as they ran in a straight enfilade and the doors between remained open except when the classes were held. A strict rule forbade our going from the "other side" to the schoolrooms and vice-versa without asking permission. Parallel to the dancing-rooms were the music-room and the round room, which served as a library, looking into the central courtyard. The windows there were of ordinary glass and the rooms seemed smaller and more intimate. On this first evening I wandered up and down and around the dancing-rooms, but their bare vastness made me feel homesick and I went to the round room. There I saw Olga Andreevna replacing some books and asked her if I might have something to read. From the first I felt a friend in her: she was the most human of our governesses, and never was called a "toad," as all the others. I chose, on her advice, *L'Histoire d'un Ane*, by Madame de Ségur. She patted me slightly on the head and said she knew I was a serious child fond of reading. Anticipating the joy of some reading before supper, I went with my book to the dining-room. It was long and comparatively narrow. The tables were laid for supper. One of the seniors was making tea from a samovar. At the far end between the stove and ikon cupboard, stood a smaller table covered with black oilcloth and not laid for supper. There was a light over it and a few big girls sat round, some reading, some working. It looked cosy there and warm; there seemed room on the bench, so I went and sat down. The effect of my innocent action was explosive. Like disturbed wasps, angry ejaculations flew at me. "What impudence!" . . . "Is she sane?" . . . "I say, are you half-witted?" . . . "Let me touch your head." . . . "You must be in a delirium." "Are you speaking to me?" I asked, though I knew it must be to no other. "To you, miserable," said the girl by name Olinka. "How dare you force yourself on our table!" I retreated, feebly protesting that I was not to be called "miserable."

A bell summoned us to supper. Going in to meals had something of a processional solemnity. We formed column by twos in the adjoining room and, when the formation was ready, walked in while the governess counted us like sheep. The counting was done before every meal, and struck me at once as absurd. Much later I learned the origin of this measure. The story had become a legend, told in thrilled whispers. I heard it when I was a senior, and it had the corroboration of the maid Euphymia or Phymoushka, as we called her. Passed from one generation of girls to another, the story had very likely got much ornamented, but it was quite true in its main lines. Some years before, a girl, referred to as " lunatic Ann," remarkable for her beauty and reckless spirits, had eloped from the school with an officer of Horse Guards, whom she first met when home on holiday. On the wall inside her wardrobe Ann had written down her adventure from day to day. She described how the young officer used to be driven by a pair of bay horses up and down Theatre Street, while she stood on the window of the dormitory and signalled to him. It always happened in the afternoon, while the pupils were in the schoolrooms. Ann, being a *pépinière*, did not follow the classes and had obtained permission to go to the other side under the pretext of practising the piano. Those who read her narrative said it was thrilling and, what was more, that there was a dash here and there to be filled in by the reader. The annals of her romance were not discovered till long after her disappearance, when the wardrobes were being repapered. With the connivance of a maid, since dismissed, Ann, disguised in maid's dress, with a shawl over her head, had come out through the pantry on to the back stairs and through the side door out into the empty street. Since that event, girls upwards of fifteen years of age never went home for the holidays except for three days at Christmas and on Easter Day. In my time all the windows looking into the street were of frosted glass.

Since that first evening, I always walked in pair with Lydia Kyasht. We had been friends since we both entered the school. There was an unwritten law of friendship according to which one girl had no right to be on intimate terms with any other besides the acknowledged. A little formality preceded forming a friendship. " Will you be my friend and tell me all your secrets ? " on one side, and a promise to do so on the other.

When prayers were sung after the meal, we all trooped down the passage to the dormitory, this time in disarray. Sedova told me to get to bed quickly as she would come and sit on my bed. Each senior girl had her favourite amongst the younger ones. The sign of favour was to sit on the protégée's bed for a few minutes in the evening ; in return, the protectress was to be " adored." Each elder had the duty of giving dancing practice in the evening to a certain number of the juniors, and it was from among those that her favourite was chosen. We all slept in the same dormitory ; it was like a vast hospital ward with fifty beds and ample room for many more. Some fifteen seniors slept in a recess at one end ; the governess at the other, her bed screened off. Over each bed hung the school number of the occupant. On that, my first, night in the school, Varvara Ivanovna paid a visit to the dormitory. In the dim blue light of a night lamp, her tall figure moved to and fro in the passage between the beds. Not yet asleep, I watched her from under closed eyelids. Her rhythmic, swinging stride, curiously light for her stature, seemed a majestic progress by the side of the waddling, motherly Olga Andreevna. She stopped before my bed ; I heard her shocked whisper, " Strange attitude ! She might be laid out in her coffin." I slept on my back with arms crossed because I thought it a holy attitude likely to keep off bad dreams. But I had a morbid dream in spite of that. I dreamt it was night and I stood all by myself in our dressing-room. The sound of steps on the stone floor behind me made me turn round and come into the passage. Someone just disappeared round the corner, and I caught a glimpse of the swaying skirts of a black coat. I followed the sound of steps, and it led me through vast unknown rooms. At times I could see the back of a man walking fast in front of me, his high boots and three-cornered hat. The figure disappeared from my sight, and I found myself before a door that I knew led through a covered bridge to the back wing, where the big rehearsal room was. This door was always kept locked. I tried it ; it gave, and I found myself back in the dressing-room wondering how it had happened. By the door stood the man in black, with his back to me. I could see that his hair was tied up with a bow. I thought I might creep through the door and back to the dormitory unnoticed, when the man turned round and I saw the grin of a skeleton. I knew one had to be the first to speak to an apparition—it gave a power over it—but I was paralysed. No words came, in spite of a desperate effort. The man spoke first. " I am one of those buried under here."

" What do you want of me ? " I managed to say. Here I woke up, shaken by Lydia saying, " Don't scream, you frighten me."

Next morning, as Phymoushka was combing my hair with a curry comb, I related with bated breath my dramatic dream, the breathless flight through the corridors, sable-cloak, skeleton and all. Phymoushka said my dream meant a change of weather.

All the girls up to fifteen were combed by maids, the seniors being trusted to do it themselves. Every morning, after the cold tap, we formed a queue by the window in the dormitory, where four maids went through the task, taking each her own clients. It was a sociable corner, and we would have tarried over the combing had it not been for all we had to do before breakfast. We had to make our beds and get ready ten minutes before the bell, to show up. The governess sat at the door of the dining-room ; and we came up one by one, curtsied and slowly turned round. The juniors got straight into their dancing kit and were wrapped in a thick blue shawl with long fringe. It became a habit with me to make it into innumerable little plaits ending in a knot. In a few days' time the whole of the fringe was thus plaited, and the completion of it coincided with the coming on duty of Helena Andreevna. She was very kind and, compared with the other governesses, quite unconventional. She noticed the unusual look of my shawl as I went up to her in the morning to show up. " What is this fancy work ? " she asked. I explained that I always liked to do something with my fingers. " Twiddle your thumbs then rather than spoil your shawl."

The morning was devoted to dancing lessons and music practice. After lunch we were taken out for a daily airing, the length of which varied slightly according to how soon we got ready. At the most, we had from fifteen to twenty minutes round and round a small garden in the courtyard. Our winter coats were voluminous. The black pelisse lined with red fox we nicknamed " Penguin " from the short sleeves let in at the waist-line ; it was gathered in folds under the round fur collar and together with a black silk bonnet, à *la* Perdita Robinson, made us not unlike a sugar loaf in shape. The feet were kept warm by high boots with velveteen tops. The fashion of our clothes belonged to the preceding century, but was well in keeping with the spirit of the institution, with its severe detachment from the life outside its walls. Vowed to the theatre, we were kept from contact with the world as from a contamination. Having to face life one day in its most alluring guise, we were brought up in almost convent-like seclusion. As I look back now upon my school years, I see that our upbringing, despite its seeming absurdity, fully vindicated its wisdom. If lacking the stimulus of actuality, we at least were spared the sordidness of life ; and the rarified air of discipline was a proper school for temperament, inasmuch as it concentrated its growth on one single purpose.

*　　*　　*　　*　　*

Twice a week parents were allowed to visit us. Brothers were admitted, but no male cousin ever passed the threshold of the reception room. The doors on both sides remained open, and the girls whose parents could not come on that day prowled in the next room, casting wistful glances at the fortunate ones. The sweets brought to us were immediately locked up by the governess, and we were allowed to have a few every day after meals. Cakes, ginger-breads, and everything substantial was expressly forbidden on the ground that the pupils were well fed at school. Some parents, however, smuggled home-made pies, which were eaten hurriedly and surreptitiously during the reception. The girl on duty at the door, posted there to call those who happened to be in the other room when visitors came, acted as sentinel, and by secret signs warned the transgressors of the governess's approach.

The joy of seeing Mother and Lev was overwhelming at first; but when I had asked about home, Douniasha and the white cat, Mourka, and told my own news, the primness of sitting in a row, making conversation, became almost embarrassing, and when they rose to go, I felt sadness and relief at the same time. Later, as I sat with my book in the usually empty music-room, its unpopularity being due to the belief that it was haunted, I could not read. In my thoughts I was much nearer home than during the reception hour. I worked the little pieces of information I had received into the familiar surroundings.

Apart from the acute longing for home that occasionally rose in me, I did not feel the régime of the school as oppressive. The fashionable attitude amongst pupils was to grumble against the seclusion of our life. The seniors in their last year used to write out in a minute hand a calendar finishing with May 25th, their last day at school. They checked it daily and proclaimed with satisfaction the number of days left as it grew smaller. The notes of exclamation, beginning weeks before the great date, multiplied to a fantastic degree. Some made their calendar into a tiny scroll with a ribbon through it, and pinned it on their fichu. It was displayed only when the governess could not see. Calendar keeping counted as a heavy offence, and even as a challenge; our education was free, and indecent haste for leaving school amounted, in the eyes of the authorities, to black ingratitude. Not till years later did I fall into that feverish anticipation of freedom. At present the life at school had all the value of actuality. Far from dull, it took the colour of romance every time a glimpse or a sound or a token from outside found its way into the precincts of our isolation. In this way any event, however prosaic, such as going to the Russian bath every Friday, was eagerly anticipated by me. We did not, of course, even then leave the school premises, but we had to pass through several courtyards; and the change from our own, with its dull little garden, took on the proportions of an adventure. From the second courtyard one could see figures silhouetted against the windows of the big rehearsal-room. Through an archway we passed into a third courtyard and turned into a small inner court, piled with wood. The bath-house, with its tiny windows, appeared unexpectedly rustic and out of keeping with the beautifully ordained bulk of the main buildings. On dark winter evenings, the feeble light of these windows put me in mind of a hut in the woods in fairy-tales. Inside it was warm and cosy. From the dressing-room we passed to the bath, full of steam, where the maids, in long linen shifts, washed and scrubbed us thoroughly on wooden benches that went along the walls. One could have a proper steam bath by going up to the top of a kind of open cupboard. Water was thrown on the red-hot stones piled in the large stove, and volumes of steam rose and clung to the ceiling.

Back in the school, we were allowed to walk about with our hair down till supper, when we had to plait it whether dry or not.

My second term at school, I was under the same dancing-master, only in the upper section. If the dancing studies were dry at the beginning, I had the great compensation of being often selected to dance in performances.

The favourite ballet with us small pupils was *Paquita*. The acme of our ambition was to dance the mazurka in the last act. White Polish surcoat with gold braid, blue taffeta skirt and white gloves (cotton) seemed to us the last word in smartness. In fact, our costumes were the exact replicas of Fanny Elssler's in *Katarina*. The mazurka was executed by sixteen couples of children schooled to dance it with the utmost gravity and precision. It was always encored after loud " Bravi."

Apart from getting us off afternoon lessons, the chief charm of rehearsals was that, brought to the theatre early, we sat in a box and watched the rehearsal till it was our turn to go on the stage. Prima ballerinas never spared themselves when rehearsing at the Marinsky, though going through parts sotto voce, as it was oddly called, was not infrequent when rehearsals were held at the school. The dark, empty theatre ; the brown holland over the seats ; the shrouded chandeliers—all could not take away the tense atmosphere of a real performance. The fascination was complete ; and in a way, undistracted by costumes and surroundings, one's vision retained the beauty of line better than in the full blaze of an evening spectacle.

That early touch with the theatre created a strain of exaltation hushed by daily routine, but unsuppressed, an undercurrent of romance and ambition. When particularly impressed with something seen on the stage, I secretly practised the steps in front of the long mirror in our dressing-room and memorised most of the parts years before my time came to play them.

One day I was fetched by Vera, the tall maid, from the music-room, where I was practising my piano piece. " Come, Tamaroushka," so she called me in an affectionate way. " Come at once. Varvara Ivanovna wants to see you." I felt apprehensive as I went along, and my first thought was that Monsieur Ternisien must have complained of my copy-book of French translation on account of many ink-blots. Varvara Ivanovna stood in her usual place engaged in conversation with a man I knew afterwards to be the stage manager of the Dramatic Theatre. Her benign smile as she turned to me was reassuring.

" Here is the little Karsavina," she said. " I think she will do nicely. You will have to present a bouquet to Madame

Jouleva to-night.* Marie Gavrilovna Savina will teach you what to say. Remember to look people in the face as you are looking at me now."

The same evening I put on my white Sunday apron and a fresh ribbon to my pigtail, and the governess took me across the street to the Alexandrinsky Theatre. It was Jouleva's farewell night. She had been a pupil of the Ballet School herself before she took to drama. Red runners were spread on the way to her dressing-room. I was given a big bunch of flowers and told to wait for her coming. The great Savina, though past the zenith of her glorious career, still reigned supreme over the dramatic stage. This was the first time I had seen her, and I approached her with reverential fear. She took me in charge; and when I asked her to teach me what to say, she laughingly remarked: "Ah, but she won't let you say anything. Her emotion will get the better of her." I understood what she meant when the presentation took place. As the portly figure of the elderly Jouleva appeared in the doorway, Savina pushed me forward. "Gracious madame, dear Alexandra Semenovna——" I began, as previously taught. "Permit me . . ." but here she clasped me to her bosom, smothering the remainder of my speech in her strong embrace. "Doushenka, my pretty child," she wailed, sobbing. "You bring me back my youth." Her genuine emotion was evident under the high pathos of dramatic tradition. When she had finished with me, Jouleva embraced everybody all round and passed to her dressing-room.

"You see, you had no need to learn an elaborate speech," said Savina to me. "God grant that she does not cry herself ill when all the deputations come," and with that she patted me on the head and asked if I liked chocolates.

Next day I received from Savina a magnificent box in blue silk with a rosy shepherd and shepherdess painted on the lid and full of chocolates. I also received a signed portrait from Jouleva. Both became relics and were kept at home. The silk box, protected by an old pillow-case, was stored in Mother's chest of drawers against the time when, on finishing school, I should keep my gloves in it. It was displayed on occasions before friends.

When home on week-end leave I was aware of increased attention. With Father I always had been a great favourite; but Mother, who seldom patted me before, became more demonstrative towards me. She devised dishes I liked, and often herself went to the kitchen to make a sweet course on Sunday, a thing not usual in our house.

CHAPTER VIII

*Moscow — Money Difficulties — Legnani — Classes — Pavlova —
Infatuations — A Worldly Priest — The Haunted Music-room —
The Tzar*

IN May, 1896, the Coronation of the new Tzar was to be
celebrated at Moscow. Some of the best dancers from
Petersburg were going there to take part in a gala performance.
The ballet prepared for the gala was an allegorical piece. Twelve
small pupils were chosen to represent cupids, and I was amongst
the lucky ones. My parents were going to fetch me at Moscow
on their way to Nijni Novgorod, where Father had accepted
an offer to produce ballets for the season. At Moscow we were
quartered at the theatre school, where two of the classrooms
had been converted into dormitories. The régime of the
Moscow school was more liberal than ours. Unlike us in
Theatre Street, the pupils roamed about the school freely. The
spirit of freedom was catching; the new surroundings gave
a feeling of something not unlike adventure, and our little party
got bold enough to ask tentatively that we should be taken to
see a famous circus then giving a performance. The demand
was thoroughly inconsistent with the whole idea of our cloistered
upbringing. The governess who came with us was a strict,
strait-laced disciplinarian, though a kind creature. She gave
an answer worthy of Delphi. " I can tell you you won't go
there to-day." We took it for a half promise, but in a few days
the same answer came, and we understood that every day
was to-day.

At the first sight of Moscow I could not believe this was the
old capital and the heart of Russia. The somewhat severe
stateliness of Petersburg left me unprepared for the homely

absurd character of Moscow, with its straggling crazy streets winding up and down for a long while to finish abruptly in a blind alley. When looked down on from the Sparrow Hills, the golden cupolas of innumerable churches, the crenellated walls of the Kremlin, the large sweep of panorama assume an unexpected majesty. These were not my feelings then. In fact, I summed up my impressions in a letter I wrote home : " All the streets are crooked and narrow. Not one would compare with the Nevsky. I am told there is a church called St. Nicholas on Chicken Feet, and the small street behind the school is named ' Passage of the Crooked Knee.' "

Nothing more was to be added to my experience and knowledge of Moscow. The remaining fortnight I spent in quarantine with nobody to share my loneliness. I had contracted mumps, and mine was the only case in the school. The only communications with the outside world were clandestine little notes that Lydia now and then pushed underneath my door. When I got out of bed I could look on a courtyard. There was a small garden in the centre of it, and sometimes I saw the girls walking there and made signs to them. Poor consolation ! There were no books in the hospital, and the unrelieved monotony of my days made me very miserable at first. Against the disappointment at missing the coronation performance, the illumination of the town and the fireworks at the Kremlin, was set the morbid pleasure of dramatising my plight, of imagining myself shut up and forgotten by everybody. I worked myself up to such a state of misery that the trivial occurrence of sitting down to a meal all by myself had the poignant pathos of utter loneliness, and I shed absurd tears over my plate.

My parents now came to Moscow, and Mother was allowed to visit me. One day she brought news of a terrible disaster at Khodynka on the parade-ground on the outskirts of Moscow. There was a distribution of souvenir gifts. Every comer received an enamelled mug with a portrait of the Emperor on it, a bag of sweets and some ginger-bread and sausage, all tied up in a printed kerchief. Father, with Lev and the maid, Annoushka, whom Mother had brought with her, leaving Douniasha to look after the flat, went there too. Fortunately for them they were delayed : the streets were thick with people streaming to Khodynka. At this period of his life Lev was very mischievous. As Mother came to this stage of her account she could not help laughing, in spite of the sadness of the story. They tried to make their way as quickly as they could, manœuvring through the crowds. Whenever Lev saw a couple walking he swiftly bolted in between, with a polite " Pardon me." In the breach thus formed rushed Father, and behind him Annoushka, whose back received all the cuffs. Before they reached their destination they met with several stretchers. Sobbing groups appeared coming from Khodynka· The story of the terrible disaster spread from mouth to mouth. Deep ditches on both sides of the ground had been covered with planks, along which people advanced towards the distribution point. All went well for some time, but as the crowd became thicker the planks gave way in several places and people fell into the ditch. The pressure from the back being great, others fell on top and buried those underneath. Mother said that on her way to me she had met several carts loaded with bodies. According to rumour tens of thousands perished.

*   *   *   *   *

The theatre in which Father worked at Nijni Novgorod adjoined the grounds of the fair. Mother went there often and sometimes took us, especially when some of the melodious old operettas were given. After the operetta came a short ballet that Father had produced. In spite of an excellent cast, the theatre did poorly ; and the payments to artists were irregular and incomplete. The situation worried my parents greatly. Supposing the impresario did not pay the whole salary, how would they get back to Petersburg ? To cut our expenses, we had moved to a small back flat in the same house. The summer was hot, and our small rooms stifling. We had three tiny rooms, and, for want of accommodation, my bed was made up every night on the narrow divan in the living-room. One afternoon it was too hot to go out, and we all stayed indoors. Mother, always active, moved about killing flies with an old slipper. She sang in her good contralto voice some snatches of gipsy ballads. Father had several letters to open. Usually he read them aloud; but now he sat silent and pondering, and it made Mother look up. On seeing his altered face, she guessed at once, with that quick power of divination which was hers, that something was wrong. "Vous avez perdu votre place à l'école," she said, and Father handed her the letter.

That night, going to bed, I heard their talk. Mother was trying to comfort Father, and some of the words she said came clearly through the thin partition of the room. "Not all is lost," she was saying. "Tata evidently is going to be a very good dancer, and that will make amends for their unfair treatment of you."

A few days later Mother said to me: "You know that Father has lost his place at the school. We will have to be careful now. I am afraid I won't be able to bring you any sweets when I come to see you."

The season was coming to an end, proving a failure. At the theatre, where no hope was entertained of full payment, the actors spoke facetiously and in time-honoured jargon about getting home somehow and some time along the railway sleepers. I had heard Mother sometimes darkly refer to Stepanovna, who, whatever difficulty arose, would "turn it round her finger." By writing to this mysterious person, Mother contrived to raise money, though at a high rate of interest, and thus enabled us to get back to Petersburg.

At the end of August I went back to school to begin my third term. Some changes had taken place. The dancing tradition handed down by French masters had hitherto been the only recognised form of teaching. Now, at the annual meeting of masters, it was decided to introduce a parallel class of the Italian school. This idea may have been suggested by the prodigious virtuosity of Pierrina Legnani. In those days the engagement of a foreign star for a part of the season was customary. This Italian ballerina, on her first appearance in Petersburg, won all hearts, and for over ten years successfully held the stage as a *prima ballerina assoluta.* By no means pretty and rather short of stature, she possessed great charm and grace ; and these qualities, together with marvellous brilliancy of execution, silenced all the antagonists of the Italian school. I do not think there was any active jealousy towards her on the part of our ballerinas. She was treated with the traditional courtesy given to all foreign stars on a visit to Russia, though some discreet remarks that our dancers were just as good were being made.

One of her *tours de force* was 32 "*fouettés.*" It has since been mastered by other dancers, but then it was only done by Legnani. The step is not unlike an acrobatic exercise and its presentation savours of the circus, by the deliberate suspense preceding it. Legnani walked to the middle of the stage and took an undisguised preparation. The conductor, his baton raised, waited. Then a whole string of vertiginous pirouettes, marvellous in their precision and brilliant as diamond facets, worked the whole audience into ecstasies. Academically, such an exhibition of sheer acrobatics was inconsistent with purity of style ; but the feat, as she performed it, had something elemental and heroic in its breathless daring. It overwhelmed criticism. All the girls, big and small, constantly tried to do the 32 turns. In the evenings on the " other side " one constantly saw figures like turning Dervishes wherever a mirror was available. We turned in the dancing-rooms, turned in the dressing-room, turned in the dormitory, tumbling down after a few turns and beginning again.

Maestro Cecchetti, though not in his youth, still danced

occasionally. With the change of policy at school a senior class was offered to him. The parallel senior class was given to Guerdt; and, to my Father's great satisfaction, Guerdt had chosen me to be eventually his pupil. For the time being, I was not of age to go to him, and worked in an intermediary class.

I worked fanatically in the class and at my evening practice, so much so that the nickname of " self-torturing fakir " was given to me by the girls who preferred recreation of sorts to evening practice. But hard work and fun both fitted into the space of an evening, and I had zest for both. After an early dinner, until supper-time we were left to our own devices, provided we were not too noisy. But it was fairly safe to indulge in a hearty rampage without being caught. Our living quarters were so vast that one could just distinguish at the end of a long enfilade a speck of a governess at her desk. By the time she could reach us she would find demure young maidens sedately promenading round and round the room by twos and threes, their hair smooth, their expression bland and meek. Provided a sentinel was posted at a strategic point, there wasn't much fear of detection, if one had the fancy to sneak into the maids' pantry, there to be regaled on fried potatoes or more often to have one's dreams interpreted by Phymoushka. She had at times need of consulting her dream-book, a much dilapidated, dog-eared volume.

Music, reading, fancy-work or, best of all, making roses out of crinkled paper for the eventual decoration of Easter cakes. Roses bigger than life size, better than real ones. Could real roses ever have had those vibrating golden antennæ or leaves of such varnished splendour?

Those avocations made a happy pattern of the school evenings. Bound with the narrow limits of a couple of hours, our evenings, through a secret known to youth only, had the generous amplitude of unhurried leisure as if time itself kindly waited on our pleasures.

Three pupils of great promise were about to finish school this year, Anna Pavlova amongst them. She was so frail as to seem, in our opinion, much weaker than the other two. The pupils' undiscerning admiration was all for virtuosity : our ideals shaped after a robust, compact figure of Legnani's type. Pavlova at that time hardly realised that in her lithe shape and in her technical limitations lay the greatest strength of her charming personality. Romanticism was not the fashion any more. The very figure of our dancers, as compared with the silhouette of those of half a century ago, clearly showed the reversion of taste from an idealised vision towards the attractions of more material charm.

In pursuit of contemporary ideals our stage lost sight of what may seem a paradox, but is a truth—that the ends of choreographic beauty are not always best served by perfect physical harmony. Some of Taglioni's most exquisite poses had their origin in the fact that her arms were disproportionately long.

Meagreness being considered an enemy of good looks, the opinion prevailed that Anna Pavlova needed feeding up. She must have thought it, too, as she swallowed conscientiously cod-liver oil, the school doctor's panacea, and the aversion of us all. Like the rest of us, she strove to emulate the paragon of virtuosity, Legnani. Luckily for her, Guerdt fully divined the quality of her talent. It pained him to see executed by the delicate limbs of Pavlova what seemed consistent only with the hard set musculature of the Italian dancer. He advised her not to strive after the effects that seemed to endanger her frail structure.

At the time of her début she suffered acutely from what appeared to her to be her shortcomings.

Pavlova was destined to bring back to our stage the forgotten charm of the Romantic ballet of the days of Taglioni.

One day at supper, Anna Ludvigovna, one of the governesses, who was fond of mystification, said that we would have a surprise this day week. Many guesses were made, amongst them that the heir to the throne would be born, and we should have three days' leave. The surprise, however, proved to be nothing so exciting. A lecture on notation of dance movements was to be given by Gorsky. We held it as a little diversion from routine, not knowing yet that the subject was going to be added to our studies. Going to the big rehearsal-room to attend the lecture was an opportunity for me to look at the old engravings that thickly covered the walls. Before the portrait of Istomina I now stood, lost in admiration. Known by heart the stanza of Poushkin : " She flies like down from the breath of Æolus " made me long ago cherish a romantic vision of " superb immaterial Istomina." A sleek, beautiful head in a wreath of roses and nenuphars, with wistful eyes and a smile half lazy, half disdainful, embodied for me a hitherto elusive image. The lecture gave a historic description of several early attempts made to find a way of writing down the movements of the body. The information that the French Abbé Tabourot was the inventor of signs for the notation of the dance puzzled me not a little. Judging by our standards, this secular pursuit was inconsistent with the cloth ; and an irreverent comparison with our priest in his long cassock, trying to compose a treatise on the ballet, was in my mind.

The present system had been evolved by one Stepanoff, now dead. Gorsky continued and completed his work. Stepanoff's system was very complete, but intricate and far from easy. To write down a movement, one had to analyse it anatomically and designate by signs like musical notes the proper action of the joints determining it. Lessons of notation were unpopular with pupils. We called them abracadabra and cabbalistics. That did not prevent my taking an interest in the subject. This work I often did surreptitiously during a drawing lesson. I had no capacity for drawing, and the drawing-master practically gave me up. By the time my colleagues were promoted to the cast of Antinous' head I still plodded over an acanthus leaf. My artistic cravings found an outlet in drawing a sketch map of the world at the geography lessons. From the box of crayons

I chose the brightest, and coloured my map with genuine ardour. Rivers of vivid blue (the suggestion had been given to me by once seeing a coloured post-card of the Lake of Geneva), the valleys emerald green, mountain chains of dragon blood and bright yellow tablelands contrasted vividly with the conventional colouring used by others. If not a complete success, my map, when I presented it to our good-looking, facetious geography master, was a bit of a sensation. " An omelette with spring onions. Ultra modern, but a bright effort," was the judgment.

The inheritance of preceding centuries was not yet entirely spent; anacreontic and mythological ballets, with a liberal dose of allegory and the inevitable apotheosis of gods hoisted by means of a trap-door enveloped in clouds, still remained in the repertoire. The younger pupils appeared, for the most part, in these ballets, forming the suite of some divinity, as cupids, pleasures, laughters, zephyrs. It was deemed important to make the study of mythology a subject apart. We had no books on the subject, and followed notes given by the teacher. From these notes all the peccadilloes of the Olympians were carefully excluded, and, when unavoidable, couched in terms that sometimes led to naïve questions on our part. The important part of the knowledge was the attributes of divinities and heroes, and these we learned to rattle off unhesitatingly.

There was much curiosity and speculation amongst us at this time as to what our new master of history would be like. The pessimists said he would probably be an old fright, and nothing better than our former master, who had resigned recently. These gloomy forebodings were entirely unjustified. From the first appearance, when the inspector of classes introduced the new historian to us, he was pronounced unanimously a " sweet." A new keenness animated the whole class with regard to history, and the tasks were carefully learned. Amicable discussions as to who would be his favourite occupied us till one day he started explaining to us the racial features of different nationalities.

The terra cotta heads of Eskimo, African, Mongol and European and of their ladies were fetched from the shelf where, for the most of the time, they stood gathering dust. From these principal exponents, the historian went on to the Balkan nationalities. Talking about Serbs, he said they were handsome people with dark hair and beautiful eyes, and looking round in search of illustration, "I should say like Mlle. Karsavina." This remark established my position as a favourite in his class. All contention was given up, and the new master allotted to me by general consent. I had to play up to the part assigned, and did it enthusiastically. No rivalry crossed my path, and every opportunity to shine was willingly given by others. Ingenious devices were found to improve the look of my pigtail which, to my mortification, was the shortest and thinnest in our class. On history days a black ribbon double the usual length was ingeniously plaited with my hair so as to swell its volume and add to the length, and the bow adjusted with special care by one or another of the girls. Proofs of my own devotion to the new master were frequently asked for. One of these proofs amounted to a small torture. A challenge was given : " If you love the historian, drink empty this carafe." I gulped down tumbler after tumbler of often tepid water till I felt a positive nausea, but neither this nor my plea that I would get a dropsy would satisfy my tormenters till the last drop was drained. Other girls as well sometimes went through this trial by water for their own objects of adoration, but I was a recognised butt of the girls' wit. The name of " wise fool " stuck to me, and I can see the justification of it in some marked oddities of character, the result of a speculative brain and lack of common sense. I was first in my class ; and, as for compositions, I used to write several versions of the same thing on behalf of friends. At the same time I was helpless and easily baffled in things practical.

Our chaplain, Father Vassily, was said to be a worldly priest, loving company and a good game of cards. Fastidious in his appearance he certainly was. His locks and beard beautifully groomed, his cassock always trim, the hand we had to kiss in church after Benediction white and delicate. He possessed no qualities of the fanatic or the martyr, but his worldly appearance framed a refined mind capable of abstract elevation and exquisitely human. A better teacher of religion could not have been found, inasmuch as he made religion living and lovable and practical to us future worldlings. He exemplified the texts by instances taken out of life and our immediate surroundings, instances often homely and humorous. His talking about the resistance of temptation was a pure gem in its comprehension of a child's world; and, exemplified, could not fail to apply to any serious conflict of conscience. " Suppose, Annoushka "—he always called us by Christian name—" it is on the eve of a holiday. The church bells toll, calling good Christians to prayer; you get up to put on your hat and coat when your Mama calls you : ' Where are you going, my pet ? ' ' I'm off to church, Mother darling.' ' Why not go to church to-morrow morning, Annoushka ? The church won't go away, and I have just made some fresh coffee, and there are cream and buns.' If you go to church," he concluded, " you have conquered the temptation."

A new production of a *Midsummer Night's Dream* was being prepared at the Alexandrinsky Theatre this winter, and I was given the part of Titania's fairy. My love of acting was now gratified beyond any hope. Since my early unaided efforts to act various imaginary situations, that histrionic strain had never left me. On some evenings, free of lessons, a few of us liked to sit in the music-room. It was the haunted room. Though none of us had ever seen any apparition in it, some tenacious legends were repeated about mysterious noises, bony hands tapping at the window-panes from outside, clasping and unclasping their fingers. A girl who had left the school some years before had been alleged, on her entering this room one evening, to have seen a fat, pale man sitting at the piano. On her repeating three times " God remember the good King David and the meekness of his heart," the ghost vanished. We all appealed to King David whenever any punishment was anticipated. On going before Varvara Ivanovna, on being called to answer a lesson insufficiently learned, the words were mentally repeated. From time immemorial, the room had been officially called " Ricci," after a singing-master. The legend had it that the said Ricci committed suicide, and that it was his ghost that haunted the room. " Ricci " was a good setting for telling terrible stories, in which we indulged rapturously. The tale of the finger was especially hair-raising. Its situations were so dramatic as to call for staging, and accordingly one of us went out and reappeared as a phantom bride. The blue shawl was all we could supply towards disguise ; it was pinned under the chin and hung back as a veil. The phantom moved with a dragging step, one arm outstretched as if groping blindly in silence. Suddenly with a cry " Give me back my finger ! " it pounced on one of the hushed audience, at which moment all screamed in genuine terror. It seems now that one finger less or one more ought not to worry somebody who is a corpse, but we had no criticism. We thought the phantom within her rights, claiming back a finger that had been cut off by sacrilegious robbers to secure a valuable ring they could not pull off. This gruesome piece was not the only one we used to perform in " Ricci." We had another lighter plot in our repertoire. We assumed characters, always the same, the wife, her mother and her husband. Without any preconceived plan this improvised comedy never repeated itself ; every time we began it anew, some spontaneous episodes grew out of the eternal conflict. My part was of the henpecked husband, always getting the worst of it. The humiliating part gave me real pangs of bitterness, and I racked my brains in the days between our performances trying to bring about the triumph of the much-abused husband, but, from the nature of the play, it never succeeded.

On December 6th, the Emperor's name day, all three Imperial theatres gave a special matinée for all the schools. Huge samovars steamed outside the stage door. The theatres were an unusually pretty sight on these days, full of children and young people, tiers of boxes tightly packed with girls in uniform dresses, blue, red, pink with white fichus. The parterre was reserved for boys, schools, Lyceum, military and naval cadets, and the gallery for popular schools. Every child received a box of sweets with a portrait of either the Tzar, Tzaritza or Tzarevitch on the lid. In the interval, tea and refreshments were served in several foyers, and the waiting staff wore their gala red livery with the Imperial eagles. Cool almond milk, deliciously fragrant, was a special feature of this treat.

Back at school we compared notes on the respective performances. We were usually given a choice of the theatre, but only few of us wanted to go to the Michailovsky, though the French company performing there was excellent. If the day of the treat fell on one of the two ballet nights, Wednesday or Sunday, we often took part in it. On one of such occasions we were taken in costume to the Imperial box to receive sweets. Alexandra Feodorovna, the Empress and Marie Feodorovna, the Empress Dowager, stood in the drawing-room at the back of the Imperial box and handed us the sweets. We came one by one, curtsied and kissed the hand of both Tzaritzas. The Tzar stood by. He asked, " Who is the little girl that danced the golden fish ? " and I stepped forward and made a deep curtsy. " How is it," he went on, " that the Tzar Maiden's ring was found on you ? " Ivanoushka, the hero of the Russian tale, the plot of which had been worked into the ballet, dives to the bottom of the seas to retrieve the ring which had been swallowed by a golden fish. I wore a fish head modelled in papier mâché, and there was a small opening in it with a lid where the ring was put. I explained how it worked, and bent down my head for him to see. He

76

smiled, " Thank you for explaining, I would have never guessed it." His smile had a charm irresistible. I have heard many times that all who came into his presence felt alike fascinated by his personality. To me it was like being lifted to Paradise.

CHAPTER IX

The Confiscated Wine—Make-up—The Grand Duke Vladimir—Command Performance for the Kaiser—Holiday Escapades with Lydia—Drama or Ballet

THE first week of Lent, when there were no dancing lessons, was reserved for devotions and communion. We fasted during this week and went to church twice a day. The unpleasant smell of linseed oil in which our food was cooked we all hated heartily. The senior girls usually started embroidering either a pall or a carpet for our church, and we juniors were often called in to help, and allowed to sit around at the privileged table while one of us read aloud the lives of saints and martyrs. Twelve volumes of this work were distributed amongst us, and all other reading confiscated during the first week. Afternoon lessons went on as usual, and on the Thursday before the Confession a spirit of Christian humility waxed so strong that of each master we asked to " Forgive us sinners."

At this period I was anæmic and so tired by rehearsals for the school performance that it worried me greatly lest I should fail to show at my best. Mother, alarmed by my thinness, brought me some tonic wine. For a time I successfully hid it, now in my locker, now tucking the bottle under my shawl and secreting it in the school form. I had to give a dose of it to other girls, and the tonic, being sweet, diminished rapidly. The bottle was discovered one day by Mlle. Virshault in my locker. She was positively scandalised with what she concluded to be a vicious propensity. On her next visit, Mother was asked to explain matters, and a compromise was reached. Subject to doctor's approval, the tonic wine was to be kept in the infirmary and doled out to me before meals. I was left without leave on

Sunday, and there the incident ended. I felt a martyr then; but now, in all justice, I must admit there was some foundation for the punishment.

When in dancing dress we pinned up our hair, but it always had to be smooth and well behind the ears. Every attempt to depart from that severe and, we thought, unbecoming fashion was particularly repressed in juniors. The seniors were allowed to raise their hair slightly on top, and on reaching fifteen we usually cut it shorter in front to effect this erection. I had a soft wave in my hair, and found it becoming to push it slightly over the ears. More often than not I was ordered to go and do away with the " bandeaux," and came back as if " licked by a cow," according to our expression. Therefore it was a great concession when, on the eve of the school performance, we were allowed to moisten our hair and make it tightly into many small plaits. Next morning we all were as frizzy as Papuan niggers, but the result was thought satisfactory.

Performance day itself, without lessons or rehearsal, seemed interminably long, and it was a great relief when at six o'clock we were sent to make up and dress. The make-up was a rudimentary one, a spot of rouge on each cheek; powder we could not use, but slabs of magnesia which we crushed, making a great mess round us, were given to whiten the neck and arms. For weeks before this day I treasured a pair of dancing shoes of a Parisian make Mother had bought for me, as the shoes given at school were comparatively rough. I had tried my treasures on now and then very gingerly, trying to keep them immaculate. When I put them on now and made some steps, my heart stood still. The heels slipped out at every jump. I could think of no remedy and began crying. A remedy, though, was at hand. A very efficacious, though not elegant, way was suggested by a senior girl. " Spit in your shoes and don't howl," she said, as she waved her arms gracefully, practising her bit before a mirror.

Adjoining the classrooms was a small theatre, the door leading to it heavily barred and padlocked. It opened to us once a year on the occasion of our annual performance. There was hardly any room in the wings, and we waited for our turn in the classrooms. All the same it was a real theatre, with footlights and several sets of scenery. It was regularly used on Saturdays by the students of the dramatic school. Their classes were on the floor above. We often asked to be sent to the classrooms on Saturday evening under the pretext of finishing some task; and, when escorted and left there, crept down the passage to listen at the keyhole. Nothing much could be heard through the thick baize of the communication door, except some occasional scream in dramatic moments, but the excitement of listening was great.

An abbreviated version of *La Fille mal gardée* had been chosen for our performance. I was in the *corps de ballet* with other small girls. Only old costumes and properties were given out of the theatre wardrobe, and may have looked a bit shabby; but to me the shabbiest costume was a glorious garment, and had the magic property of charming away all self-consciousness. Four of us did a little dance with others grouped round, and this was thought a great distinction. The audience at our performance consisted of parents, masters, artists and both ballet masters, Petipa and Ivanov. To our disappointment none of the Imperial family could come this year. Baron Friedrichs, the Minister of the Court, came instead, and accorded us three days' leave.

The usual high standard of sedate behaviour seemed to be forgotten that night, leniency the order of the day. After the end of the performance, as we stampeded down the passage, no attempt was made to repress our high spirits, and screams of joy on account of leave granted. Crowded by the door of the dancing-room near the passage we watched our audience go away. Some of the artists stopped to say a few words of praise. The great success of that night were three seniors leaving that year, Pavlova, Yegorova and Lubov Petipa. Guerdt came amongst us, looking proud of his pupils, and brought news that these three were given a début after Easter.

On the following year our performance brought me into some prominence. I was given one of the chief parts by Guerdt, whose pupil I became. For the first time it was decided that our performance should be repeated on a big stage, at the Michailovsky. Many so-called *balletomanes*, subscribers and devotees of the ballet, gained admittance that night. The Grand Duke Vladimir, with his family, was present. He was looked up to as a great patron of the arts, and the Grand Duchess, his wife, was President of the Academy of Art. Exceedingly handsome and of commanding presence, he usually spoke very loudly, evidently not conscious of it. " Who is that ? A sparrow, what ? " His spontaneous remark boomed out suddenly when a very small girl came on to do her solo dance. Suppressed laughter ran through the audience, and the sparrow heard it too, and was put off for a second, until a loud " Jolly good ! " put her at ease. After the end, the Grand Duke came down to the school and had supper with us. His gruff kindness encouraged the girls, and they thronged round him and chatted freely. I own I was shy, and became more so as he pointed to me saying, " She will beat them all in time." At supper he called me to sit by him. It had been my turn to say the prayers before the meal, and he now praised me for good elocution, and asked if I was good at everything. I confessed I was rather bad at calligraphy. " You don't say so," he said, and called for a bit of paper. A menu-card was produced, though it announced only cold meat and cream ice : in itself it was an unusual refinement. He made me write my name on it, and looked at my scribble with an expert eye. " I call it unusually good," he said, and told me to put the date as well. That was the first incident of a long series of kindnesses shown to the shy, reserved child that I was, by one who was well known never to swerve in his sympathy.

Ever after, the Grand Duke always sought me out to say a

few words whenever he came near us. It appears that on speaking to the director, he praised me as a future hope, and ordered my photograph to be sent to him. Varvara Ivanovna, to whom the order was transmitted, was in a dilemma how to obey it, and at the same time not turn my head with this unusual favour. Accordingly we were all taken down and photographed. The whole story I learned much later.

In the late spring a Command Performance was given at Peterhof on the occasion of the State visit of the German Emperor. An open-air performance of the ballet *Peleus* had been elaborately prepared. Another spectacle was in readiness to be given at the Theatre in case of a wet evening. On the morning of the performance the news from the Observatory was reassuring, and it was decided to give the ballet. The spot chosen for the performance was a small island on the Peterhof lake. On this island an amphitheatre had been built backed by ruins, constructed in a previous reign, and reminiscent of a picture by Hubert Robert. The stage backed on to the lake, which stretched level with it as far as the eye could see. On a tiny islet out on the lake a high rock had been built up, with a cave of Vulcan in the centre. As the curtain rose, Vulcan, in his forge, was hammering the armour destined to be worn by Peleus. The inside of his cave was weirdly lit; sparks flew from under his hammer. The elements played their part in the general effect: summer lightning from time to time lit the sky, and a faint rumbling of far-away thunder was heard during this scene. The prologue finished with the appearance of Mars and Venus, with their suite on top of the rock. Peleus, kneeling, received his armour and befeathered helmet from the god's hands. Rosy light now flooded the stage, and Thetis surrounded by nymphs was seen gliding over the water. This beautiful illusion had been effected by a simple device—a raft with a mirror surface. Another effective entrance was that of Venus, throned high on a gilt barque and attended by cupids, pleasures, laughters and nymphs. I was one of the cupids. We embarked some way off on the other side of the island behind the amphitheatre, and for a time drifted out of sight. At a given signal, the barge, hung with garlands of flowers, sailed into sight and landed Venus and her cortège on the stage. The arrival of the barge was well timed with the music; the whole of the performance went without a hitch. The transparent stillness of a " white night " cast a spell of unreality all round, that curious sense of detachment from time and place. A more wonderful setting for the fête could hardly have been imagined, and the spectacle would have been fit for the Court of the Roi Soleil himself. One thing, however, worried the performers a good deal. Owing to the damp night air, all our elaborately curled wigs got somewhat dishevelled, but it could hardly have been called a serious drawback to the effect of the whole.

All the details of that day I remember very well. It was a red-letter day, marked by a new experience. Brought to Peterhof early in the morning for the rehearsal, we remained there the whole day and had our meal in a restaurant. The idea of it thrilled us, and we had brightly coloured visions of seeing the smart world. Taken straight to a separate room, where we were served, we did not, however, see much gaiety. After the meal we walked through the park to where the fountains played. It was a hot day, and we had our parasols of brown holland. From what aberration of taste this clumsy article was to me an object of care and pride, I cannot think. Probably because I never had one at home, Mother considering such things superfluous, or because in a novel I had read long ago the heroine " turned her head and drew arabesques on the sand with the point of her parasol " as an answer to the words " my life and happiness are in your little hands." Somehow in these days a parasol was to me a symbol of elegance. I kept it open even under the deep shade of the venerable oaks planted by Peter the Great, and I drew some arabesques as we sat on the bench. At Marly, a small toy palace, the kindly custodian took us to see a square pond full of gold-fish. He rang a hand-bell and the fish splashed up for crumbs.

* * * * *

At home there were preparations on foot for going to the country. The blue set of the sitting-room, under holland covers, was crowded into one corner. The dining-table, with all the sewing paraphernalia, had been pulled out of the recess and dominated the room. The sun poured freely through the dismantled windows. Father said repeatedly he preferred the windows bare, without the " rags and hangings." " Really, Platon, you ought to live in barracks," Mother exclaimed impatiently. She had spent much of her time in crocheting a set of window-curtains in Meander pattern. Every summer the curtains were taken down, washed, dipped in weak coffee and stored away till winter. Besides Aunt Katia, helping with sewing, another member of Father's family was in attendance on Mother. I never could separate the appearance of Uncle Vladimir from some mysterious goings on. After some hushed instructions from Mother, Uncle Vladimir would depart on an errand, with a bulky parcel under his arm. With the same air of mystery, he would come back without his bundle, but with some money he discreetly remitted to Mother. The mystery, though, could not deceive anybody. I knew Uncle's errand meant that some of the winter wardrobe had gone to a pawn-shop.

On the first of May we were still in town. Father thought it a proper day for the release of his birds. He was fond of siskins and their gay chirruping ; he also kept a starling whom he taught to whistle tunes and say " The Christ is risen." In the spring he always let his birds out.

> " Winged songsters, my airy prisoners,
> As up you soared your silvery notes
> Prayed to heaven for me,"

Father declaimed as he wrapped up the cages. Our destination being Ekaterinhof, we started early. " By fancy prompted, although not by need compelled," quoted Mother. " Why trundle all that way and have your ribs elbowed by the crowds of workmen ? As if you could not let the birds free in the summer garden. Look at that." From the window we could see that the horse-trams running on the opposite side of our canal were overcrowded. Everyone was going to a popular fête with *carrousels* given at Ekaterinhof that day. But I would not be put off : my heart was bent on this expedition, and accordingly we started with our cages. We came to the edge of the park, where it thinned down to a struggling group of aspens and weeping birches. " Here is an ideal spot," said Father. " The water is close by." He let me open the siskin's cage. The little bird ceased hopping ; timid and mistrustful at first it stood still for a moment, as if holding its breath. Then, with a sudden shrill chirrup, darted out swiftly. The starling looked wise and deliberate. He crept out on the door, warily looked round, his head on one side, and flew off decorously without hurry.

My sworn friend, Lydia Kyasht, came with us to Log. Being an orphan, she had no regular home to go to, and Mother gladly accepted the charge of her during holidays. Lydia had an inexhaustible inspiration for pranks and the irrepressible spirits of a young puppy. Neither scolding nor punishment she ever resented. Nor did it affect her very much. Her good nature and real affection for us all always disarmed Mother, and only on one occasion did she provoke Father's rare and violent wrath.

After early dinner at noon we two enjoyed unrestricted freedom. Nobody ever worried as to where we were, as long as we came home in time for supper. There was, however, one restriction ; we were not to use the boat without either Father or Lev going with us. The boat was padlocked on a heavy chain, but the key hung ostentatiously on the nail by the kitchen door. One day, when Father and Mother were both away from home, Lydia saw her opportunity. Possessed of the key, we went down to the lake and rowed ourselves to the other side, five kilometres off, to pay a visit to some friends. The initiative was Lydia's; and, though cautious at the start, I fell into the spirit of the adventure. We enjoyed our visit greatly, had a large tea, games of leap-frog and corners, and set off rather late. The wind was now against us, and as the dusk gathered we still struggled, not yet half-way across. The boat leaked, and we often stopped to bail it out; in doing so, one oar slipped down into the water. With the remaining one we manœuvred desperately, trying to rescue the other. The moment was of great agony. "Kneel down and pray," stipulated Lydia. She always professed a belief in my sanctity, a belief born in her mind when at school I had a badly blistered toe and would not give up working. "She is a saint," repeated Lydia, relating the incident to my Mother, "and a martyr." In the meantime some anxiety had been felt at home at our not being back for supper. Inquiries had been made; and, on somebody's mentioning that we had been seen setting off in the boat, a great alarm started. A rescue party set off and found us still taking turns in chasing the oar and praying. The scolding we got was such as to stop us from ever repeating the experience, but our spirit was undaunted. Its next manifestation was our "Planter's" exploit. This was another emanation of Lydia's fertile brain. We were out gathering wild strawberries on a hot day. "Let us take off our clothes for coolness," suggested Lydia. Our large straw hats we kept on, and both agreed we looked like negroes on the plantation. The little wood was close to the road, and we were seen by a lady neighbour who happened to be driving home from the station. Greatly shocked, she went to Mother and complained of our offensive behaviour. It was Mother's turn now to take us in hand, and she did it most efficiently by forbidding us to go beyond the garden. During the enforcement of this measure I felt very miserable. Luckily it was removed in a few days, and Mother allowed us out on "parole." I felt happy again. Those were halcyon days. An almost pagan love for woods and open spaces grew stronger in me every day. I used to forget time and lose the sense of my identity in a delicious drowsiness.

The country was safe. No tramps were seen on the roads, no robberies heard of. There were bears in the forest all round ; but, according to the peasants, they fed on oats, and were harmless and even timid during summer, except for the she-bear, who might attack if she had her young with her. One day Lydia and I wandered far into the woods after mushrooms. I had just found a whole family of them and knelt down to pick them before a group of trees. The trees clustered together so as to form a kind of bower. Within it, something like a gigantic ant-heap caught my eye. I called to Lydia, and she came to look at it. Suddenly the ant-heap moved, and against the opening between the trees we saw a head with pricked ears. I will never forget our wild run. Fortunately, Lydia had a sense of direction, and we soon came to the road. When home, we breathlessly related our escape. Lydia professed to have heard the sound of broken brushwood as the bear followed us ; it was more than I did. Highly incensed by Lev's sceptical attitude, she swore she had seen the marks of a bear's paw on the road. Father said it must have been a year-old bear, who is usually left at home to mind the babies while the parents go in search of food. The peasants call them *pestun*, which means a male nurse. " The *pestun* is not actually ferocious," Father explained, " unless interfered with." We both resented the minimising of what we thought a terrible danger, Lydia especially whom Lev, by his sly remarks, could work into a frenzy of incoherent argumentation. They were always at war ; the daily skirmishes over lessons of spelling, of which she stood badly in need, were entertaining to witness. It was not easy to pin Lydia down to a task ; she apprehended the approaching danger and displayed great cunning in keeping out of her mentor's way.

Once Lev locked her in the room over a task of copying so many times a word of five letters in which she had made three mistakes. When, with facetious admonitions, Lev unlocked the door, he found the room empty. His rebellious pupil had long ago jumped out of the window, leaving a defiant message : " Lev, silly ass, I despise him," scrawled on a bit of paper. Unfortunately for the sting of that invective, the word " despise " had also several spelling mistakes in it ; so Lev had the last word after all. Already, then, he had that nimble wit and direct power of spontaneous retort which, in after-life, made him a formidable opponent to his learned colleagues. Though he was then, or thought himself to be, a free thinker, there was not a trace of priggishness in him. Totally free of superstition himself, he would earnestly discuss with gipsies their witchcraft and black magic, being always inclined to humour rather than to combat errors.

It was this summer that Mother's occasional heart attacks became very alarming. They were usually preceded by days of great moral depression. One particularly bad attack may have been brought on by heavy thundery heat. Dry storms raged far away. Of evenings the sky trembled with summer lightning. It was harvest time. In distant fields some stacks caught fire. The smell of juniper from burning forests like heavy incense rose thick and suffocating. No rain came to relieve the tension of many days. One evening we sat at supper on the balcony when, with a sudden, piercing cry, Mother fell down from her seat. Father carried her in and laid her on the bed. She now tossed in a fit of hysteria, throwing off the cold towels we were applying to her head, now would lie exhausted, moaning. The attack lasted for hours. It was terrible to witness. At one moment I lost my head completely ; shutting my ears, I rushed out and ran wildly, not knowing what I was doing. An elderly couple, our neighbours, were just coming in to have an evening chat. They stopped me. By this time I was quite incoherent. The old lady led me off. She gave

me some valerian drops and then went into our house to see if
any help might be given. She returned to fetch me when
Mother came round after her fit.

Both our neighbours belonged to the theatrical world.
Yurkovsky himself was one of the producers of the dramatic
stage, she a retired actress, once celebrated. Her husband's
devotion wrought an unfading romance round their life. The
bucolic names of Philemon and Baucis, by which my Mother
christened them, could not have been better applied. I have
met with some beautiful old people before, but Maria Pavlovna
was the unique example I ever knew of a pretty old woman.
Malicious sparks in her eyes and a suspicion of moustache over
a tiny pouting mouth had the grace of youth at once roguish
and demure. No hectic struggle to cheat time can ever have
entered her life; her old age was serene and dignified. Her
dress was reminiscent of the early 'sixties, and she wore her grey
hair piled up in plaits like a crown, after the fashion of her
youth. Her husband taught his little grandchild to address her
as " Beautiful grannie."

Yurkovsky clearly thought me on the wrong track in choosing
dancing. His interest in me dated from my acting in *Midsummer
Night's Dream*. I often called at their house at Log. The old
man usually called me to his study and made me recite to him.
I knew no end of poetry, and he left the choice to me. He sat
in his chair, a tall, slightly bent figure, with a long grey beard,
and listened to me, his eyes shut. After a slight pause, he
would speak and explain to me how to modulate my voice.
" You ought to be on the dramatic stage," he frequently said
to me. " There is undoubtedly a natural quality of lyrism in
you ; " and then he added, " You would serve a more intellectual
art." We sometimes engaged in long talks. He opened my
eyes to many of my fallacies ; one of them was that acting, to
be great, must be inborn. He shook his head. " I know that
is current coin of the stage, but it is not true. Ristori never
conceived a single part by herself. It is the power of assimila-

tion that is essential to a great actor, from whatever source he receives his inspiration." This remark of Yurkovsky about serving a more intellectual art, though used with all gentleness, unsettled me greatly. I was sad to feel my chosen art needed an apology. I could not yet understand the infinite possibilities of the whole art of dancing. I merely felt the sheer joy of movement and the determination to persevere. Instinct was to hold me on my path, till understanding came to prove the path a right one.

Mother often said Lev took after her, and I was " Father's daughter all through." Now about to finish the gymnasium, Lev was shaping as a serious scholar. His intellectual strain and his wit Mother maintained to have come through her inheritance. She spoke with pride of her great Uncle Homiakoff, poet, religious philosopher and one of the great leaders of the Panslavist movement. She fondly believed Lev was to perpetuate his fame.

On the low shelves of the book-cabinet in town, amongst cardboard boxes kept, with other odd rubbish, on the principle " You never know when it will come in handy," I had found one day several of Mother's notebooks. Entitled " Pensées et maximes " they contained observations, reflections on events, criticisms of books read. Most of them were written in French. It was not affectation ; the pupils of the " Smolny Institute," where Mother had been brought up, addressed " Maman," as the directress was called, in French, it being the established language for conversation. If now Mother could not afford an intellectual pursuit, the habit of thought had been formed in her. She kept singularly apace with the interests of Lev and the young friends he now often brought to the house.

CHAPTER X

Cartwheels—Prince Volkonsky—Methods of Rehearsal, Guerdt—
Progress—" Little Lopokova "—Kosloff—Johannsen—My First
" Love Affair "

THE twenty-sixth of August, a week before the classes
started, was the day usually appointed for getting back
to school. The theatres reopened on the first of September.
Apart from rehearsals and morning practice, there was not much
to do during this week. Some work, though, was distributed
to us—hemming handkerchiefs or unpicking the seams of blue
kashmir dresses that had passed their prime and had to be turned.
A new dress was given to us every year, but only to be worn
on Sundays. For everyday wear we had the old one neatly
rearranged and lengthened, but slightly faded.

Our morning practice by ourselves often turned into ram-
pagious games whenever the governess left the room. A smart
feat which we tried one after another with varied success, was
to get far back into the corner of the room, run across and leap
horizontally on to the piano in an impeccable arabesque, as we
had seen the ballerinas caught in a final leap by a partner. Lydia
had the wild idea of making some " lifts " with me. An
ignominious fall, when she first dropped me and then fell on
top, was the result, as well as my bruised knees and elbows. I
had a trick of my own. " ' Tooska,' show your acrobatics,"
the girls urged me, whereupon I turned cartwheels and walked
on my hands. This conversion of my name, I remember,
shocked Varvara Ivanovna. When she overheard my being
called so, " For shame, maidens," she would say, " hers is such
a pretty name. Tooska ! Just like a mongrel puppy." The

name stuck to me nevertheless. " Toossinka " was the affectionate modification of it.

In 1898 Prince Serge Volkonsky became Director of the Imperial Theatres. The grandson of the exile Volkonsky, that alone surrounded him with a halo in my eyes. We all were curious to see the new Director, and thought the chance would be one of the dress rehearsals of the Opera or Ballet to which we usually were taken. We did not have to wait long before we saw him. One morning, another girl and I sat at the piano in the round room. A volume of overtures for four hands in front of us, we struggled through the " Matrimonio Segreto," when a sound of the opened door made me turn my head. Volkonsky very swiftly walked in, making for the opposite door leading to the dancing-rooms. Something impetuous was in his tall slim form as he moved determinedly, his head slightly bent on one side. The elongated elegance of his shape, his sleek head with a parting *à l'anglaise*, in my spontaneous admiration I could only compare them to the tailors' plates. He stepped short and bowed in answer to our curtsy. The music on the stand caught his attention. He fixed his eyeglass, " ' Cimarosa,' I see ; please go on." I noticed a slight nervous twitch in his face, and his exquisite hand as he stood by the piano lightly tapping on the lid. " It should be taken in a quicker tempo, when you have learned it," he said and then asked if there were any dancing-classes in progress. Answered in the affirmative, he passed on to where the junior girls were now at work.

To show how unusual to us girls it was so suddenly to come into direct touch with the head of the theatres, I must explain that Vsevolojsky, the former director, never showed any interest in the school. A distant imposing figure, we only saw him from afar at dress rehearsals, surrounded by the numerous officials attached to him, or in his box during performances. Whether I concluded rightly, I do not know, but I think his feeling towards the ballet must have been as towards some very narrow speciality ; and so our artistic education was entirely left to masters, who presumably knew their job. Nothing more was required of the ballet than a perpetuation of tradition and a high level of execution. From time immemorial the ballet had been surrounded by a luxury of *mise-en-scène*. Vsevolojsky, a great student of the eighteenth century himself, did all the designs for the costumes of the *Sleeping Beauty*. They were admirable in their documentary fidelity to the period of the Roi Soleil. With all that, the ballet at that time was accepted as more of an amiable toy, than as an art on equal terms with others.

At home, where a little gossiping newspaper was read for reason of its giving the fullest accounts of the ballets, I got some idea of the budget allowed to the threatre. Much indignation had been recently expressed by that paper concerning 40,000 roubles, a sum enormous then, spent on the production of a new ballet. Two new ballets were produced every year with great lavishness; real heavy silks, velvet of the best quality, hand embroidery were used for costumes. Stencilling was not thought of yet. Our chief costumier, Kaffi, at times found some ingenious economical devices; for instance, the ostrich feathers in the *Sleeping Beauty* were all made of wool. They looked rich and even more theatrical than the real ones. The head-dresses and wigs thus ornamented were heavy to wear, but artists did not grumble against them. At that time the costume of a dancer considerably hampered the ease of movements. We wore tight corsets, stiff boned bodices, packets of tarlatans coming well below the knee.

Our new Director often came to watch our lessons. Music, declamation, and pantomime he paid special attention to. He was a fine musician himself. Twice a week Guerdt gave us lessons in pantomime. He taught us by his own example. He first acted a scene himself, and then let us repeat it, correcting us as we did it. We acted scenes from actual ballets in the repertoire and from the old ones that lived in the memory of our master through either the glory of their interpreters or because these scenes offered an opportunity of a highly dramatic or of a comic situation. Few, if any, accessories were used. The main features of the scenery were easily supplied by benches and chairs. Two chairs with a space between would represent a door ; a bench would be placed to be a couch, if absolutely required by the situation. As for properties, they were imaginary. We poured wine, plucked flowers, stabbed, span, knocked at the door—all without accessories. The movements necessary for these simple actions were to my mind the most difficult to find, the dramatic ones easy enough. We were constantly corrected by the master. " You don't write a letter by simply wobbling your hand. Press, form the characters." Or, "That is not the way to hold a rose." Out of his pocket would come a handkerchief. Folding it in imitation of a flower, he gazed lovingly at the piece of cambric, and rapturously inhaled the imaginary fragrance. No theoretical explanation, no attempt to define a law determining the means of expression were given to us. A purely intuitive actor, Guerdt was hardly conscious himself of the two quite different elements of the present ballet acting. Mimed narrative had by now established itself firmly. A scene acted in a past tense, in which the actor had to explain what took place off the stage, necessarily called for description or entirely conventional gestures. In other ballets such as *Giselle*, *La fille mal gardée*, the action came spontaneously from the core of the plot. It unfolded itself from the situation by means of emotional gestures or acts direct to the purpose.

Pantomime lessons as given by Guerdt were an admirable example, but not a teaching based on any clearly understood principle. I think that consideration must have been in Volkonsky's mind when he, frequently present at our lessons, set us some problems to work out. The little plots he gave us were simple and circumstantial. From a skeleton of a plot we had to imagine the situation and devise the action. Without an example before us we often failed. Here Volkonsky would prompt us by suggestions : " You see the villain going off the stage; his malignant smile convinces you of his villainy. Turning to your Mother you say—' it is he that has stolen my letter '—how will you do that ? Look at the person you are addressing and point to the one of whom you speak. In a gesture of accusation, turn down the palm of your hand. The contrary will imply invitation, demand, address." By these remarks he made us depend on the understanding of the principle of acting and not merely on copying a demonstrated exercise.

I was going to be fifteen in February. I now enjoyed all the privileges of the seniors, except that of belonging to the select set of Pensionnerskaya. The dressing-room of the seniors was so called. Its window looked on Theatre Street. Seen from the street, our windows, divided by twin columns, with wreathed and garlanded metopes, were perhaps the most beautiful feature of the building. The harmonious pile took the whole length of the street. But to us inside only the frieze of the opposite building, identical to ours, and a bit of sky were visible. Our windows were all of frosted glass except the top panes. When the first rumbling of wheels broke the snow-hushed silence of winter, we could not resist the longing to behold the signs of spring, be it only some trays of geraniums carried shoulder-high by hawkers. One could get a glimpse of the street by the acrobatic trick of standing on another girl's shoulders.

Pensionnerskaya was large and high-ceilinged. Bare but for a tall mahogany cheval glass, it was nevertheless a cosy place in winter because of the always lit stove. Built-in wardrobes lined the walls. The inmates of Pensionnerskaya enjoyed the privilege of an extra ten minutes after the curfew bell.

The closer the time drew to my fifteenth birthday, when I was to live at school altogether, the more I treasured my holidays. They were spoilt only by my dread of the approaching separation. No one suspected the intensity of my feelings. From my undemonstrative ways Mother concluded that life away from home made me a stranger to their interests and worries at home. She thought me aloof. She often said, " Lev is the one that understands all I have to go through."

We were living through hard times. Father was singularly unfit for the increasing competition in his profession. He abhorred modern dances. *Pas d'Espagne, Hongroise, Pas de quatre* became the fashion, but he still kept his pupils on lancers, minuets and polkas. No wonder that younger teachers superseded him and that he had but few lessons now. One permanent employment he still retained ; twice a week he gave lessons at the Charity School of Prince Oldenburg. The salary was meagre, but continuous. The school was right outside the town at Lesnoy, and it took Father nearly all day to get there. In mid-winter Father dreaded his trip. The conveyances were slow. A street car pulled by horses would take him outside the town ; there he changed for a steam tram. In spite of some straw put underneath the benches his feet grew numb with cold. What he dreaded most was coming back. His stiff shirt quite moist with perspiration, a tail coat being *de rigueur* for a dancing master, he felt the cold intensely. He used to come home quite chilled and famished. A glass of vodka warmed him, but from constant exposure he contracted a permanent cold. He used to sneeze so many times that we lost count. He told us how once in the street he was obliged to stop in one of his prolonged fits of sneezing. A passer-by, attracted by the unusual number and might of his sneezes, stopped to look at him. " Bless you," he said politely. The sneezes continued, " Bless you," he repeated. " Oh, bless you, bless you, bless you. Are you never going to stop." The polite stranger could not wait till the end of the sneezing fit. Saturday was one of the Lesnoy days, which meant I saw very little of Father during my leave. He was growing deaf, and Mother sometimes got irritated at having to repeat her words. He did not like to own to his weakness, and said that most people with a musical ear were blunt to ordinary sounds.

Baboushka now lived with us. She was over seventy and

visibly failing. But her amazing vitality had not been lowered by age; she was the first to stir in the house, and late at night one could still hear her moving about in her room. The sound of drawers being pulled out and shut invariably indicated that Baboushka was looking for something. Most of her time was spent in searching. Her few belongings played hide and seek with her. Great had been her annoyance when she had to miss the solemn occasion of a prize distribution in Lev's school. Lev had been awarded a gold medal, but Baboushka could not see her favourite receiving it; she had hopelessly mislaid her best chignon, and fastidious as she was about her appearance, she would not show in public without it. " Here I put it," she repeated, coming to the same place over and over again, expecting the lost object to be there. " You have had your play; send it back my way," she often addressed the invisible forces whom she suspected of playing mischief on her.

When a vacancy at the widows' house at the Smolny Convent was offered to her, Baboushka went eventually to live there. Years later I went there to see Baboushka. The white and gold beauty of Smolny soothed one's aching thought of destitute old age finishing in an alms-house. In the big church, graceful as a festive hall, there was a felicity almost secular. Pensionnaires' rooms opened on the vast corridor with a fine gallery round the top. Baboushka shared a room with a relative of hers, Aunt Olimpiada, a giantess with a small birdlike head and a thin little voice. In a loud " aside," Baboushka told us that Olimpiada had just sold her Voronej estate and had heaps of money in her stocking. It was the last stage of Baboushka's life. She remains in my memory a singularly consistent figure. As in a book, the events of her life grouped round her into patterns of romantic interest. Penury left no taint on her childlike simplicity.

*   *   *   *   *

I was now in the class of Guerdt. I like to dwell on that time, a spring time amongst the seasons of my calling. To my beloved master, I owe a debt of never ending gratitude.

Ephemerae of a brief summer, great dancers leave no record but a pious legend. Only careful hands can transmit the intangible treasure ; only the inspired tend the spark of reminiscence till it flames again. Guerdt was a chosen instrument for handing down to us the wealth of the art of dancing, such wealth as he had gathered during his long career. He had witnessed in his youth a romantic florescence never to be repeated in its pristine vigour. Guerdt was not searching for new ways ; he was a jealous guardian of a glorious tradition.

The most interesting part of his lesson began when the necessary routine of exercises had been got through. He then worked the steps into short consecutive dances. Often he reconstructed the parts of old ballets long gone from the stage. Great dancers of the past lived again, evoked by him. Some kind of spell there was for me in coming into the succession of the great art revealed through my Master. When, the lesson finished, a maid would come in with a large handbell, it was unwillingly we trooped out all steaming hot, looking forward to to-morrow, when perhaps " the dance with a shadow," the Masterpiece of Cerito, would be gone through again.

My last two years at school were devotional and happy. Full of a single purpose, every day revealed to me new heights to strive for. It was not conscious of restricted freedom. Unlike other girls, I did not feel those were years struck out of life. The time in front of me seemed short ; apprehension rose sometimes that it might not be long enough to achieve all I wanted.

Every Sunday afternoon, we, the seniors, were taken to the Alexandrinsky Theatre. We liked dramas where one could have a good cry. In Pensionnerskaya, where I belonged now, we liked to act what we had seen, imitating the actors very closely.

Lessons in elocution and acting were given to the seniors by

an actor of the dramatic theatre. We chiefly kept to monologues and poetry. Sometimes he gave us some scene to act.
In my Father's time there was no separate dramatic school.
Pupils of the theatrical school were trained according to their
evinced capacity, though dancing was compulsory for all.
Slavina, one of the leading mezzo-sopranos, had been trained
for the ballet first. Singing classes we also followed, though
there was no hope of another Slavina amongst us. For the
examination in the spring we now were preparing nothing less
ambitious than *Mary Stuart*. The classroom, crowded with
desks, was found inconvenient ; so eventually we went to the
Little Theatre for our dramatic lessons. There was a little
foyer at the back of the auditorium, on the walls of which hung
frames with photographs of all the pupils who had finished the
school. From these photographs one could see that our dress
remained for ever unaltered, only the coiffures being different ;
the hair crowned on top of the head and a fringe was a much
prettier fashion than our hair scraped behind the ears.

The whole school was usually taken to the dress-rehearsals of
operas, forgoing afternoon classes. *Freischütz* was being
revived this year. The scene in the wolves' valley, where Caspar
comes to cast his bullets, especially appealed to us. To repro-
duce the stage tricks—thunder, lightning, flight of evil birds—
we had no adequate means. All the same Pensionnerskaya
being large and we full of invention, we got up a performance
to our great satisfaction. " First," sings Caspar, the get-up
being skirts gathered and tucked into velveteen boots in imitation of trousers. " First, first, first," echoed voices from various
cupboards. The same effect of reverberating echo is repeated
at the casting of the second bullet. " Third," echo roars.
Towels, boots, articles of clothing shower from the cupboards,
representing the flight of evil birds. Thunder rumbles as the
iron stove is banged with tongs and pokers. Witches creep
out with shrill cries. The wolves' valley was only played when
the governess was at the " other side." At times the din and

roar would reach her. According to who was on duty there would be either mild remonstrance or lost marks. Marks lost for behaviour meant that one might be called before Varvara Ivanovna for a thorough rating. For repeatedly lost marks we were left without theatre, and the most dreaded punishment of all was the dress of ticking. I was left without theatre for a small offence. I had pushed Lydia's head into a pail of soapy water left after the washing of the floor. Not that she minded it very much; she even asked my forgiveness for causing me to be punished. Yet at the time she could not help screaming; the governess coming in, I had to confess. I missed the theatre sadly. The school looked deserted on Sunday afternoon. The play given was *Treachery and Love*, where I knew there would be ample occasion for emotion and a hearty sob.

When the school year was terminated, the senior pupils moved to a little country house on the Kamenny Ostrov. On summer evenings the islands teemed with smart carriages. All that remained in town of the world of fashion thronged in summer to the Elagin Ostrov, an island approached by shady drives and opening in a point to a sudden wide view of the gulf. People went there to watch the sunset. Right at the bridge leading to Elagin, where all the carriages crossed, stood our wooden mansion. A two-storied barrack, it turned its back to the fashionable villas. All the windows looked into the garden. High palings barricaded the house on all sides. Like a comic little stronghold of innocence, there it stood, shabby and demure at the very gate of worldliness. Moving there simply meant a drive of about three-quarters of an hour. The accommodaton of our *datcha* was very simple, just sufficient. The largest room, not very big at that, had a mirror and bars. Every morning we practised in it. Every day one of us took the lead in setting steps. We were tenacious, striving to overcome technical difficulties. The remainder of the morning we sat on the covered verandah; while one of us read aloud, others unpicked the old blue dresses. This summer we read the history of the

Middle Ages and the Renaissance. The book gave a very complete picture of that period, but all I remember now is that the plaited coiffures of Florentine ladies were often made of silk thread. The two hours of educational reading was not, of course, our own device. The governess usually sat with us, doing some handiwork of her own.

The Islands, fashionable in the cool of the evening, were deserted in the afternoons. So of course we were taken for walks in the afternoons, and we met not a soul on our walks, except policemen, a few prams, and occasionally some timid lovers who could be seen keeping to the shady paths. We invariably walked by twos and were kept to an unbroken step. One day we came across a man sitting on a bench. He rose at our approach; a shabby drunken figure reeled towards us. " Goodness," it ejaculated, " I thought the blue Cuirassiers marching—only girls."

Far more attractive than the well-kept park of the Elagin was to me the interior of the Kammeny Ostrov. Its alleys even at noon were bathed in subdued green light. Green were the ponds, green the canals smothered by weeds. Melancholy looked the dwellings far apart, most of them nondescript; but here and there a fine façade, a verandah with wooden pilasters half hidden by overgrown lilac bushes, stood resigned and pathetic, waiting for decay to set in. Life had ebbed away from this once fashionable spot. The opulent new villas stood by the riverside.

*   *   *   *   *

In the autumn of 1901 I received the " white dress "* and entered the upper remove of Guerdt's class. Our group worked in the big rehearsal-room which communicated with our wing by a bridge. This passage was cold in winter, and

* The junior pupils wore brown ; pink was given as a mark of distinction and the white dress was the highest of all.

to traverse it we pulled our velveteen boots over our dancing shoes. The rehearsal room was much larger than any of our dancing classes, and the rake of the floor corresponded exactly with that of the stage. I took it as a good omen that my place at the bar was underneath the portrait of Istomina. My master was pleased with me. " There is a new something in your work," he said once, " it becomes artistic." He conferred an unprecedented distinction on me by adding a plus after the highest mark he gave me at the end of each week. " Your future is safe ; you are a lucky one," the girls used to say.

The last years at school were a foretaste of the future career. Though the senior girls appeared much less in ballet performances than the small ones, we were known from the school display ; we were talked of amongst the artists, and the coming out of promising pupils was anticipated. Within our school world, reputation shaped already. I forgot the pain when our dentist said to me : " Have patience ; a future prima ballerina must have pretty teeth." Amongst ourselves we often talked of the future with youthful optimism. We distributed among ourselves all the best parts. Ethics forbade to choose a part that another girl had claimed first. It had been decided amongst us that Lydia should have *Coppelia*. I was assigned the dramatic ballets—a futile and happy occupation. We stood in the anteroom of the stage, waiting to step in and conquer. No thought of difficulties on the way to success ever crossed our minds.

One out of the group of the small pupils given now into my care was little Lopokova. The extreme emphasis she put into her movements was comic to watch in the tiny child with the face of an earnest cherub. Whether she danced or talked, her whole frame quivered with excitement ; she bubbled all over. Her personality was manifest from the first, and very lovable.

A pupil of the Moscow School, Theodore Kosloff, had been transferred to our school for his last year's training. There was an occasional exchange of artists between Moscow and Petersburg. A rivalry and a schism existed between the two schools.

In Petersburg's ballet, the opinion prevailed that at Moscow the dancers sacrificed tradition to cheap effects—" dancing to the gallery," it was termed. We were reproached with being too academic and stale. A certain difference in execution was obvious. Less correct, at times untidy in their poses, the Muscovites displayed more vigour than our dancers. At the same time, contrary to our principle of making any difficulty appear easy, they emphasised every *tour de force*. The main feature of the male dancers of our stage was an extreme simplicity and reserve. They put themselves deliberately in the shade, leaving to the ballerina the display of graces and smiles. Their Moscow rivals lacked all restraint ; forcible expression, too elaborate grace and overacting characterised their dance.

Kosloff was given an informal début at our small theatre. I had been chosen to do a *pas de deux* with him. Though my good luck created no jealousy, it was a shock to the girls finishing school that year. I still had two years more. The *pas de deux* chosen for us was from *The Wilful Wife*, an old ballet once danced by Zucchi, entirely gone from the present repertoire. Curiously enough, in that first serious test I did not feel any stage fright. An overwhelming excitement surged in me. The moments before my appearance were intolerable in their suspense. I was told that I went deadly pale in spite of the rouge on my cheeks. There was nothing unusual in this. When, after a strenuous class, the girls became the colour of beetroot, I only went paler than before. Pallor was a sign of emotion with me as well.

Christian Petrovitch Johannsen was present at this performance. He was a very old man close on ninety, blind in one eye. Johannsen held a class for the dancers, a *classe de perfection*. A respect amounting to veneration surrounded him. On that occasion he could not be trusted to find his way across the building. After the end, I saw him leaving the stalls supported under each arm by the brothers Legat. My father was in the audience. He went to greet his former master. Afterwards

Father repeated to me the words spoken by the old man. " Leave this child to herself, do not teach her. For God's sake don't polish her natural grace; even her faults are her own." In these words the glorious veteran blessed me on the threshold of my career. Two years later I became his pupil.

The criticism of Maestro Cecchetti had been reported to me by the girls of his class : " *Una bella fanciulla,*" he said, " but still a weakling."

At least a month before the performance my master started training me. He spared neither time nor zeal. Every afternoon he came expressly for me. What he gave me was far more than a mere technical training; with loving care he tendered the frail fabric of a yet unconscious temperament. He had now a new manner towards me. An affectionate adieu took the place of the impartial nod of a master dismissing his pupil. Such apparently trivial details as the warm shake of the hand or occasional pat on the shoulder he gave me at parting moved a world of gratitude and affection in me. A timid neophyte could not more reverence the high priest at the door of a temple than I did this beloved master. No words will adequately describe the sweet delirium of that phase. The days of Lent, with the ever vibrating sound of church bells; the heart meek and devotional; the ascent of light of the approaching spring; the opening petals of a new-born ecstasy; a fading, receding sense of reality; an ever-increasing enchantment. I stood in a luminous world; a magic circle closed round me.

My first " love affair " was an immediate result of this informal début. Easter followed close on the school performance. We had three days' leave. The nervous and physical strain of the last month had undermined my strength. A slight cold, that otherwise would have passed off easily, made me very ill. On my return to school I was sent straight to the infirmary. My illness was not infectious. Girls ran in to see me from time to time when coming to the dispensing-room. Lydia even managed to sneak off unnoticed during intervals between lessons.

She was fearless, and very seldom got caught. On one of her visits she triumphantly told me that Kosloff was in love with me. He had danced with her at the ballroom class and charged her with messages for me. How she enjoyed her rôle of confidant. She devised a scheme of correspondence between us and carried it on *con amore*. The rehearsal room had a gallery along the upper row of windows. The gallery served as communication with the boys' quarters. From the gallery there was an access to the stairs leading into an ante-room, usually empty in the morning. There, under a small water tank Lydia decided that the letters should be put. She managed to fetch them. How she could do it under the vigilant eye of a governess I cannot understand to the present day. She did, and revelled in it. Half a dozen letters on both sides, an Easter egg, a bunch of carnations, two or three meetings at home in the following summer, constitute the brief story of our romance. I was still at school when Kosloff became a member of the company. No mention was made, when we met in after years, of our childish infatuation.

On the plea of acute anæmia following my illness, Mother obtained leave for me to spend the summer at home. She wanted to take me to the seaside, a plan which carried great weight with Varvara Ivanovna. But Mother could not fulfil her plan. Father had found work at a private summer theatre in town. He could not go away; and keeping two establishments was beyond our means. Mother took a little villa in the " Old Village." The front houses stood on the bank of the Neva, opposite the Elagin Ostrov. Further away from the river squalid dilapidated villas stretched along the dusty road, their gardens profaned by heaps of rubbish and washing hanging on the lines. We lived in the back row, close to the cabbage fields. Though islands were near by, just over the bridge, Mother advised me not to go there, because of the risk of being seen by the school; the deception about my being at the seaside had to be kept up.

Lev spent most of his time over his books in the attic. He plied me with serious reading, being greatly worried with, to his standard, my insufficient education at school. He called it " penny learnings." I mildly accepted philosophic essays, liked the Iliad in beautiful translation, but revolted against a popular astronomy that Lev tried to force on me. He had bought a second-hand rusty telescope and occasionally climbed up on the roof to watch the stars. Astronomy, with its string of inconceivable figures, bored me; Lev's persuasions left me cold. Our tastes met over a series of monographs of painters and draughtsmen. Amongst these the illustrations of fairy tales by Schwindt became my favourite. The charm of quaintness was first revealed to me in this book. The undulated halo of hair, invariable coiffure of ballerinas in any part, had hitherto been my admiration. Now, looking at the little princess with a smooth parting and plaits coiled over her ears, I had a premonition of a grace different from the accepted standard.

I could not read the text in German. Very likely it would not have added much to the first intuition of style which the illustrations opened for me, awakening a train of thought destined to be of incalculable value to me in after years.

CHAPTER XI

Teliakovsky—Lydia's Diphtheria—The School Performance—Chinese Theatre at Tsarskoe Selo—Final Examinations—My First Trousseau—My Début—Farewell to School

WHEN I returned to school in the autumn, Varvara Ivanovna met me with the remark, "You do not seem to have improved in health. Evidently your holiday at home did not profit you much." Our school doctor also was pessimistic about my health when the usual overhauling took place. I was greatly upset when he shook his head and said that in his opinion I would never be strong enough for a dancer. Nevertheless I was getting stronger as time went on. Regular hours, plain, wholesome food, airy rooms, periodical courses of tonic—the whole régime of the school helped me to overcome my anæmia. I was now in the uppermost section. The spring would see me through the educational classes, but still under the age to leave school. Leaving school at 17, as I would be in the spring, was unprecedented, the regulation age being 18. Varvara Ivanovna inclined to keeping me for another year as a *pépinière*. It meant following only the study of the arts—dance, music, singing, acting and fencing. My parents naturally wished me at home. Besides the motives of pure affection, a consideration of my salary as a help in our straitened circumstances was taken into account by Mother. She went to see the Director. In conversation with him my Mother evidently used a wrong argument. "Your Excellency will not strike a year out of my daughter's life from a mere consideration of precedent. She has the highest marks, and is fully qualified to be on the stage." "It surprises me, madam," he answered, "that you think the school years do not count as life. Why, an extra year will give her the benefit of further perfectioning her art." My Mother could not obtain a definite answer, and the question remained pending, subject to the decision of a conference of masters.

A new director, Teliakovsky, was now at the head of the theatre. Prince Volkonsky had sent in his resignation. A man of refined intellect, great gifts and extensive knowledge of art, loyal and amiable, Volkonsky was greatly regretted. With him the prestige of a great name went from the figure-head of the Imperial stage. His successor had to cope with the mistrust and partiality of public opinion. He was unpopular at the beginning. Years of sound policy gradually brought about the recognition of his merits. Teliakovsky followed a distinctly national orientation. During his directorship, operas by Russian composers began outnumbering the foreign ones on our stage. A great vogue of Italian opera, until recently subsidised by the government, had almost entirely banished the taste for serious music amongst opera-goers. Teliakovsky had practically to force the operas of Rimsky Korsakoff on an unwilling audience. But in spite of unfriendly criticism, the productions of the new director stirred the theatrical world. Genuine interest, sneering curiosity, vehement protests all whirled in the wake of Teliakovsky and of his modernising influence.

Don Quixote, after a long oblivion, was revived this year. Costumes and scenery, a riot of colour, were painted by the Russian artists, Golovin and Korovin. Curiously unaware of the new tendencies, conservative within, walled in by the never-changing public of *balletomanes*, our ballet stood bewildered at this breaking away from the stale tradition of quasi-realistic scenery, of accepted canons of costumes. Ballerinas regretted their voluminous tarlatans, starting from the waistline. The new costumes were cut on different, softer lines. The body, no longer encumbered round the hips, appeared supple and elongated. It was the reform of a dancer's line. It was compulsory that in this ballet everybody should dress their hair in

Spanish fashion, smooth with a side parting and *accrochecoeurs.*
It was novel to the eye at first, but not half so strange as it is
now to look at the photographs of ballerinas in the costume of
Pharaoh's daughter, a lotus flower perched upon hair waved and
arranged in the latest fashion.

Gorsky came from Moscow to produce *Don Quixote.* An
entirely new element made itself manifest in his handling of the
action. Hitherto, the *corps de ballet,* apart from the actual
dancing, remained passive or vaguely responded to the acting
of the principal characters. As Gorsky used it, the *corps de
ballet* was no longer confined to executing separate items; it
became an organic part of the plot.

I was given a charming little part in *Don Quixote.* In the
garden of Dulcinea I appeared as a Cupid in a short silver tunic
and fair curly wig. The part was conceived as that of a mischievous little god and led to amusing scenes. At the end I
had a whole dance at the head of a swarm of smaller Cupids,
the tiniest pupils. The girls criticised my costume "Like a
gingerbread angel from a Christmas Tree," but I was quite
enamoured with my part and the costume. I felt quite heroic
when commanding the evolutions of my little army of Cupids.
Lydia and I were going to take the part of the Cupid in turn,
but illness prevented her from having her share in the good luck.
Christmas was near, and with the prospect of three days' leave
before her, she tried on the policy usual with us of concealing
any indisposition. Rather than miss leave by being kept in the
infirmary, we had recourse to our own remedies. A drastic cure
existed for a sty. "Spit in my eye when I do not expect it,"
one girl asked me. Surprise was supposed to be potent medicine
for a sty. For several days Lydia had a sore throat, the usual
cures did no good. She asked me to look at it. We retired
into the privacy behind a cheval glass in Pensionnierskaya.
"Your throat is full of white spots," I said after the inspection.
"It must be angina." "Scrape them off," she suggested.
With the aid of a hairpin, wrapped in cotton-wool, I succeeded

in removing some of the white spots. She said she felt relieved and could swallow now, and could I let her have a bite from my apple? We bit in turns, share and share alike. The same night she woke me up, saying she felt ill. I gave her a drink from the tumbler of water we had between us by the bed. In the morning she gave herself up. The doctor diagnosed diphtheria, and she was taken in an ambulance to the hospital for infectious diseases. It was thought advisable to break up the school at once, and in consequence we had some extra days at home. No one else had caught the infection. Varvara Ivanovna gave me a sinister warning, " I should not be surprised if you got diphtheria too. You two were so intimate."

My parents had moved from the old house on the canal. A smaller and cheaper flat had been found opposite the Church of the Intercession of the Holy Virgin. The flat was absurd. The biggest room in it had no windows ; a feeble light came in if the door remained open. I somehow could not feel quite at home, and I think Mother too must have felt some nostalgia for our old house. Uncertainty as to whether I was to finish the school this year annoyed my Mother. It was time to begin my trousseau. I had no wardrobe of my own as yet, and went about in Mother's clothes when on holiday. As a result of the hints my Mother had gathered and of her own conviction that I wouldn't be left for another year at school, Mother decided to begin my equipment. A pedlar woman from Yaroslavl used to call periodically at our house, her wares strapped to her back. Mother ordered a piece of extra good hand-spun linen and some lace from her. From some recesses of her chest of drawers Mother brought out a filigree *porte-bouquet*, the one she had on the day she left Smolny. It was the only trinket she possessed.

Of what went on behind the scenes at our school Mother learned now and then from Oblakoff, the School Secretary. Round Oblakoff's tea table, in the large low-ceilinged room of the entresol, in Theatre Street, the air was impregnated with bits of information. His flat was just above the boys' quarters. His wife, a former dancer, still kept in touch with her ancient colleagues. The fond conclave mapped out a victorious career for me, Anna Ilyinishna, a woman of energetic speech, often repeating to my Mother that, once on the stage, I would make them sit up.

In Lent my Mother was informed that, as an exception to the rule, I would be allowed to come out that May. Though this issue had been anticipated, the prospect almost frightened me. For years I had lived in such an intensity of preparation that, without fully realising it, that time of preparation had ceased to seem transitory ; it had become my very life. Besides, I realised that my present means were inadequate to attain the high ideal I had set myself ; I had thought to leave the school and appear on the stage equipped with full mastery ; only much later did I understand that the stage is a school in itself, a cruel one perhaps, and at times unsparing, but the only school to temper the mettle of the artist's soul.

Time went from now on at an accelerated pace. Events of importance to me came in rapid succession. Lent sped on in rehearsals for the school performance ; it was to be at the Michailovsky Theatre. Both of the principal dancing masters, Guerdt and Maestro Cecchetti, were to produce separate ballets. *In the Kingdom of Ice* was the name of the ballet that Guerdt put on. Lydia and I had the principal parts. Mine was slightly dramatised, though the whole lot remained very slender.

Palm Sunday had become a traditional day for our performance. Palm Week is a break from the long monotony of Lent ; an anticipation of Easter, of all the holy days the holiest in Russia. Noisy bazaars swarmed in the streets, their chief wares grotesque toys, whistles, golden fish, big roses made of bright tissue paper, Oriental sweets and wax cherubs—heads and wings only. The profane and devotional mingled to produce the sudden light-heartedness and religious expectation of Palm Week.

Through the solemn service of Saturday night one fervent prayer constantly surged in mind :—" Lord, help me to dance well to-morrow." If I feel strong to-morrow everything will be all right, I repeated to myself. Lack of strength hampered me greatly at that time. I did not realise that on the morrow we would be judged not so much for what we gave as for the promise showing through our necessarily imperfect execution. The benevolent mood of the audience reached me across the footlights. The severest critics made allowances for inexperience, and the timid ardour of youth could not help moving the hearts of the spectators. Only a limited number of ballet subscribers could obtain seats for our performance. Parents, masters and artists were first invited. The lucky ones amongst the *balletomanes* considered it a privilege to be present ; each wanted to be first to proclaim new talent, to witness the first steps of future dancers. I felt fit and, but for a small lapse, would have been in the seventh heaven after the end of the performance. When I had finished my difficult solo and retired into the wings, I felt such an immense relief that it produced a curious reaction in me. I completely forgot that I had to come on again for an insignificant bit of dance. I stood in complete beatitude behind the scenes while my music played and the stage remained empty for a short time. When I realised what I had done, I felt almost crushed under the enormity of my fault. All the glory of the evening faded away. Nobody, of course, except my master and the girls realised there was anything amiss. My master only laughed good-naturedly in answer to my stammering apologies ; he was pleased, very much pleased with his two favourite pupils, Lydia and me.

The future smiled on me again. An overwhelming luck fell to my lot. A gala performance was being prepared for the expected visit of the French President, Loubet. The best artists were selected for this performance. Geltzer was going to come from Moscow to share the honours of the evening with Mathilda Kshessinskaya. Whether Geltzer fell ill or simply shirked a performance of which the chief part was given to another dancer I did not know. What mattered to me was that she did not come. Teliakovsky, free from hierarchical prejudice, ordered that I should take her part; the instance of a pupil appearing in the same rank with distinguished dancers was without precedent.

The ballet given was *Lac des Cygnes*. I appeared in a *pas de trois* with Fokine and Siedova. In early days at school she had been my protectress and mentor. She accepted me kindly, and helped with technical advice. Siedova by now was an unofficial prima ballerina. She was unsurpassed in virtuosity.

During rehearsals, Preobrajenskaya took an interest in me. The palm of supremacy in grace belonged to her. To infinite charm she added an unusual clear-headed judgment. She always knew the wherefore of perfection. She was very witty, and an excellent mimic. " Now, young beauty," she would say, " Step off ! Fire away ! Control your arms if you don't want a partner minus a few teeth."

The gala performance took place in the Chinese Theatre of Tsarskoe Selo, which stood in the Chinese village, a graceful whim of Catherine the Great. Built in 1778, the theatre was kept in good repair. It stood among ancient pagoda-like fir trees. Inside, it was of rare charm—lacquer panels ornamenting the boxes, red and gold rococo chairs, bronze chandeliers with porcelain flowers—all the precious *chinoiseries* of the eighteenth century.

All through the evening there was no applause. The be-jewelled audience remained mute, passive as a *tableau vivant* in the light of innumerable candles. The Imperial Family and the Court were present. Every artist afterwards received a present from the Emperor, as was always the case with Imperial performances. The excitement of the Chinese Theatre being scarcely over, my master told me I was granted a début on the closing night of the season. Débuts as a rule were given sparingly : there had not been any for several years. Guerdt's choice fell on a *pas de deux* that had been created by Virginia Zucchi. It was called *Le pêcheur et la perle*. Fokine, who was by now a first dancer, was to be my partner.

My mind was now divided between my coming début and preparations for the final educational examinations. Up till now I had passed from class to class on the strength of my marks. Learning had been extremely easy to me, the only apprehension I had being on account of mathematics. My mind shrank from figures, and when it came to mental addition I had recourse to Nature's adding machine, and grew very dexterous at working it under my alpaca apron. We now formed groups for training : one recited the lesson, the other followed the book. I crammed with Elena, the clever girl of Batioushka's parable. She was conscientious, and came every morning to wake me up before the bell. We would go to Pensionnerskaya to read through the task of the day. We all believed in the good old precept of putting the book under the pillow every night.

I passed all the examinations successfully. Even my mathematics didn't let me down. A first prize had been awarded to me. It was to be a book, and I was left the choice. I asked for *Faust*. My wish slightly perplexed the council of masters. Varvara Ivanovna expressed the opinion that *Faust* was hardly a book for a young girl. Mother related to me the deliberation on this subject as told her by Oblakoff. Eventually I got my *Faust*, a beautiful presentation copy, complete with commentaries on the second part and with many plates ; it bore an inscription on the flyleaf, " To Tamara Karsavina for her excellent progress in learning and her exemplary behaviour."

The examination over, we were allowed three half-days' leave each for shopping. The foretaste of freedom was intoxicating. The marvellous freshness of unspent sensations invested the simplest acts of life with splendour. My own happiness was the key to the world's gentlest mood. The world met me kindly.

The shopman of the Gostinnoy Dvor was highly sympathetic; he discussed the scheme of pink voile and écru lace with Mother, and approved of it as suitable for my complexion. The girl at the milliner's shop endeared herself to me for her helpful advice. It had been difficult to decide upon a hat; there were two that suited me particularly. A small incident occurred on one of my shopping days, a trifling incident not worth mentioning, but for the sudden revelation it brought to me of the fundamental goodness of the human heart. On leaving school, each pupil received 100 roubles for equipment, good money in those days; yet I had to be clothed from head to foot. To make the money go the longest way, Mother decided to look for a second-hand coat and skirt in the Alexandrovsky market. She knew of an honest Jewess, who dealt in second-hand clothes of good provenance. I had heard of the Jewish market, but never yet been inside it. The shops on the front arcades were sedate and full of good plain clothes of an extremely conservative cut, such as were worn by tradesmen's wives and people of humble class. Inside, there was a glass-roofed rotunda, well deserving its name of " Bustling Market." The Jewish proprietors kept on the alert ready for a sally at the sight of a prospective buyer. Speaking in voluble jargon, they tried to secure clients by forcible means, the boldest even pulling at one's skirt. In much later years I came to love this place. Far more attractive than the salons of ambitious antiquaries, where all things have their prices, their neat labels and their history, were these dingy little shops.

On that first visit to the Jewish market I was quite bewildered. A direct appeal to me seemed to require at least a polite refusal. Mother laughed at my apologetically declining the proffered goods, and told me not to waste time. In the little shop where we entered, everything was orderly. Minna, a good-looking woman, took us up a ladder to a tidy garret. One by one she took dresses off the hangers and brought them for our inspection. Mother chose a dark blue tailor suit. To me it looked quite new; there was the name of Redfern on the label sewn inside.

Minna's elderly husband sat in the corner making entries into his book. He looked up and watched me trying on a fluffy opera cloak. There must have been rapture on my face; I caught the glance and the kind smile Minna gave to her husband. She said a few words to him that I could not understand. Minna turned to me, translating his answer. "Abraham says you have a lucky face. Some day you will have all the finery you may wish for. You won't then come to us any more," she added with a little sigh. "And what then, wife," rejoined Abraham a little sternly. "May the young lady's luck come true. We shall be glad of it." There was great sincerity in these words. The old Jew looked suddenly dignified. I was moved; the world met me kindly.

My acquaintance with Minna did not stop there. Not for some time could we afford to order new evening dresses for me, and for some years Minna remained my costumier. When no more in need of second-hand dresses I still revisited my friends occasionally, looking for old lace and curios. I became fond of them both. They were patriarchal Jews, family-loving. The sincerity of their kind wishes, at that time only felt instinctively, was proved many years later. In 1927 I was touring in Scandinavian countries; during my stay at Helsingfors I received a visit from Minna, then a refugee, having lost Abraham. She lived with her married daughter in some small Finnish town, and undertook a long journey with the sole purpose of seeing me and talking of old times.

On shopping days Mother and I usually found time to go home for an improvised meal of coffee. At that time Lev had some fellow-students coming daily to read through the course with him. This system spared students considerable expense. One book did duty for several of them. On my fleeting first visit home, I rushed into Lev's room to show him my exciting purchases. I did not expect to find company. I realised at once that my interruption was welcome. Smoothing their hair, hastily pulling on their jackets, the young men sprang to their feet from the nonchalant attitudes in which I found them. Lev told me afterwards that all of them were *balletomanes.* He suspected that their clubbing with him must have been determined by the fact that he was my brother. These boys adopted a highly chivalrous attitude towards me. When an ice-cream man happened to be down in the yard, I was offered a treat. Many a poem was written to me ; while I admired the verses, they were subjected to the merciless criticism of the other boys, who would try in their turn to produce better ones.

The 1st of May, 1902, was the night of my début at the Marinsky. My *pas de deux* was introduced into the last act of *Javotte.* On the eve of the performance, Lydia reminded me to cut my finger nails short, " not to scratch your partner." She had had her début with her elder brother previously to mine, and could now speak from her own experience. I felt eager, yet strangely light-headed, and my limbs trembled slightly. Guerdt kept by me in the preceding interval. " Don't stand still. Warm yourself up," he advised. " Courage ! " He made the sign of the Cross over me at the first notes of introduction and hurried to the first wing to watch me from there. My parents and Lev were in the audience. Douniasha came with them, but had to be led out on account of her loud sobbing when she saw me.

Between that night and the present day lies a gulf. Through many stages, countless avatars, stretches the whole distance from half-conscious ardour to the lucidity of ripe artistic means. It is like speaking of somebody else, who is not me any more. Impartially and with only a vague amused tenderness, I can see now a form half graceful, half awkward, limbs appearing too long, smooth black hair framing a childish face, pale and intensely grave ; and an unconquerable habit of raising the eyebrows in *accent circonflexe*, as my Mother termed it, which gave a look of wonder to the rare smile. Mother unsuccessfully tried to break me of this habit, saying it would give me wrinkles.

I think there must have been something appealing in that surprised look of mine; the enthusiastic reception I had on that night was more than my technical skill deserved. The audience was partial to me, to my youth and my demure naïveté. " An ovation, my child," Anna Pavlova nodded to me on the way to her dressing-room.

The theatres closed for the summer, the examination over, there was still more than a fortnight to wait for the " Act," a ceremony marking our coming out on the 25th of May. The days got out of shape, long from inactivity and yet too short for dreams. We spent most of the time in our little garden, talking or reading. My mind constantly wandered away from the book. The little calendar scrawl thinned down rapidly; it ceased to exist on the 24th of May. On the eve of the great day we were late in breaking up the last evening in Pensionnerskaya; we put our hair in curl papers; gave favourite imitations of masters; boldly sang prohibited couplets of farewell, poor rhymed efforts of our collective brains.

Up betimes long before the morning bell, my first thought was for my pale coral dress waiting for me in my wardrobe. It had to wait for a while yet. For the last time we dressed in blue serge and plaited our hair. There was a church service in the morning and thanksgiving. After a hurried lunch we assembled in the big dancing room in the presence of parents and masters. Father Vassily said a farewell word. We came forward to receive prizes and certificates from the Inspector of classes.

Farewell to the " toads " and masters; farewell to Varvara Ivanovna, all skirmishes forgotten—tender farewells on both sides. Farewells to the friendly maids; furtive adieux to all the rooms, nooks and corners; a short bit of prayer before the dormitory ikon. Secular garb, affectionate vows of eternal friendship—the last page of school life was turned.

Yet unwritten pages were to be bound in the same book. Theatre Street remained a consecrated ground of daily work, a link in the chain of continuity. A nursery of creative search, a haven of repair. The mirror-image of yesterday had vanished ; the same mirror, unsparing, unflattering, guardian of zeal, will reflect the shape of to-morrow. Before this same mirror, under the same roof, in the aloofness of Theatre Street, began, continued and faded a dancer's career.

PART II

THE MARINSKY THEATRE

CHAPTER XII

The Marinsky Theatre—A Benefit Night—Increasing Popularity of Ballet—The "Balletomanes"—The Brothers Legat—Johannsen —Social Life

AT the time of which I am speaking, the ballet company comprised about 180 persons, with a preponderance of women. The ranks were as follows :—*corps de ballet, cory-phées*, second and first solo dancers and ballerinas. Salaries went according to rank. Promotions were given every spring and announced by the *Journal of Orders*, an official weekly gazette. The page of the journal dealing with the ballet troupe held a central position in a frame, together with announcements of rehearsals and other matters for general information. Every morning, artists, before entering the rehearsal room, tarried on the landing to scan the page of the journal. Remonstrances, fines, honourable mention and scanty words of gratitude appeared on that page. With a feeling of great satisfaction, though I knew it already, I read the confirmation of my being received into the troupe as a *coryphée* on a raised salary of 720 roubles (£72) a year. It seemed a lot for the first year, as compared with the usual 600 of beginners. At home, my monthly £6 made a welcome addition to the budget. As a matter of course I brought my money straight to Mother ; she gave me my fare every morning. It was all the pocket money I had. In consequence I never could buy anything, though I liked to look at the shop windows and sometimes wished for things, but without any bitterness or regret. I lived at that time in a complete unconcern of money, in a blissful poverty. The world gave me plenty ; I felt myself a centre of it. My happiness took a pensive hue at times, but it was ever present.

The Marinsky Theatre invariably began the season by *A Life for the Tsar*, a patriotic opera. The first Sunday of September the ballet opened. About a fortnight before the season the company assembled. The first day was more in the nature of a review of troops. We reported to the *régisseur* and went home till a notice of rehearsal summoned such as were wanted. The whole service of notifying the company was carried out by five couriers attached to the staff. They usually went on foot, each working his assigned district. A telephone was not installed at the rehearsal-room till much later.

My first part was in a group of solo dancers. I was put together with Pavlova, Siedova and Trefilova, then virtually ballerinas.

The tedious grind through which many a dancer went before reaching any prominence had been spared me. From the very beginning I was placed amongst the chosen. My career began under good auspices. The policy of the new director was favourable to the young; every opportunity, every encouragement were given to those who showed any promise. In the first year Lydia and I kept apace. We were paired in most of the parts. In some ballets, special dances were introduced to make us appear together, for the sake of the contrast. Each of us had her own enthusiastic crowd of theatrical admirers. When both on the stage together, the two camps joined forces, making a formidable noise, sometimes even to the annoyance of our elder comrades.

Theatre—Janus with two faces—your frown was yet hidden from me. Wise heads gave warning. An elder dancer, prominent on account of her wealth and connections, took a fancy to me. Nadejda Alexeievna never aspired to any fame. Indisputably elegant, she was well pleased to be in the first line of the *corps de ballet*. " Do not be too confident," she used to say to me. " The theatre is a hotbed of intrigues. Why do you think she made you a present of this costume ? " The costume in question I thought most beautiful and the gift most generous. " Fancy you in dark mauve ! " she went on, " A pall for a coffin, not a costume for a child."

Nadejda Alexeievna was genuinely fond of me. It pleased her to form me according to her own ideas of wisdom and elegance. I was an exasperating pupil, oblivious to my own appearance, and my friend insisted that I should come for her inspection before going on the stage. Later on, she arranged for me to dress in her room. " You look like nothing on earth," she often exclaimed in despair, hastily rearranging my hair. " If it were not for the face you've got on you, the public would laugh at you."

Nadejda Alexeievna thought it all-important to be on good terms with the public. She assumed the rôle of my sponsor. In those days I secretly believed all supper parties at restaurants to be wicked. To her house, however, I often went, though with apprehension. I shied from meeting the formidable body of *balletomanes*. She was always at home to callers. The élite of this very specific world of *balletomanes* gathered in the salon of Nadejda Alexeievna.

There had been a period when, by the majority of the public, the ballet was regarded with scepticism and the lovers of it thought eccentric. Now, no longer the Cinderella of the stage, the ballet had become fashionable. A competition for seats, for the right to be a subscriber, well proved the interest it aroused. To obtain a seat, a petition to the Chancery of the Imperial Theatres had to be filed ; the chance of success was so small that big premiums were constantly offered by advertisement to the original holders of the stalls. The subscribers held tenaciously to their prerogative. No outsider could ever penetrate into the first row of stalls without a Sesame, a favour of a *balletomane* friend. Even then, a new face would be looked upon as an intrusion and eyed suspiciously by the neighbours. The seats were handed down from father to son, the name of *balletomane*, once given in derision, was becoming almost an hereditary dignity. Having picked up the gauntlet,

the *balletomanes* bore their name proudly. Whatever there may
have been of personal motives in the attachment of some of them
to the ballet, the cult of this delicate art was always uppermost.

A very knowledgeable, exacting, somewhat dogmatic and
conservative public, *balletomanes* were capable of high enthusiasm.
They were conservative in the extreme. A new venture, the
slightest variation from the old canons was heresy to them;
an occasional modification of a step an irreverence as well as a
disappointment. There were some favourite steps eagerly
awaited. One could feel from the stage how the whole audience
stiffened in breathless expectation of a favourite passage. The
passage well executed, the whole theatre burst out clapping in
measure to the music. Artistic reputations were made and
undone by casual remarks of the leaders of the stalls. A foreign
celebrity, in a series of performances, displayed a sound virtuosity.
She was round-shouldered. " A flying turkey," drawled
Skalkovsky. His remark had been caught and repeated all
round. They were a tyrannical public, those *balletomanes*, and
pig-headed to a degree; if once they pronounced a dancer
lacking some quality, no amount of evidence to the contrary
would dispel the prejudice. They classified and ticketed the
dancers as graceful, dramatic, lyrical, and did not encourage any
attempt to develop qualities beyond those originally assigned.
But they were enthusiastic. On no account would they miss
a performance. When Mathilda Kshsessinskaya went to dance
at Moscow, the first row of stalls at the Marinsky emptied;
her faithful had followed her.

Less pontifical, but hardly of smaller importance, were the
lesser *balletomanes*, the pit and the gallery. They also crowned
and dethroned. Erudition and the terminology of the ballet they
may have lacked, but in spontaneity of admiration, in fanatical
transports of young enthusiasm they far outstripped their
colleagues of the stalls. While the stalls preserved a certain
decorum, the gallery spared not their throats. Long after the
stalls had emptied and the lights gone down in the auditorium,

the gallery raved. The safety curtain crept down, dust sheets were brought in; the gallery still shouted. A last rite was to be performed yet—waiting at the stage door. Manifestations at the stage door varied in proportion to the popularity of each artist. They ranged from silence to delirious outbursts. Sometimes a group of young people would follow their idol, keeping at a distance, a silent escort. Up in the gallery, or paradise as it was called, the admiration for artists was idealistic. The young generation showed an exaggerated mistrust of the smart set of the stalls. My comparative aloofness, which in the opinion of Nadejda Alexeievna might deprive me of a powerful support, was my best introduction to the favours of the gallery. It was repeated that I never went to suppers, and my reserve was glorified. The gallery made a pet of me. All this idealism and exuberance is not to be wondered at in young people. They were mostly students, schoolboys, young people of modest means. They had, though, their veterans and even a grandfather. When an address was to be presented by the gallery to an artist on a benefit night, the grandfather headed the deputation. He was a clerk in some Ministry, a shy, bearded little man in a neat uniform.

Only a certain number of seats in the gallery belonged to subscribers. The rest went on sale. The box office opened at eight o'clock in the morning. Even in the bitterest cold the queue round the theatre started overnight, though a ten hours' vigil by no means ensured a ticket. Eventually the ballet opened to wider circles, even non-subscribers being occasionally able to gain admittance. Old *balletomanes* disapproved of this measure ; they grumbled at missing a performance but would not demean themselves by going to other than subscription nights. At this time, however, the measure was not even anticipated; for a while yet the Chinese wall enclosing the ballet world—a very curious world with its own culture, its narrow range of interests, professional gossip, its wilful ignorance of intellectual progress— stood unbreached.

A playful familiarity reigned at Nadejda Alexeievna's parties. I felt no firm ground under my feet amongst the elderly set of *balletomanes*. The constellation of generals at her table intimidated me, and I may have cut an awkward figure there. Though the actual school restrictions were left behind, the habit of reserve and the code of modesty remained. My subconscious ear still heard the dread swish of Varvara Ivanovna's skirts.

Though I felt ill at ease at her parties, I liked my self-constituted chaperone, and was quite happy when she decided not to be at home to anybody, and to have tea with Mamma. Mamma's rooms on the mezzanine were lumbered with wardrobes, hat boxes piled on top. The old woman addressed the company as " Little Brothers." She never missed making the sign of the Cross over her mouth when yawning. Two schoolboys, Nadejda Alexeievna's son and ward, appeared occasionally from some inner recesses of the capacious flat. After tea Mamma either played a game of solitaire, aided by us all, or told fortunes from the cards.

An outstanding event of each season was the benefit night of the *corps de ballet*. Months before, every seat in the theatre was bespoken. This year a ballet master from Milan had been engaged to revive the *Source* of Delibes. His first production proved his last one on our stage. Coppini had a good reputation as a ballet master at the Scala; his methods must have been those actually used by the Italian stage. If this production could in fairness have been taken as an example of the taste of the Italian ballet, no doubt would have been left in one's mind as to its complete decadence. The production of the *Source* was an unconscious and biting caricature of the classical tradition as it may become in the hands of a totally unimaginative producer. To the delightful music of Delibes, Circassians twiddled their rifles, Naiads marched and countermarched. For his grouping Coppini made a large use of stools. Square blocks were ostentatiously brought on and placed in the desired formation. The back rows mounted on them to effect a bulky group. A change of group, and the blocks would be carried to another point of the stage. Fully admitted in the ballet, stools never yet had been used so tactlessly. Petipa also used blocks, though with discretion ; they would be carried in under cover of a compact group in front. The ballet stage of necessity had to be flat, and a good effect could be got out of elevated construction of grouped masses, provided all clumsy preparations were disguised. These minor effects worked faultlessly at the Marinsky. The chief property man, Lebedeff, had a considerable staff under him. At the performance the whole body of scene-shifters wore costume. Lebedeff usually marked the places with chalk. He designed on the floor arrows and diagonals for the orientation of his staff. The signs were rubbed off in the evening, leaving a faint trace of chalk not visible from the audience.

After several months of intense rehearsals, the production was ready—tawdry, stilted, impotent. The marvellous dancing of Preobrajenskaya alone accounted for the ballet remaining in the repertoire. Even her superlative artistry could not redeem the absurdity of the plot nor save it from ridicule. The ballet might have passed as a parody of charades played by children. An old witch casts a spell over the Princess from some motives not clear to the producer himself. Witches may work mischief from restless wickedness ; the situation is acceptable : all that an un-sophisticated spectator asks is that they at least should do it adequately. The Princess becomes petrified, and is carried off the stage in a coma. Her lover seeks the protection of the benevolent fairy of the spring. Whether the spell was not a proper one, or whether there was some natural improvement in the comatose state of the beauty, the puzzled audience beholds her in the last scene walking on to the stage. She is being supported by her lover and making for the spring. Either from need of exercise or from sheer viciousness, she avoids the shortest route to the spring situated at the back of the stage She moves instead down to the footlights, petrifaction having settled by now in her face and slightly impeded her step. Along the footlights and up the stage, the princess in a roundabout way arrives at the spring. She is being propped against the rock during a parley with the fairy. This latter, being herself in love with the *jeune premier*, shows some reluctance, but gives in and revives the princess by touching her forehead with a red tulip. The Circassians come on to celebrate this miracle; the fairy calls her butterflies; for a while all dance, till the fairy makes up her mind to die. She does it eventually in time for an apotheosis on the blocks.

We of the ballet were uncritical at that time: there was no intellectual fermentation as yet amongst us. Comparisons were drawn between different productions, but the principle of staging remained unquestioned. However, the arrant absurdity and bad taste of this production awoke a somewhat ironical attitude amongst the artists. Not that this attitude in any way affected the will of doing one's best; discipline was ingrained in us. We indulged in some parodies of the different scenes and of the ballet master's outrageously turned-out toes. The prestige of Marius Petipa, at all times high, now rose supreme. The artists more than ever realised his exceptional gifts. Petipa certainly had a distinct leaning towards processions interrupting the action. His ballets verged on *féeries*; they were all constructed after the same formula, with inevitable happy endings and a *divertissement* in the last act. Nevertheless, Petipa was a great master and had a perfect command of masses. The intricate but always precise pattern of his grouping developed with facility and logic. He had unerring tact in the use of *coups de théâtre*, a true sense of stage effect.

The *Source* gave me a very good opportunity. Lydia and I were among the principal butterflies and had a solo each. Coppini addressed me affectionately as " Bambina " and was evidently pleased with my eagerness. In these early days especially, each new part was a joy, every rehearsal a sacred duty. The chief interpreters and solo dancers were often called to evening rehearsals, a call which with the majority was unpopular, interfering with their plans. I looked forward to it as to a party; it was a new and delightful sensation to be received as an equal by the artists before whom I so lately trembled.

Two brothers, Nicolas and Sergei Legat, were the leading male dancers then. Both talented dancers, they were also very good draughtsmen. An album of caricatures was just being started by them and was eventually published. Nicolas had a caustic strain in him; some of his unpublished caricatures were not without a sting, but he never told tales out of school and was very popular with the artists. The real blue-eyed boy of the troupe was the younger brother, Sergei, who was beloved by all; so handsome, so irresistibly good natured. A true and generous comrade, he had a rare sense of humour which never became offensive. There always occurred intervals at rehearsals when, not actually wanted, we could sit in a far corner. I became friends with both brothers; they usually beckoned me to join them. Nicolas worked at his drawings, Sergei told anecdotes, of which he knew no end. He made me repeat them, which I never could do; I usually forgot the point, which only made him laugh the merrier. Sergei used to mimic my first appearance in the class which all the solo dancers attended daily. He was late that morning and rushed in to take his place at the bar without as much as looking round. "Heavens! A funny little object drops a deep curtsy to me." He made a mock bow in answer. This incident started our friendship. My primness was a constant joke to him.

I was rather helpless in the class. The old man Johannsen never got up to show the steps; he indicated them by vague movements of his shaky hands. For a long time I could not make out what he wanted, and made constant mistakes. Besides, I was frightened of him; it made me doubly shy. There was no way of hiding behind others. Johannsen had only one eye, but Argus might have envied him, and my manœuvres never escaped him. As a penalty I was ordered forward all by myself, the cynosure of all eyes, the butt of the old man's choler. A Swede by birth,

Johannsen spoke broken Russian intermingled with French. He had a vocabulary of oaths of uncommon wealth. "Pity you are weak-minded," he addressed me after each failure. "What a dancer I could have made of you but for that." He pointed to his forehead and then tapped the back of his fiddle. Epithets like "cow on the ice" rained on me. Once he was pleased with me, so much so that he called to Marius Petipa, who at that moment came in, "Come and see her *jetées en tournant*." While I exhibited my *jetées en tournant*, Johannsen muttered sadly, "What a pity! She could dance, but such a fool." Johannsen gave us very intricate steps, very difficult to fit to the music. He laid his fiddle across his knee and played pizzicato, using the bow only to point towards someone faulty, nine times out of ten to me. "I see you. Don't you imagine I can't see your bumbling feet." A small tragedy happened once; more than usually exasperated, he threw his fiddlestick at me and called me "Idiot!" On the point of bursting into sobs, I turned my back and left the room. Sergei followed me. "Come, angel, come and ask his pardon; the old man loves you. Be sensible." He led me up to Christian Petrovitch. I apologised. For the first time I saw him smile. "I taught your father," he said to me. He took my hand; it was wet with perspiration. "Clammy," declared he, "your blood wants purifying. Drink Hamburg tea. Where have you been last night?" "At a charity ball, Christian Petrovitch." "A ball indeed! We never went to balls. That is why you stumble like an old crock. No balls for a dancer."

Such was my docility that I drank Hamburg tea, and it upset me thoroughly, so much so that Father advised me to leave it off, as it was a well-known horse medicine. I realised in time that Legat must have been right; it was not persecution on the old man's part. He seemed to be constantly worrying about me. It became his habit to call me up before him to ask whether I had been to a party again and to touch my hand.

Whenever he saw me in difficulties, Sergei took me apart

for coaching. He was protective to me and infinitely gentle. On his own, he sometimes gave me practice in lifts. An untimely tragic death was soon to take away everybody's darling. Not a soul but felt a blank left in our midst, a sunshine gone out of life.

The spirit of comradeship was stronger in those days than later, when the advent of new ideas brought dissension. In these humdrum years there had been unrepeatable sweetness. I feel glad I was in time to see that phase of our ballet.

The benefit night was an opportunity for paying tribute to our *corps de ballet*, greatly esteemed as a wonderfully disciplined body. It was also the fashionable performance of the year, a parade of jewels and toilettes. The performance was followed by a banquet at Cubat, which afterwards became an institution. This one was the first ever given to the whole troupe : it was also my first night at a restaurant. Restaurants were synonymous with wickedness in my mind. To the last moment I hesitated whether it would not be better to sneak away by the back door and return home. Nadejda Alexeievna teased me. " Why do you fret so ? Nobody is going to abduct you. Is that what you are afraid of ? " I suddenly realised I was being ridiculous. The last feeble argument I used was that it went against my principles. " Come on," she said gaily, " and bring your principles along." In spite of the principles, I could not help enjoying the party ; the compliments I received, the attention paid to me, the lights, music, gaiety, the food, the like of which I had never tasted, well-nigh turned my head. Besides, nobody seemed to want to abduct me ; so where, after all, was the wickedness ? Little pricks of conscience I felt at times, though Mother fully approved of my going. The truth was that I was a prude and a prig at that time ; I had my own scheme of life built up during the years at school. I was to be a priestess of my art, uncompromising, spurning worldliness. Some fatuous Russian verses to an actress that I had read long ago impressed me by their sentiment, and I took them for my device. Translated into English, they would be something like this :—

No rhymes of languid poets,
No melting sighs of swains
The fortress of her heart can storm ;
Her art alone there reigns.

At that banquet the foundation of an unwavering friendship was laid with Box No. 25. That box of the *bel étage* belonged to a group of subscribers, all friends. I received a standing invitation to come to the box whenever not dancing. Lydia and I went there very often. I never had better, more faithful friends than these. The box was easy to single out, as two of its front occupants had Assyrian beards that were real museum pieces. There was also a lame, fire-eating aide-de-camp who had been hardly prevented from challenging a male relative of a ballerina who had used some ugly words at me. A frequent visitor to this box was a sailor who went by the name of Lieutenant Furioso. Between cruises, the Lieutenant wrote articles on drama and ballet. He became a constant visitor at our house, perfectly content to talk to Mother for hours when I happened to be away. He was a rabid reactionary, my Mother a Liberal ; so politics always led to heated discussions. Otherwise she liked him and chaperoned me willingly to theatres with him. The Lieutenant was a frantic organiser of parties. Before leaving for a cruise, his activities intensified and we never felt secure from his sudden appearance in the evening with some scheme or other. His bustling, rotund figure, his insistent eagerness neither of us two could resist. We were worn to shadows after a round of these gaieties, and sighed with relief when he was gone. From thousands of miles his roving spirit reached and disturbed us. Telegrams arrived in the middle of the night to convey to us that the sky was blue at Malta or that affectionate thoughts greeted us from the other hemisphere. Cases came with tinned fruit or full of hay that had once been rare flowers of exotic origin.

CHAPTER XIII

*My First Leading Rôle—A Criticism—Additions to my Reper-
toire and Promotion—First Appearance of Bakst—Kshessinskaya
—Volkonsky's Resignation*

BEFORE my first year on the stage was out, I received a first
leading part in a one-act ballet, *The Awakening of Flora.*
I set to work with a joyous heart. There was no dramatic plot
in this ballet, the part being purely a dancing one requiring a
certain amount of technical virtuosity of a higher level than I
had hitherto attempted. A year of Johannsen's rebukes had
not been spent in vain. I could now master considerable
difficulties.

Being spring, the smart season was over. That consideration didn't worry me; my spirits were always higher in the
spring. All went well. Marius Petipa was pleased. " Très
bien, ma belle," he said. All went well; that is, till the very
rehearsal. I must have overworked myself by that time; my
toes were blistered, and my strength began failing me. The
approach of the performance brought a sickening fear, a frame
of mind due, perhaps, to the fact that my friends on the
stage wanted to impress me with the importance of success;
some, less well-disposed, said it was much too early for me to
have a responsible part. Both encouragement and discouragement were equally pernicious to my mental balance. Once the
idea of possible failure had been put into my head, it began
working ravages with my self-control. It hypnotised me. On
the eve of my performance, some trivial discussion arose at
home. I was highly strung; Mother lost her temper with me.
I cried the best part of the night, and woke up in the morning
with aching head and swollen eyes. Lev gave me some small

change for a cab to get a blow. By the evening I was in a wretched state; there was a lump in my throat. I came on, feeling I was on my trial. All was dizzy before my eyes; I was unsteady, couldn't get my balance, and my legs shook. At the end applause roared, and bouquets filled the stage. It didn't cheer me up; I had sentenced myself as a failure. One hope lurked in my mind—perhaps the audience had not noticed my slips; they were cheering me so.

The leading critic of the ballet was then Skalkovsky. He believed in my future. He was an educated man with a Parisian veneer, a genuine lover of the ballet and author of several books on the art. His real essence, romanticism, he disguised under a sneering wit. The long article he wrote after my début in *Flora* left me undecided whether to be pleased or annoyed. It was witty. Some of it I remember to the word " . . . Balleto-manes arm themselves with opera-glasses. They crane forward in their stalls not to lose sight of a trap-door at the back of the dimly lit stage. It slowly rises; the young dancer comes on with a timid step. All eyes rapturously follow her attitudes, her inimitable grace of a young fawn, Byzantine eyes and supple arms. Karsavina, by her descent, belongs to the people who had created gods and heroes, whose present sons carry on a small traffic in sponges and Rahat Lakum. . . . It is prema-ture to pronounce a final judgment on the dancer's abilities. She gives a generous promise; whether she fulfils it, time will show. It amused me to watch the attitude of the public, and especially that of the gallery towards their favourite. It puts me in mind of a reception given to a new governor of a district by a leading country squire. A gipsy choir came in to sing after the banquet. The eager host flew to the governor. ' How would Your Excellency wish them to sing ? With a whoop or without ? ' ' With,' came the condescending answer. The reception of the young dancer that night was a continuous whoop from start to finish; before she starts her dance, she is greeted with clapping and shouting. Whenever the nervous débutante misses her pirouette, the frantic cheers double in strength."

My further chances of promotion were not affected by what I considered my failure. Nothing could have been kinder than the attitude of my Chief towards me. The Head of the Chancery, the director's right hand, called me one day to have a talk. " It would be deceiving you to maintain that you were quite adequate to the occasion. We all realise that it was mainly due to nervousness and want of stage experience. There is not the slightest doubt about your capacity. In consequence we expect much from you."

Next season another ballet was given to me, *The Trial of Damis*. The double part gave an opportunity of acting. This took my mind off the technical difficulties. Moreover, the ballet was composed in the style of the eighteenth century, in which I felt instinctively at home. I did not know much about the period then, but even as a child I had had some intuition of it.

A one-act ballet, *Graziella*, was added to my repertoire. There, too, was ample field for acting in charming comic situations. Sergei Legat was adorably funny as a jealous lover. The spontaneity of his acting was contagious, and helped me to a better understanding of my part. By now I had some tentative methods of my own towards the conception of a rôle. I imagined the looks of my heroine ; the more different it was from my own self, the better it helped me. When I succeeded in giving a body to the part, I stepped aside and looked on to the visionary figure that went through all the evolutions of dancing and acting. As yet I had a very small knowledge and no advice as to the artistic side of my profession. Stray impressions of things seen, echoes of unrestricted reading, the habit of imagining involved stories round other people and myself were the only sources that my imagination fed on in those times. Graziella appealed to me by her name ; it conveyed a graceful girl with sloping shoulders. The head of the princess looking out of the travelling carriage, as seen in my favourite illustrated book of Schwindt, fitted her exactly. It was not a far guess for the ballet of 1850's. My ringlets raised some doubts in the mind of Nadejda Alexeievna. My shoulders now took to drooping at odd times, and Mother remarked that I mustn't get into the habit of stooping. Some critics marked a sense of style in *Graziella* as well as in *Damis*. I also retained the ballet of *Flora*. By now I had partly overcome my stage fright, and my success was still on the increase.

In the third year of my career I was promoted to be a solo dancer of second degree, my salary raised to 800 rubles (£80) a year. A rather spiteful dancer remarked that the increase of salary must come handy to me, considering the expense of keeping a *claque*. As far as I know, there was no organised *claque* at the Marinsky. The gallery had too strongly manifested likes and dislikes to make it possible for a small group of hired clappers to forge a success. Some instances were quoted of dancers having had the services of a claque, but I can hardly believe it. It is true that there was a man in the gallery, Vinogradoff by name, originally the cashier of a summer variety theatre, who was the supposed leader of the claque for foreign artists. I did not know Vinogradoff at that time, and it was only much later that he attached himself to me from motives of disinterested devotion. He was a simple, uneducated man, adoring the theatre, a blend of cunning and enthusiasm, rather a pathetic figure at the end.

I have already mentioned that our director, Teliakovsky, did much towards encouraging national art. Hitherto, the same official painters had done the scenery and costumes year in, year out. Teliakovsky now adopted a policy which required much courage, and meant going against the grain of traditional, self-contained organisation. Painters from outside the small official circle, such as Golovin and Korovin, were appointed to the theatre, and shortly Bakst was to make his début as a stage painter.

These artists, together with Alexander Benois, Doboujinsky, Soudeikin, Lanseret, Somoff, formed the nucleus of a rebellion against the stale standards of art. By the untiring energy of Diaghileff they were united into a separate group, under the name of *Mir I*ʒ*koustva*, the " World of Art," which entirely severed itself from the academic group.

In the same year, 1904, Bakst made the scenery of *Oedipus* for the Alexandrinsky Theatre, and that of the *Fairy Doll* for the Ballet. I met him for the first time at a dress rehearsal, a dandified young man in appearance, pernickety in his ways. Bakst won through at once ; the success of both his productions was acclaimed by all parties.

Consistent in his policy, Teliakovsky discontinued the invitation of foreign ballerinas. None of our dancers had been abroad yet ; Pavlova still belonged to our stage. There was a rare abundance of talent in the ballet at that time—adorable Trefilova ; frail, exquisite Pavlova, who brought back the almost forgotten fragrance of " Giselle "; Preobrajenskaya, witty and accomplished, the darling of the audience ; brilliant to audacity Mathilda Kshessinskaya, Siedova covering the stage in a few leaps; beautiful Marie Petipa ; Egorova. . . . Round them grouped the spring garland of young dancers—the reserve. The *corps de ballet* was justly famous for accuracy and discipline. Nor was the discipline allowed to slacken. Such paragraphs as these appeared in the *Journal* now and then. " His Excellency the Director wishes to express his disapproval of the *corps de ballet* for their getting out of line in the last act of the *Sleeping Beauty.* . . ." " A severe reprimand for wearing jewels with peasant costumes to artists " ; names followed. I had the mortification once to see my name, and also Lydia's, in the rubric of fines. I had miscalculated the day of the week, and did not appear to take my place in the ballet act of the Opera ; it was on one Friday night which I thought to be Thursday. Lydia, my understudy, felt too confident on my reliability, and did not go to the theatre either, though, according to the regulations, all understudies had to be present at the performance. We both were fined to the extent of a month's salary, to be deducted by instalments in the course of a year. The deducting went on for some time, and then the Head of the Chancery sent for me. Talking about other things, he, as if casually, advised me to send in a petition for the lifting of the fine. Not only was it lifted, but the money deducted was restored to us at the end of the year " in consideration of their zealous fulfilment of duty." I must say that such leniency was not a usual proceeding ; fines were not meant as jokes, but towards us both at that time there was a kind and protective feeling on the part of the authorities. I remember an incident of another fine, rich in consequence. It happened during the directorship of Volkonsky. Mathilda Kshessinskaya one night wore her own costume, disregarding the express wish of Prince Volkonsky' that she should put on that designed for the part. She was fined the next day. She took it ill and obtained a retribution ; a few days later the *Journal* displayed an order from the Minister of the Court cancelling the fine. Prince Volkonsky immediately sent in his resignation. He was much and justly liked, and society resented the slight on one of its members. Hostile manifestations towards Mathilda took place in the theatre ; she paid dearly for her short triumph. As an artist, she was then at the best of her wonderful personality. Her virtuosity was not inferior to Legnani's, while her qualities as an actress were supreme.

Mathilda timed her appearances to the height of the season, allowing herself long intervals, during which she left off regular practice. In her holidays, she became untiring in the pursuit of pleasure. Fond of parties, cards, ever laughing, amazingly bright ; late hours never impaired either her looks or her temper. She possessed a marvellous vitality and a quite exceptional will power. Within a month preceding her appearance, she completely subordinated her life to her work. She trained for hours, ceased to receive and go out, went to bed at ten, weighed herself every morning, always ready to restrict further her already frugal diet. Before the performance she stayed in bed twenty-four hours, taking only a light meal at noon. At six o'clock she was at the theatre, allowing herself two full hours in which to make up and practise. One evening I happened to be practising on the stage at the same time as she; I noticed a feverish glitter in her eyes. " Oh ! " she said, in answer to my inquiry, " I have been simply dying for a drop of water the whole day, but I won't drink before dancing." Her fortitude impressed me greatly; I was in the habit of occasionally walking home from rehearsal in order to save my fare for buying a sandwich between the acts. I decided there and then to give it up. While at school, I always admired Mathilda, and even treasured a hairpin I had picked up after her. Now I took her every word as a law.

She showed me great kindness from the very beginning. It was in the autumn of my first year that she sent me an invitation to spend a week-end at her country house at Strelna. " Don't bother about bringing smart frocks," she wrote. " We are quite rustic down here. I will send down to fetch you." Consideration of my insufficient wardrobe had troubled me; she must have guessed it. She had another considerate thought, that I might not know her secretary at the station. To spare me looking for her, she came down herself to fetch me. A small party of friends was staying in the house. As a hostess, she was at her best. The garden was quite big, and close to the sea. Within the paddock lived several goats; a pet one, who made her appearance in *Esmeralda*, knew Mathilda and followed her like a dog. The whole day Mathilda kept me at her side, and had endless little attentions towards me. At dinner she saw me in difficulty : not dexterous enough to carve a snipe in jelly, she took my plate, saying, " Never mind, you have ample time to learn all those tricks." I had the impression that all round her fell under the sway of her gaiety and good nature. Yet, even to my uncritical mind it was obvious that there was a good deal of flattery on the part of her sycophants. Placed as she was, a great artist, rich and influential, that was to be expected. Jealousy and gossip were at all times busy with her name. I had a sense of bewilderment all the day ; it did not seem possible that this charming woman should be the formidable Kshessinskaya alleged to be an unscrupulous intriguer, ruining other people's careers. What completely won me over to her side were little human touches of her character ; there was more in her kindness than the attention of a hostess towards a shy girl under her roof for the first time. Some teased her on my account. " You have turned out a real chaperon, Malechka." " I am going to," she returned, " Tata is such a pet."

" Should anybody try to harm you, come straight to me. I will speak for you," she said to me later. She was as good as her word. Later, there arose an occasion for her to intervene on my behalf. I was getting considerably fewer parts ; it was found out that the impression had been given to the director that the work was too much for me. A prominent ballerina, not, I fear, among my well-wishers, had shown an unexpected anxiety for my health, and begged the director not to overwork me, as I was consumptive. The director accordingly, deceived no doubt by this admirably acted solicitude from a quarter where it was not indigenous, had, from genuine consideration, gradually lessened my work.

Next morning I went back to town, marvelling at what the world can hold of brilliant gaiety. The previous night I had been initiated into a new world. The garden had been illuminated with lanterns ; the house had rung with music and laughter. There was a renewed zest in me as I hurried to Theatre Street, trying to be in time for my lesson. On that bright, mellow morning of early autumn, happiness almost choked me.

CHAPTER XIV

Illness—Visit to Italy—Beretta—Nicolini—Performance at the Court Theatre—Chaliapin—Progress—Nijinsky's Début—" The Eighth Wonder of the World"—An Unfortunate Incident

SHORTLY before the close of the season, in May, 1904, I fell very ill. For some time I had been sickening; my strength often failed me, and my dancing got much weaker. I still enjoyed the partiality of the gallery, but some warnings were given by the critics. In their accounts of performance I was sometimes mentioned as lacking precision. For some time I tried to overcome my illness; it came and went with inexplicable suddenness. When Mother at last called in a doctor, he found an acute malaria. After several attacks, following close on one another, I was left exhausted. The doctor said a change of climate was necessary, and gave the name of a place in the Italian Tyrol, well known for the cure of malaria. As an immediate step towards my improvement, he ordered all the flowers and plants away from the room, where I lay for many weeks. There had been constant inquiries about me; I heard the bell tinkling and voices in the ante-room, but I was not allowed visitors. Mathilda had been very sympathetic, and, on meeting my Mother once, asked her if she could be of any help. I was grateful that Mother did not want to profit by her kind offer. A subsidy as well as a loan had been granted to me by the Chancery; that made it possible for Mother to take me abroad. Two months in Roncegno rid me of the fever. It was time to return to Petersburg for the beginning of the season, but I had lost ground during my illness, and it also had been my dream to work with Signora Beretta of the Scala in Milan. Trefilova and Pavlova had been to study with her; their amazing progress sent Beretta's reputation high among us, so we decided to profit by my being abroad and go to Milan.

We paid a preliminary visit to the Signora in the Via dei Tre Alberghi. We found her at her meal. A leg of chicken in one hand, Signora Beretta, with a stately flourish of the other, waved us towards her sitting-room, where we waited for some time till a ludicrous little figure waddled in. Fat and short, her pyramidal shape was emphasised by a very small head with a meagre blob of hair on top. From the look of her it was unbelievable that she should have been a great star of the Scala. Dry laurel wreaths, an enlarged photo on an easel draped with fringed ribbons, a quantity of smaller photographs showing the Signora in her youth, always rather plump, firmly and correctly planted on her toes, made a pathetic display round a lonely old woman. She was very courteous. It was agreed that I should join her class in two days, the time allowed for her servant, Marcella, to make my tarlatans and bodice. Towards the end of the interview, Signora Beretta got communicative; she took me round her little sitting-room showing me her photographs, giving the names of her parts. We parted friends; she chucked me under the chin. " A dopo domani, giovanina."

Beretta held her class in one of the practice-rooms at the Scala. We were about fifteen, myself the only foreigner, all fairly accomplished dancers except a niece of Beretta's, a weedy little creature, who could not keep up adequately with the very strenuous work of the class. She invariably broke into sobs sooner or later, whereupon the Signora suddenly got ferocious, banged her stick and shrilled out " Piangi, piangi, maladetta." For the rest of the time she remained imperturbable; she never got up from her arm-chair to show the steps set for each day of the week. Even on hot days her knees were wrapped in a rug, a red cushion under her feet. " Marcella," she called now and then, and the old servant came to chafe her feet. We filed up to her after the end of the class; she held her hand out to be kissed; sometimes she embraced us. From the door of the dressing-room the pupils still called affectionately: " Grazie, carissima Signora."

The methods of Beretta were those of the Italian school, which does not care for individual grace of movements, but is implacable as to correctness of attitudes and *port de bras.* Exercises were set in the systematic pursuit of virtuosity; the class was forcible, not a second of rest allowed during the whole bar practice. The result of it for me was a considerable degree of endurance and amplitude of breath. It was hard at the beginning. I had been used to milder practice, and during my first lesson I fainted at the bar.

The dancers were very devout—they called on " *Madonna mia* " at every difficult step—and occasionally invited me to go with them to a small chapel at which the statue of the Holy Virgin was the Protectress of dancers.

The season at the Scala had not begun yet, so I did not see the Italian ballet. From the pupils' talk, I understood the *Excelsior* was the *clou* of their repertoire, and that it was a magnificent show, with a thousand performers on the stage and live elephants.

While in Milan I went to the shoemaker, Romeo Nicolini. At the Marinsky our dancing shoes were usually furnished by the theatre, and were of Parisian make. Those who preferred Italian shoes could get them on their own, touching their shoe money at the end of the year. There was a gradual scale in the distribution of shoes. The *corps de ballet* were entitled to one pair each four performances; *coryphées* received a pair each three performances; second solo dancers for two; first, every night; ballerinas, each act. I stood for a long time in his shop before I could approach him; he was engrossed in the discussion of some acade iic point with two girls, all three gesticulating fiercely. Their hands did beautiful *entrechats* and *cabrioles,* and it was easy, without a word of Italian, to follow the discussion closely. One of the dancers stepped into the middle of the room, gathered her skirts and executed a series of neat *renversées*, while Nicolini nodded approvingly and said " Ecco."

I stayed two months with Signora Beretta ; at parting she embraced me fondly and congratulated me on my progress. I had undoubtedly improved considerably under her tuition ; my jumps were higher, my " points " were stronger, and my general standard of precision had improved beyond all measure. I was now ready to justify the expectation of all those who had pinned their faith on me.

I incurred the slight displeasure of my Chiefs for not returning in time. Some of my parts had been given to other dancers in my absence ; I had to wait for the opportunity of showing my new skill and effacing the impression of weakness I had left behind me. A first chance to do so offered itself in *Pachita*. There was a *pas de trois* in the first act, one of the accepted masterpieces : my appearance in it marked a new stage in my career. A new brilliance and precision had been noticed, as well as the fact that I had to encore a solo which hitherto had been classed as a dull one. In our self-centred world, where no other topics were discussed but those of the successes or failures of the night before, my newly acquired vigour created some stir. The judgment of fellow-artists was more feared than the adverse criticisms of the newspapers, especially the judgment of the *corps de ballet*, where one met with the impartiality of professional knowledge unbiased by personal ambition. Seniority of age, respected from schooldays, made it possible for an obscure dancer of the *corps de ballet* about to retire to give advice to Preobrajenskaya. " Olinka," the former would say, " don't hunch your shoulders. I noticed you did so last night." The advice was accepted gratefully. I remember Maestro Cecchetti telling me once about the famous Ferraris ; she used to place a stage hand in the stalls while rehearsing, who was to criticise her in return for a glass of beer. Adverse criticism did not lose him his drink.

My fellow-artists, through thick and thin, had a generous

belief in me.   At times I was sorely in need of their confidence;
in those early days I was severely criticised by Svetloff, the
leading critic.   I know now that he did it in good faith, and
in later days I had no warmer eulogist than him, but at that time
it wrecked my self-confidence, of which I never had a great
share.   I knew agonies of sickly fear, discouragement beforehand if I had to reappear in the part for which I had been
mercilessly torn to pieces.

*   *   *   *   *

Every year there were several performances given at the
Court Theatre of the Hermitage, where the stage was spacious
enough for the production of any ballet or opera.   The pick
of the cast was nominated to take part in these performances.
On these occasions the *corps de ballet* would be suppressed, and
solo dancers take the ranks.   I remember especially the night
of a fancy-dress ball, when the entire Court wore historical
Russian dresses.   That of the Empress Alexandra Feodorovna
was the genuine saraphan of the Tzaritza Miloslavskaya.   Being
on that night only one of the *corps de ballet*, where comparatively
little concentration was required, I was entirely taken up with
the splendour of all that I could see in front of me.   I strained
my eyes trying to distinguish figures in the semi-obscurity of
the audience.   Those three in front, the Tzar and both Tzaritzas,
one could see distinctly.   The young Empress, in a heavy tiara,
put on over a gauze kerchief entirely concealing her hair, looked
like an ikon of rigid beauty; she held her head very stiff, and
I could not help feeling it would be difficult for her to bend over
her plate at supper.   I had a better view of her in the interval
while peeping through the hole in the curtain, for which there
was great competition; her dress of heavy brocade was sewn
over with jewels.

In the dressing-room, where several of us were getting ready,
I was reprimanded for putting on old shoes.   " Can't you

produce better ones for the Imperial Family, you born raga-
muffin?" The whole of the dressing-room supported the
ironical remark, and I was made to wear a brand new pair.

As a pupil at school, I had danced at the Hermitage before.
Then we were taken straightaway at the end, and missed the
best part of it—the supper. One or other member of the
Imperial Family would come to have supper with the artists;
most often, as on this occasion, it would be the Grand Duke
Vladimir and his sons, who inherited their father's great love
of the theatre. After the Grand Duke left, we still remained
at table. I sat at the far end, where we were all young people.
Sergei Legat made me laugh with his jokes. I leant across the
table answering him by some nonsense; the noise being formidable, I had to shout. Suddenly there was silence; only my
voice rang. Startled I looked up and saw Chaliapin from his
end stretching his arms towards me in a comic attitude. All
looked at me, smiling at some joke of his at my expense. I
was dumbfounded with shyness. In after times, when we had
come to know one another well, I could laugh at his wit, his
imitations and pithy narratives; but now I was ready to cry
from self-consciousness. This was not all. Profiting by a
moment when everybody's attention was turned elsewhere, I
had crept to the door. A strong paw caught me, and the
marvellous voice soared over the hubbub. Soon all were
listening with bated breath. "In love and hate, believe,
Tamara, I'm supreme," sang Chaliapin.

This year's Hermitage presents were made after the design
of Alexandra Feodorovna herself. I received a brooch with
her cipher in rubies and diamonds.

Not for two years yet was I to reach the summit of a dancer's
ambition—the leading part in a five-act ballet. Looked at
broadly, these years were a steady ascent; considered closely
they constituted many failures of unripe understanding, the
whole unavoidable purgatory of doubt. Now, no more a

precocious and petted child of the public, I had reached the stage
where much was asked of me—the justification of the faith
formerly given to me on credit. Exacting demands now
replaced indulgence. I had to readjust my position, and found
it difficult. Above all, I was not equipped with the practical
sense. I was as unfit for scheming as for defending myself
from the inevitable rebukes of jealousy. I had a great, singularly abstract ambition and a total lack of *carriérisme*. I had no
personal influence with critics or influential admirers; and for
that very reason, I believe, Teliakovsky took active care of me.
In the circle of my own age, where jealousy never came to spoil
the mutual affections of schooldays, I was often sent as spokes-
man whenever new tarlatans were wanted or some small privilege
to be obtained. Once I went to see Teliakovsky on account
of some part which brought on me the unfavourable comments
of the critics. With a heavy heart I came to renounce my claim
on it. "Don't pay the slightest attention to the papers," said
Teliakovsky. "You never go to supper with the critics;
hence there may be ill-feeling towards you. Personally, I
think the part suits you, and I wish you to keep it."

Another small incident showed me how much I owed to
my Chiefs. I asked to be relieved from appearing in an opera
under the pretext of a sore toe. I did not care for the part;
that was at the bottom of my move. The same day I was seen
rehearsing away, using my toes unsparingly. Nothing was
said officially, but at the next performance, while I was waiting
in the wings, the Chief of the Chancery took me aside. He
rebuked me mildly for caprices, and concluded by saying:
"You must not spoil our policy by such unreasonable acts."

I received my first great part, that of *Tsar Maiden*, in 1906.
The day was to be the 13th of January. I remember it very
well, as the day seemed to me of bad omen. Teliakovsky had
not been present at my performance; some new production
required his visit to Moscow. He sent for me on his return.
"I am told you were very good the other night, but I would

like to know what you feel about it." He was rather surprised at my self-depreciation, and it was afterwards said that he could not make head or tail out of my account. This part established my positions of rising ballerina, but it was not till the next year that I was given another big part, that of Medora in *Corsair*, a part which stands out as a milestone on my way. Blind groping was left behind; I could now see my way clear down the long path to my ideal.

*   *   *   *   *

Nobody was aware as yet of a sensation about to come. It is curious to note that in the sphere of our stage so closely revolving round its orbit, so watchful of the advent of new talent, the star of Nijinsky had not been hailed before. He was going to finish the school in the coming spring of 1906, and he wasn't talked about yet. In the crowd of other boys, now carrying the train of the Queen, now one of the tormenting spirits in the *Vision of Raymonda*, there moved, unnoticed, the Eighth Wonder of the World. I came across him accidentally. Now, following upon the death of Johannsen, Madame Sokolova had been appointed the teacher of dancers, and held her class every morning in the big rehearsal room. A few of us, wanting to carry on the precepts of Christian Petrovitch, worked separately under Nicolas Legat, his favourite pupil. We were a migrating body, sometimes working in one of the girls' dancing-rooms, but in the mornings, when none were available, proceeding upstairs to the boys' quarters. I always felt uneasy when our small group filed along the narrow gallery overhanging the rehearsal-room. Legat, as if flaunting a comic defiance to the official class down below, walked first, picking out absurd tunes on his fiddle. It seemed to me the eyes of Madame Sokolova looked up at me with furtive reproach: I felt guilty; Father particularly wanted me to work with her, saying a woman, and such an artist as she had been, could be invaluable to me. Eventually I became her pupil.

One morning I came up earlier than usual; the boys were just finishing their practice. I glanced casually, and could not believe my eyes; one boy in a leap rose far above the heads of the others and seemed to tarry in the air. " Who is this ? " I asked Michael Obouchoff, his master. " It is Nijinsky; the little devil never comes down with the music." He then called Nijinsky forward by himself and made him show me some steps. A prodigy was before my eyes. He stopped dancing, and I felt it was all unreal and could not have been; the boy looked quite unconscious of his achievement, prosy and even backward. " Shut your mouth," were his master's parting words. " You fly-swallower." " Off with you all now." Like peas falling out of a bag, the boys rushed off, their patter a hollow repercussion in the vaulted passage. In utter amazement I asked Michael why nobody spoke of this remarkable boy, and he about to finish. " They will soon," chuckled Michael. " Don't you worry."

Recognition of Nijinsky's wonderful gifts could not fail to be unanimous from the moment he came on the stage; there was some reserve, however, in the appreciation of his personality. " He is not much to look at, and will never be a first-rate mime." The troupe as well as the audience misjudged the unique quality of his talent; had he tried to follow an approved pattern of male perfection, he would never have given the full measure of his genius. In later years, Diaghileff, with that clear perception of his that was almost uncanny, revealed to the world and to the artist himself the latter's true shape. At the expense of his better self, Nijinsky valiantly tried to answer the requirements of the traditional type till Diaghileff the wizard touched him with his magic wand. The guise of a plain, unprepossessing boy fell off —a creature exotic, feline, elfin completely eclipsed the respectable comeliness, the dignified commonplace of conventional virility. Special dances were constantly introduced for Nijinsky; I was almost invariably his partner. A *pas de deux* from an old ballet, *Roxana*, was our first dance together. A painful incident in connection with it is still vivid in my memory. We had rehearsed by ourselves wherever a free dancing-room was to be found ; the first time we danced before the whole company was at a theatre rehearsal ; I was aware of the intense interest of all the artists ; I felt a scrutiny, not unkind, round us both, and was more nervous than at a performance. We finished ; the company clapped. From a group in the first wing, a sanctum reserved only for primas, an infuriated figure rushed up to me. " Enough of your brazen impudence. Where do you think you are, to dance quite naked ? . . ." I couldn't realise what had happened. It appeared that the strap of my bodice had slipped off and my shoulder had become uncovered, which I was not conscious of during my dance. I stood in the middle of the stage dumbfounded, helpless against volleys of coarse words hurled at me from the same cruel mouth. The *régisseur* came on and led off the Puritan. By this time a dense crowd of sympathisers had surrounded me ; my chronic want of handkerchiefs necessitated the use of my tarlatan skirt to wipe away the tears. Preobrajenskaya, stroked my head, repeating : " Sneeze on the viper, sweetheart. Forget her, and think only of those beautiful pirouettes of yours." The scandal spread rapidly, and an ovation met me at the next performance.

CHAPTER XV

The Russo-Japanese War—Preobrajenskaya—A Provincial Tour
—Strange Reception in Warsaw

DURING the Russo-Japanese war of 1905 the performances
at the Hermitage were naturally suspended; the regular
life of the theatre went on as before. Within, *battements* and
entrechats and *pirouettes* remained of paramount importance; art
was snugly sheltered, oblivious of the storm already gathering.
From outside, the reverberation of the distant war penetrated
but faintly into the auditorium; empty stalls here and there
reminded that officers had gone to the war; in the intervals the
latest telegrams were sent for. The disastrous war hardly over,
great troubles broke out in the country; our little world was
still at its pursuits, eagerly looking forward to the benefit night
of Preobrajenskaya.

Her road to success had been a hard one. She had begun as
a *corps de ballet* dancer and gradually worked her way to the
top. Her virtuosity she owed to Cecchetti, her master, and
perhaps even more to her own undaunted courage. Cecchetti
was busy at the school the whole morning, she daily at rehearsal
and nightly at the theatre, taking part not only in every ballet,
but almost in every opera where there were dances. The
performance over, she went to take her lesson with the Maestro;
it lasted far into the night. Artists respected her greatly for her
perseverance and loved her gentle ways. Her ultimate success
was greeted with enthusiasm by all.

Preobrajenskaya had fixed her benefit for the 9th of January.
I was not dancing, and sat in the stalls. She had chosen her
masterpiece, *Les Caprices du Papillon*. Towards the last act,
alarming rumours ran in the theatre—riots had broken out in

the town; the mob were on their way to the theatre; they had already broken into the Alexandrinsky and stopped the performance. Panic spread. The theatre quickly emptied. On the stage the performance never so much as flickered. Our discipline was good; it was to be tested more severely still in days to come. After the end I went behind the scenes. All were hurriedly changing to get home quick. I lived close to the theatre; at the stage door I found Lev waiting for me.

I never liked using the theatre carriages except on rainy days. They called at various places to deposit their loads, so that it took me twice as long to drive as to walk. Besides, I had a passion for wandering and looking into people's windows. I had favourite spots in the district which I knew as my own ten fingers. Strong associations were attached to these places. As a child I had invented stories about the people living inside, stories told to myself in instalments, each walk a new instalment. In a lane at the back of the Church of the Archangel Michael there was a wooden house, whose panelled gate had two urns on its pilasters; the small architrave and window cornices were ornamented with carved wreaths pierced by an arrow. The place bore the melancholy name of Cancelled Lane. The windows of the lower storey came level with the ground; at the last window a young seamstress, a Jewess with pathetic eyes and a skin like a camellia, sat working. I passed so often and looked so intently at her that, at the end, we smiled and nodded to each other. One day I missed her in her usual place; she did not reappear any more. Her story shaped like this to me: She was in love with a Christian; all was agreed between them; she was going to renounce her faith; her father discovered her plans and turned her out with a curse. . . .

Slightly out of my way, but I made a détour sometimes, was the shop where we used to buy penny books, and where I had bought once a much-coveted box fringed with tissue paper. Nowadays I went to look at my photographs sold there as postcards. On my way to the theatre I liked to call at this and other favourite places to take my mind off the stage fright; it was soothing and restored my mental equilibrium.

On that night we reached home safely. The streets were quiet and empty. Lev was telling me what he knew about the disastrous day; it had been on that morning that the priest Gapon had led the workmen to the Winter Palace to present a petition. Had the Emperor been in town, the tragedy might have been averted.

*   *   *   *   *

Lydia's brother, Yegoroushka, a dancer, had planned a provincial tour for us for the summer of this year. He was many years older than Lydia, and acted as her guardian. To me he showed the same rough kindness as to her; but we were both slightly afraid of him. Previous to the provincial tour, he had taken us to Warsaw, where one of the regiments was celebrating its jubilee. We danced at the Grand Theatre; the gallery packed with soldiers suddenly burst into laughter when I spinned my pirouettes. Every time I stood on my toes, the other leg up, in a ballet pose, roars of laughter from up above shook the theatre. Towards the end I heard only suppressed giggles. There was a banquet given to us after the performance, and I took the opportunity of asking the officer next to me what had made the soldiers laugh. It appeared that some disapproved of the ballet on the ground of decency; others, the hilarious section, had merely been expressing, in the way usual with simple people, their astonishment at the novel sight of someone standing on one leg. "The Barishnaya no doubt knows her job," one had said to the officer, "but, poor little lady, she is underfed." "Stands on one leg and whirls like a peg-top," giggled another.

Yegoroushka accepted invitations for us and went to parties as our chaperon; when going out on his own, he locked us up. "Safer: too many young men about." Lydia and I shared a pretty room on the attic floor of the old-fashioned Hotel Brühl.

For the summer tour Yegoroushka got together about fifteen dancers. We had to furnish our own costumes, though some of mine had been lent me by the kindly wardrobe mistress of the Marinsky. The loan was unofficial, granted under a vow of secrecy. On the top floor of the Marinsky, room after room was filled with wooden chests and hampers. She let me choose from disused ones, of which there were quantities. Some of the names I knew faintly ; some I had never heard of. I almost forgot the purpose of my call, wondering what could have been those ballets with titles so ponderous and quaintly graceful. Now, as in my childhood, names and words had an uncanny power over me ; they ruled my actions by inexplicable magic. As a child I had come across Madagascar in one of my books, and often repeated it under my breath ; it had all the quality of an incantation. I asked to look into " Roxana, the Beauty of Montenegro." Nothing suited me out of this hamper, and I turned next to the " Reward of Virtue, or Liza the Milkmaid," and found a *paysanne* dress which took my fancy (in ballet jargon we still referred to peasants as *paysani* and *paysanki*). Some dresses we made at home, Mother helping me with a Spanish costume for *Paquita*. I made myself a fillet of golden thread, working it as I used to net hammocks as a child. Our home-made costumes must have been pretty clumsy, but they were the apples of my eyes. As I possessed no trunks, I travelled with my costumes in my hand, wrapped up in the old Bokhara shawl of many hues.

From the programmes our repertoire looked ambitious, but, in fact, the ballets were very much curtailed and, adapted to the small means of our company, could be but a poor show. In a few of the big towns the theatre and orchestra were good, and the performance went on creditably ; when we came to out-of-the-way little holes of the western district, our shows became precarious. The first fiddle of the Marinsky came as conductor on our tour. Nothing having been organised beforehand, the valiant soul would go out in the morning to collect musicians ;

collecting was done by means of canvassing pedestrians in the main street. " Can you play some instrument ? " he addressed people at random. Not many of them could, but they often gave information as to where one could find a small band. In this district, where the population was almost entirely Jewish, no wedding festivity would be complete without some band. At Kishineff there was an especially disastrous performance ; the unexpected sounds raised by the band (nervousness was to be taken into account) only faintly resembled the well-known music, and at times silence fell but for the obbligato of the double bass and the voice of the conductor singing loud the melody till the musicians, one by one, picked it up.

Yegoroushka, in making my salary 25 roubles (£2 10s.) a month, laid great stress on the fact that experience was what I needed most. A rough and tumble, it was indeed an experience of sorts. The enthusiasm I felt for these parts, unattainable to me on our stage, hardly suffered from the tawdriness of the surroundings. The restraint and timidity I had felt for a long time at the Marinsky, where the thought of the severe judges watching for my mistakes sometimes set me trembling, now left me. However naïve my conception may have been, I achieved much towards feeling the parts.

CHAPTER XVI

A " Ballet " Revolt—Pavlova, Fokine and Myself as " Revolutionaries "—Tragic Death of Sergei Legat—Lovat Fraser

THE autumn of 1905, the autumn of the attempted revolution, I remember even now as a nightmare. A cruel October wind from the sea, chill, sleet, sinister hush in the town. For several days trams had not been running, the strike gaining rapidly. My heart was heavy as one night I was going home from a political meeting which we artists had held that day. I chose a roundabout way, avoiding pickets. My thin shoes let in water. My feet were numb, my mind bewildered. That artists, so conservative at heart, usually so loyal to the Court, of which we were a modest part, should have succumbed to the epidemic of meetings and resolutions seemed to me like treason. Meetings were being held everywhere ; autonomy, freedom of speech, freedom of conscience, freedom of the printed word— even children at school were passing these resolutions. Whether in full conscience of the cause (I have reason to think it was not so) or following a few leaders, our troupe also put forward claims and chose twelve delegates to negotiate them. Fokine, Pavlova and myself were amongst them. Our President was a man from the ranks of the *corps de ballet*, a student at the University, a man of high integrity and limited vision.

The light was cut off that night in the whole town. I groped my way upstairs ; our flat, as usual, was lit by petrol lamps. Mother met me aggressively ; she had been much against my going to the meeting at all. " It will land you in a pretty mess, those meetings. Mark my words."—" Let the child say first what has happened." Father's tolerant intervention gave me an opening. Keeping as much as I could to the words of our

orators, I explained that it was decided " to raise the standard
of art to its adequate height." " How are you going to raise
it ? " from Mother threw me off my high horse.   During our
meeting I could not make out how it would benefit art if we were
to rule ourselves.   Not only was there no conviction in me as
to the righteousness of our motives, but all my love for the
theatre, its atmosphere, its loyalty to our upbringing, felt deeply
wounded.   My feeling at the meeting was that of a meditated
sacrilege, but words had failed me.   I fell in, however, with the
wishes of the others, and put my own feeling down to my faint-
heartedness.   And now, like repeating a lesson, I told them at
home that we were going to ask for autonomy, choose our own
Committee to decide artistic questions and questions of salary ;
do away with the methods of bureaucratic organization.   My
words sounded hollow to my own ears.   " So you are in arms
against the Emperor who gave you an education, position, means
of livelihood.   Don't you go raising any standards.   You will
bring your art to a high level if you become a great artist,"
summed up Mother.   She was for using her parental authority
and forbidding my going out till all was quiet again.   Lev had
his word.   In his opinion, though it was all nonsense, I had to
stand or fall with my friends.   " You can't wish her to be disloyal to her fellow-artists," he said to Mother.   " Where is your
fairness of mind ? "   Poor Liberal little Mother was silenced by
his argument.   Father was for temporising and pretending an
illness.   I meant to go through, but was miserable.

A resolution of the meeting was being elaborated at Fokine's
flat.   I fancied that the porter at the front door cast a glance of
disapproval at me ; there was no greeting, none of that familiarly
respectful chat which constitutes the code of *bienséance* of such
folk.   The somewhat forced cheerfulness of the members present
was a relief to me ; I felt almost ready to believe they were in
the right.   It occurred to me too that they would not have
faced the risk without some potent reason ; the reason must be
the righteousness of the claim.   So I went on thinking thus till

we came to discussing the demands for raising our salaries. There the ghastliness of what seemed to me to be blackmail flashed on my much tortured mind. I believed I could yet prevent our doing wrong, and asked Fokine to have a talk with me apart. We went out on the landing for privacy. There, groping for my words, humiliated by what might appear apostasy, I told him my doubts. He listened sympathetically. Nothing he said served to allay my scruples, but in the emphasis of his conviction, in the pathos of his words I saw an honesty of purpose. " Whatever happens," he concluded, taking me by the hand, " I will be for ever thankful we stood side by side in this crisis."

One by one the belated members arrived, bringing some fresh information. The railways had stopped ; to prevent a meeting of workmen on the Vassily Ostroff the bridges had been raised. Fokine picked up a receiver to see if the telephone was still working. No reply from the exchange. He continued to listen. " Confusion on the lines. . . . Bits of information swim pell-mell. . . . Nothing more heard." Two little dancers, mere boys, came in all flushed and excited ; they constituted themselves scouts. Their honest admiration for our actions would not allow them to keep quiet. " We saw some detectives outside," they bubbled, interrupting each other, " must be detectives, both in pea-green overcoats and goloshes." At all times the obviousness of our secret police, their goloshes in all weathers, were everybody's joke. According to the scouts, the performance was going to be stopped at the Alexandrinsky, the actors would harangue the audience from the stage.

The whole day passed in desultory tension ; an improvised meal was served, and in the evening it was decided to go to the Alexandrinsky so that we might act in concert with the dramatic troupe. We found the performance going on in much the usual way. Karpoff, the *régisseur*, took us to a small entresol room behind the scenes. Properties for the week's repertoire were stored there, and the room was much lumbered with stage garlands, portraits of ancestors, halberds, helmets and furniture, but there was nobody in it. Karpoff pulled up a curule chair for me and retired to the fanlight window. The dramatic troupe was to strike till its claims were satisfied. He spoke hurriedly, looking at his watch. Bells rang for the " all down." He rushed on the stage, finishing on the way, " Bear in mind, we are striving for an honourable freedom. Not long ago the Russian actor was a serf . . . Now is the moment. Pull up the skies, you up there "—the last words addressed to the stage hands. We left him busy with the usual routine of the performance. On the morrow we were to hand our resolution to the authorities. Next day, coming at the appointed time, I found my fellow-delegates walking up and down Theatre Street. The first arrival had found the door of the vestibule locked ; from within, Andrei, the porter, had refused admittance. Much indignation was felt at this affront. When all had gathered, we went into the Chancery. Teliakovsky being away at Moscow, the Chief of his Chancery received us. All through the speech delivered by our President, his face bore a pained expression. A former officer, he clicked his heels with a dry bow and, without any comment, he remarked that the resolution of the troupe would be handed to His Excellency on his return from Moscow ; the audience was at an end.

The next step was to try and prevent the matinée performance at the Marinksy. *La Dame de Pique* was being given ; a considerable number of dancers appeared in it. My duty was to go round the ladies' dressing-rooms and call the dancers off. The task was distasteful to me, and my eloquence not of the most persuasive. A few left the theatre ; the majority refused to strike.

Within the next few days the circular of the Minister of the Court was made known to the troupe. Our action was qualified as a breach of discipline ; all who wished to remain loyal were to sign a declaration. The great majority signed, leaving us, their chosen delegates, in the lurch. We represented nobody,

yet continued to gather either at Fokine's or at Pavlova's flat.
" Well, you have played your little game," said Mother one
night, " you are no more members of the troupe." She had
been to gather information as usual at Oblakoff's. I believed
what she said was true, though no direct notice had been given
to us. There were more alarming events happening than the
mutiny of a few artists ; on the 16th of October a mass meeting
on the Vassily Ostroff proclaimed the Republic. Whether the
morrow would bring arrests or a revolution nobody ventured
to say.

Twelve of us were gathered as usual ; we clung to each other
those days—suspense was easier to bear in company. The door
bell rang. Fokine went to open. A few moments later he
staggered back into the room. " Sergei has cut his throat," and
broke down sobbing.

Sergei Legat, bitterly against his will, had been nagged into
signing the declaration. The soul of loyalty, he felt himself a
traitor. " I am a Judas to my friends." The same night he
raved, " Marie, which is lesser in the eyes of God, that I should
take your life or mine ? " He was found in the morning, his
throat cut with a razor.

*   *   *   *   *

Many years later I came across one who reminded me of my
lost comrade. My friendship with Lovat Fraser was of necessity
of short duration ; I met him in 1920, barely a year before his
untimely death. I was planning the production of the *Nursery
Rhymes* and wanted him to design it. With all due deference
I approached the much admired artist, Hugh Walpole acting as
mediator. Next day Lovat brought me some of his designs for
our ballet, and at the same time with our work started a great
intimacy that bound me to him and Grace, his wife ; it needed
no preliminaries.

Lovat the artist or Lovat with an inexhaustible fund of meek humour, I do not know which was dearer to his friends. The artist in him was inseparable from the man; there were no watertight compartments between the two. Lovat needed no isolation, no working himself up for the intensive productiveness of his last years. He would sit hunched in a basket chair in an attitude snug, but hardly suggestive of draughtmanship, and at times use an odd implement—a nailbrush applied savagely on a finished design. Neither his small daughter crawling over him as he drew, nor William of Orange, with contented purr settling on his knee, would provoke any sign of impatience from him; he went on working just the same. A big kitchen table, hopelessly littered, stood by him, and one wondered how his clean beautiful colours could have come out of all those bottles that, from the look of them, might have contained boot polish. Talking of a curious toy he had seen in a shop, a tiny pedlar woman and her diminutive wares, Lovat put off the drawing of the Industrious Pirate to see what he could achieve in the way of a small picture. " I'm making you a birthday present, Thamar." A square inch of masterpiece—marching soldiers, their banners flying—was soon ready. But he decided he could do a better one : a tiny fair came next, and " The Charm of the English Countryside " (a tree, a cloud, a cottage the size of a pea), crowned his effort.

The production of *Nursery Rhymes* hardly over, we started planning another. The collaboration was not to cease if we could help it. During one of the Saturday suppers I had in my house, we conceived an ambitious scheme of uniting English composers and artists to establish periodical seasons of ballet. None of us had sufficient money for the undertaking. We thought the idea might appeal to the British public, and decided to circulate what we joyfully called a " manifesto." This manifesto, besides Lovat and myself, was signed by Arthur Bliss, Arnold Bax, Eugene Goossens, Lord Berners, Holst, Paul Nash, Albert Rutherston and others. We expected generous support, but got none. However, the getting up of the document had afforded us much merriment. These parties at my house went on far into the night and were often marked by " serenades," as Harriet Cohen, to all " Tania," called the musical surprises she arranged for me—I was not to know beforehand what they were to be, whether Eugene Goossens would play or Mademoiselle Colignon sing ; most often it would be Tania herself playing Arnold's compositions.

In good faith and joy of heart we were preparing another production. Arnold Bax having orchestrated a ballade of Chopin as a present, we were staging it and also *Jack in the Green*, for which Holst let me use his St. Paul's suite. Lovat was taken ill. On the eve of his operation he sent me his last drawing ; strength was failing him ; only the half of the figure was drawn, but his thought dwelt as ever on his work. Unselfish and considerate to the end, he added explanations for the best and cheapest execution of the costume.

Lovat's death left a great void in the life of his friends ; in his presence one felt better and happier. There was no stern, forbidding virtue in his character—only the gentleness that radiated from him and seemed to keep all evil things at bay. Unfaltering kindness lit by crystal gaiety : what power for good there is in such as Lovat Fraser and Sergei Legat.

* * * * *

On the 17th of October the Ukaz creating the Duma was issued. It included an amnesty for strikers. In a few days life resumed its normal current, and our inglorious *épopée* finished with a fatherly admonition. Teliakovsky assembled the delegates : as far as our resolution was concerned, he exonerated us ; the attempted strike was an act of flagrant insubordination, and he pointed out that it might have fared far worse with us had there been no amnesty. He mildly qualified the policy of the troupe as misguided. The position of artists, he pointed out, was that of a privileged body, receiving a free education and provided for to the end of their lives; was this strike a grateful return for all these benefits?

Amongst the artists actively involved in our brief trouble there were some who hinted darkly at the prospect of a covert persecution on the part of the direction as a result of the events of October. The subsequent career of Pavlova, Fokine and myself clearly showed that there was no such intention in the mind of Teliakovsky. For a time an antagonism was felt between the two factions of the troupe, but that soon wore out. The funeral of Sergei first brought us all together in a common grief. I felt thankfulness when resuming work; the theatre became dearer than ever to me, the world I had almost despaired of living in again.

The gallery, true to its hero-worship, manifested its approval of what it judged to be the courage of conviction, and the former delegates of the troupe were loudly acclaimed. I personally was much weakened by the strain, nervous and physical; the long journeys on foot in rain and bitter wind, protracted vigils, abandoned practice, occasional, if any, meals —all told on me now. When I first reappeared after the last weary fortnight, my execution was poor; I was on the point of fainting when I came off the stage. With daily work I recovered fairly quick and in time to meet the important events of my career.

CHAPTER XVII

The Rhythm of Theatre Life—Petipa—The Beginning of Fokine's Régime—Isadora Duncan—Fokine's Creative Efforts—" Cleopatra "—Prague

THE life of the theatre obeyed the same rhythm, day in, day out. With performances only twice a week, there was ample time for preparation, for thought, for one's own life. Occasional gaiety, escapades now and then—for the rest my own life was subordinate to that of the stage. Before nine o'clock I left the house with my diminutive Gladstone bag, containing my shoes and some dancing apparel. The mood of the day was determined by the degree of my satisfaction over my practice; the day loomed bright if my pirouettes and *entrechats* were neat; depression set in when I could not master difficulties. Quiet and concentrated was the atmosphere of our big room in the morning—it was an academy till noon; then the whole stairs and dressing-rooms filled with chat, gossip, laughter as the whole *corps de ballet* arrived for rehearsal. For those in the ranks, the daily routine of rehearsing was no more than a conscientious duty. Sedately seated along the walls, some with knitting, some drinking tea, they gossiped about the latest scandal, talked of the price of living, servants, and all the trivialities of life, till interrupted by a call. To us, the ambitious ones, all other interests were submerged by the one great undertaking. We could not sit quiet. At the back of the room several of us would practice steps and try some *tour de force*. Most often, seeing I would not be wanted for some time, I liked to escape; finding some empty room in the Babylon of the Theatre School, undisturbed by noise and by the critical remarks of onlookers, with the mirror for judge, I became daring. I plunged headlong into difficulties yet inaccessible, often failed, sometimes succeeded. Neither falls nor failures ever discouraged me, so long as nobody witnessed them; I had unlimited daring. In the lonely, happy pursuit time flew; often the head of a courier, whose duty it was to watch that the artists should be in their places when needed, would peep round. " Tamara Platonovna, please to come down."

The duty of coaching us in the current repertoire devolved on the *régisseur*, Sergueieff. He was an adherent of the system of notation, and had written down many ballets. Still, a favourite method of reviving forgotten parts, and the one used by artists, was that of recalling the dance by memory while the music was being played. " Music prompts," we used to say. Prompting often came from unexpected quarters. Some one of the older dancers, of the grade we surnamed " Near the Water," would call out " No! No! that is not the step Brianza did in this part, I remember." Here she would indicate the forgotten step. A piece of water so often figured in the background of the old type scenery that it gave its name to the back rankers.

I would leave my tarlatans in the dressing-room, but the mental luggage of my day's work I brought home from Theatre Street. While driving in the omnibus, I often became aware of the amused smiles of people sitting opposite. In utter confusion, I then realised that I was mentally going through my dances. My face must have worn a ludicrously ecstatic expression, as my head waggled and bowed to the music running in it. I moved, ate, dressed and spoke to an irrepressible obbligato of ballet tunes, to the sway of dance rhythms. Taking only perfunctory care of my clothes, I spent my evenings at home in darning and breaking in my ballet shoes, mending tights and making tarlatans. A book before me, I read by snatches and worked. " I see you are running through your new variation," Mother sometimes startled me. We all sat of evenings round the dining-table. Nominally independent, I was as much under Mother's rule as when a child. I never dreamt of going anywhere without asking her permission. An occasional walk home alone from Theatre Street was all the freedom I needed. When let free earlier than usual, I would take a circuitous route home. Walking through the colonnades of Kazan Cathedral, I counted the columns on both sides. I had once suffered from persistent insomnia, and Mother had advised me to fix my mind on counting these columns, but lying awake I could not visualise them at that time. And now, dreading the recurrence of my complaint, wanted to provide a ready cure. I seldom missed going in to offer my votive heart and a penny candle to the miraculous Image. The next stage on that route was a hunchbacked footbridge with four lions. I hesitated between smart, lovely Morskaya and dreary Kazanskaya ; in the latter there was a shop window with popular prints of biblical and patriotic subjects. Parables of Lazarus, Daniel in the lions' den, the Battle of Poltava, the storming of Erzerum, I could not define what attracted me in those cheap pictures. It must have been the naïve intricacy of episodes grouped round the chief medallion.

I was far from realising at the time that we were witnessing the close of a glorious epoch of our ballet. The force that had built the formidable structure was ebbing away. Marius Petipa, close on 90, had retired. In the history of our ballet he will stand a providential figure of titanic strength. His genius was unquestioned during his lifetime, but the wealth of his inheritance could only have been appreciated retrospectively in connection with the new movement. The force of Petipa's creations reached out far beyond his lifetime and is not yet entirely spent.

Fokine, in spite of passive disapproval on the part of the elder members of the troupe, began his career of ballet-master under good auspices. The first ballet produced by him was for a charity performance. The initiative of asking him came from a group of men dancers of a distinctively higher intellectual level than the majority of our troupe. They were members of the committee of a grammar school for peasant children founded and maintained by our ballet. The cause being patronised by the authorities, the stage, orchestra and costumes were given free by the theatre. Fokine chose his interpreters among his supporters. Pavlova, himself and I had the leading parts in *The Vine*. This ballet had been given before, but was soon shelved partly on account of its music, considered too symphonic. The music of Rubinstein certainly differed from the favourite type of ballet music, a string of obvious tunes squared up in 32 or 64 bars to fit an amount of steps considered the limit of a dancer's endurance. From Father I had heard that there was another reason for the disgrace of *The Vine*. According to the plot, a party of revellers, after excessive libations, fell asleep in the wine cellar; the Spirit of the Vine appears in their dream, and the scene becomes a bacchanal. As it had been performed at a gala celebrating the wedding of a Grand Duchess, the subject was found coarse and unsuitable to the occasion; the ballet was disapproved.

By his choice of this piece, Fokine established the first point of his creed :—" Music is not the mere accompaniment of a rhythmic step, but an organic part of a dance; the quality of choreographic inspiration is determined by the quality of the music." The whole outward attitude of Fokine towards the steadfast canons of tradition was that of antagonism; he stood isolated from the majority of the troupe. A few, and those the younger ones, grouped round him. My mind could not easily discard the beliefs in which I had been brought up : Fokine's intolerance often pained and shocked me, but his enthusiasm, his impetuosity, subjugated my fancy. My belief in him was deeply rooted before he actually began producing. Through casual remarks of his, through tirades steeped with a feeling of a crusade to be led against the smug and the Philistine, there loomed new shores, there called glorious exploits.

> New Argonauts in quest of beauty,
> Our soul we pledged to the sea.

As soon as a sonorous stanza would fit in with my feeling, all my doubts dispersed.

The great sensation caused in the artistic world by the first appearance of Isadora Duncan was still fresh when, in the spring of 1907, Fokine produced his *Eunice*, this time for inclusion in the repertoire.

Isadora had rapidly conquered the Petersburg theatrical world. There were, of course, always the reactionary *balletomanes*, to whom the idea of a barefoot dancer seemed to deny the first principles of what they held to be sacred in art. This, however, was far from being the general opinion, and a desire for novelty was in the air.

I remember that the first time I saw her dance I fell completely under her sway. It never occurred to me that there was the slightest hostility between her art and ours. There seemed room for both, and each had much that it could learn to advantage from the other.

Later, in Paris, I viewed her from a more critical angle, because she had developed her now well-known theories and explanations of her art. I could no more see her as an individual artist, but as a militant doctrinaire, and moreover I could feel many discrepancies between her ideals and her actual performances, though her theories were for the most part nebulous, and had little real connection with actual dancing on the stage.

She had all the sentimentality of the New Englander, so incompatible with the rôle of a revolutionary.

" It is in the unopened flower that I find the inspiration for the new dance . . . dancing must be something so big and so beautiful that the beholder says to himself, ' I see before me the movements of the soul, the soul of an opening flower.' "

In her strictures on ballet, which she termed a " false and artificial art," Duncan blindly attacked the essential element of all stage art—artificiality. Like a child who knows the alphabet but cannot yet read a book, in her limited sectarian vision, she laid down the principle that the art of dancing must return to its natural state, its very alphabet. Whoever said that nature never produced a symphony by Beethoven or a landscape by Ruysdael answered her arguments with finality. However, a great artist can be an indifferent theorist, and the perfectly genuine impulsiveness of her bodily movements should have been sufficient reason for her art unaided by far-fetched arguments.

Her art was personal by its very nature, and could only have remained so. Through my own experience I realised that teaching is not the conveying of your personal knowledge to the pupil, neither is it to model the pupil after your own individual shape. Teaching of art can only be based on what the consecutive achievement of the ages has built up—technique, in fact.

Duncan's thesis was completely overpowered when Fokine, equipped with all the technique of balletic form, made *Eunice* as a direct tribute to her, with a far greater range of movements than those at the command of Duncan or her pupils. It was possible for us with our training to have danced as she did, but she, with her very limited vocabulary, could not have emulated us. She had created no new art. Duncanism was but a part of the art to which we had the key. All the amateurs, who to-day seek a short cut to success as dancers, and seek to express themselves by prancing about in Greek costume, are the result of these mistaken doctrines.

My admiration for the artist herself has not diminished in spite of my critical attitude. I have retained two vivid impressions of that season that to me sum up both the shortcomings and the sublime qualities of that remarkable artist.

As was her custom, before the curtain rose on her dances to the music of *Tannhäuser*, she addressed the public to explain her interpretation, and she told them that she considered that the climax of the Venusberg music was too mighty for expression by the dance, and that a darkened stage and the spectator's imagination could alone supply the necessary intensity of feeling.

But when she interpreted the *Elysian Fields*, then her artistic means were not only adequate, but raised to the same level of supreme and absolute beauty as the music of Glück itself. She moved with those wonderful steps of hers with a simplicity and detachment that could only come through the intuition of genius itself. She seemed to float, a complete vision of peace and harmony, that very embodiment of the classical spirit that was her ideal.

In truth, *Eunice* was a compromise between our tradition and the Hellenic revival embodied by Isadora. The leading part, taken by Kshessinskaya on the first night, displayed in its texture an almost complete vocabulary of classical ballet. Pavlova, looking as a figure out of a Pompeian frieze, from her first appearance to the end, was consistent and exquisite; she infused a definite sense of style into *Eunice*. She and the whole of the *corps de ballet* had bare feet or make-believe ones. Tights were not to be discarded; ten toes pencilled in had to suffice to the illusion. After the first night, Kshessinskaya gave up her part to Pavlova, and I replaced the latter.

A perspective of years between this first creative effort of Fokine's and his later mastery shows how timid was the initial manifestation of his rebellious spirit. " Lord help me," exclaimed a robber when he made the sign of the Cross previous to looting a church. In his ikonoclastic campaign, Fokine performed the old rites of devotion to the orthodox forms of dance. When in full possession of his means, in the ripeness of his talent, Fokine still remained, whether consciously or not, a logical consequence of the epic Petipa. No more could be added to the serene grandeur of the cycle completed; the modern mind, of which Fokine was the expression, criticised previous methods : rhetoric, the empty pomp ; the ready-made formulæ. In the colossal fabric of Petipa's ballets, the subject was treated abstractedly, a mere vehicle for the dance. No more padding lame action with mimetic monologues ; no more conventional gestures, like the language of deaf mutes : Fokine brought the dramatic plot to a logical simplicity, to the three unities of Greek drama. But while his choreographic invention was woven after finer designs, its tissue was worked on the same loom as that of his great predecessor. A " balletic " form of dance was termed classical from time immemorial. Fokine used classical dance as the basis of his choreography. He embroidered new patterns on it ; he invested it with the style of any given epoch into which he made excursions ; but his starting point was always the virtuosity of the classical ballet, and he made use of the rich material accumulated in its treasury. *Eunice* excluded, the majority of his productions needed a high degree of virtuosity on the part of the interpreter. What he could not stand was the obviousness of difficulty, an exhibition of technical tricks. " Why all these long preparations ? You are not going to burst into *fouettés*." In the course of the same rehearsal he would be moved to transports alternatively of admiration and fury. Because of his earnestness, of his demanding of the best one could give, we his followers were devoted to him, though he was extremely irritable and had no control of his temper. At the beginning it used to upset us ; in time we grew used to chairs thrown about, to his leaving rehearsals in the middle, to his vehement harangues. At theatre rehearsals he sat in the stalls to see the effect of his staging. Over the heads of the orchestra, his voice, hoarse with shouting, opened at intervals a machine-gun fire of imprecations. " Putrid execution. Loose, untidy. I won't stand carelessness."

In time, when not only a comparatively small group was at his command, but the whole of our company abroad respected a leader in his person, he grew even more dictatorial. I remember an incident at Monte Carlo. He was taking the rehearsal of *Giselle*. The same evening I had to dance the part and naturally spared myself, only marking the steps and the chief moments of the acting. The ensemble lagged ; Fokine waxed wrath ; suddenly he flew at me. " How can I blame the *corps de ballet* if the star herself gives a bad example. Yes ! your example is corrupting, shameful, scandalous." He rushed off. The same night he fondly hovered round me, giving a touch to my make-up. He smiled blandly when I poured out my grievance against the morning scene, and commented on my last act of *Giselle*. "You seemed to float in the air. . . ."

Immediately after *Eunice* Fokine produced *The Egyptian Nights*, later known as *Cleopatra*. A considerable part of our troupe, the "first subjects" especially, manifested undisguised hostility towards our work. As a prospective ballerina, I shared the dressing-room of the stars. I felt in an enemy's camp at times; some grotesque and funny imitations were given there, deriding our efforts. I could not argue very well : the law of seniority was in force on the stage as it had been at school. The youngest member of the upper caste, I was shouted down, admonished for my "swollen head," my "antics." I stood in need of a much greater amount of fortitude when, on my becoming sole leader in Fokine's ballets, I had to face the prejudice of the conservative element amongst the audience and the critics. Wilfully overlooking the fact that, parallel with my new parts, I steadily moved upwards in the classical ballets and worked incessantly, my critics charged me with being a renegade to tradition. But as suddenly as the persecution began, it left off.

* * * * *

Back from a voyage round the world Lieutenant Furioso emerged as fertile a plan-hatcher as ever. He was now scheming an engagement at Prague for me. He had made friends with the Panslavist leader in Prague. This matter was somehow being instrumental in bringing about my engagement. Not till I received a formal invitation from the National Theatre at Prague did I take his plan seriously. Even then I could not realise I was to dance abroad; the venture seemed a leap into the unknown. I could find nothing in my experience capable of giving a body to my future surroundings. I could not house my imaginary self into a definite picture; a vague nostalgia, as of a homeless spirit, mixed with my pride and elation. I was not to start for a couple of months. One of the items of my preparations was the polishing of my French. My correspondence with the director of the National Theatre, M. Schmoranz, had been carried on in that language; I concluded it was to be the official medium. Madame Florence, recommended to me by some friends, not only polished my halting speech to fluency; she warned me against the loosely worded translation of Russian thought, very common with us. She spoke beautiful French; her sentences had some of the cadence of rounded literary periods. I wrote essays, read and conversed; we became great and lasting friends.

On my arrival at Prague, I was met at the station by the Panslavist himself, as Furioso had planned. He conducted me to a little inn of patriotic name and squalid appearance. Next morning, on my mentioning my address, Monsieur Schmoranz seemed very upset. The same day a suite in a modern hotel was put at my disposal. I began feeling a " star " which did me good, ridding me of some of my timidity. My first interview with Schmoranz put me in good humour. On my being ushered into his study, he met me half-way, bobbed an abbreviated curtsy over my hand, and conducted me to an arm-chair. He assured me I was to be their guest and everything at the theatre at my disposal, down to his own box. I expressed the hope there had not been too many spelling mistakes in my letter to him, and felt at once my remark irrelevant. He maintained the same line of high courtesy; might he send a car to take me out that afternoon; he would be proud to show me the marvels of Baroque churches, in which Prague is rich. To keep up a clever conversation, I remarked, frightened at my own boldness, that I could not admire Baroque; Renaissance was the style of architecture I liked best. I was fairly ignorant of both. In the course of my stay at Prague my director drove me out every free afternoon. I saw under the best conditions all there was to see. My guide was a serious scholar ; his speciality had been the history of architecture before he became director of a theatre. Sight-seeing was made a thrilling study through his erudite love of his subject. Few had been my initiations into the domains of enlightened observation up till now ; scarce my knowledge, but my aptitude strong. Schmoranz showed me the intimate beauty of the town—old streets in which every door had a sign, a narrow lane called " Golden " after the alchemists who had lived there. Down worn steps that might have led to the Inferno we descended to see an *oubliette*. He drew my attention to the inscriptions carved by prisoners, with a nail maybe ; to the remains of an improvised pack of cards, figured in blood.

" Juste pour vous, qui aimez le frisson." Each day turned for me a new page in the book of wonders. From something old-maidish in his manner and appearance, from his out-of-date meticulous courtesy, his funny little idiosyncrasies (he would neither motor nor telephone), Schmoranz was all the more lovable.

He had high ideas of propriety, and appointed a duenna for me. Signora Viscussi, wife of the Italian ballet-master, always made a third in our excursions, and sat with me in the box put at my disposal every night I didn't dance. During my stay in Prague I never missed a single performance ; and my day would invariably be brought to completion by an evening at the theatre.

I had heard that every seven years the human being enters on a new phase of existence. I was now beginning the fourth of these cycles, and became aware of a great change in myself. Five years of stage experience in Petersburg had failed to give me self-possession. The Petersburg critics had the facetious precept that praise was dangerous to the young and might stop their striving for perfection. As applied to me, this policy increased my natural diffidence ; and at best I was a timorous and self-depreciating performer. Here in Prague, the absence of repressive criticism entirely freed my mind from a timidity bordering on obsession; here former mistakes were not recorded against me; for the first time the dark, ominous gap called audience ceased to prey on my mind. Because I was received as a star, I believed myself to be one, and threw off the veil of diffidence that had muffled my self-expression. The first season at Prague saw the end of the schoolgirl and the beginning of the artist.

May was cloudless; cherry orchards dressed in bloom covered the hills round Prague. In a close-fitting amazon-like dress and a hat with drooping feathers I thought I looked fatal and mysterious. My mirror sent me back a happy smile in which there was no mystery. After the first night on which I danced *Casse-Noisette* I was offered a prolongation of my contract, and signed for the following year. A happy idea of Schmoranz, who had constituted himself my good fairy, was to give me a part in a ballet of Czech folk-tales. My appearance in this ballet went straight to the hearts of my audience and gave rise to my popularity. I was now recognised in shops and out in the street. This and the presence at Prague of a real balletomane, one of the " Assyrians " from Box No. 25, who had come to follow my performance, flattered my vanity. On the morrow of my first night, Schmoranz, with great delight, translated some notices. One styled me *diva*; Schmoranz fondly dwelt on a sentence comparing my steps with the leaps of a young gazelle.

For ever after I treasured a talisman given to me by Schmoranz. On my last night, attached to a bouquet, I found a little case. A small piece of wood set in garnets in the form of a brooch was inside; it was a piece of the sycamore under which the Blessed Virgin had reposed in her flight to Egypt. Many precious remembrances I took away, too, of the brave, unsophisticated little crowd piously doing their work of artistic propaganda in their none too rich, homely theatre. The National Theatre could afford only a small ballet troupe. The operatic and dramatic artists gave a hand in the non-dancing parts of the ballet. I left friends behind. " Your portrait is bought by the Manet gallery," wrote to me the artist who had painted it. " But I have kept the etching of you, the one in the hat with blue feathers " (the fatal hat). " My Mother mended the shawl you have given me." The companion of my early ramblings, wrapper of my costumes, the Bokhara shawl of many hues had caught the fancy of the artist; I left it behind as a gift.

CHAPTER XVIII

Sokolova—" The Swan Lake " and " Corsair "—Svetloff

FOR a long time I had meditated leaving the class of Nicolas Legat. The decision was not easy ; I was afraid he might take it as disloyal. In our profession, where a master takes infinite pains to form a pupil, exerting himself in demonstration, there are ties of gratitude binding the pupil to him. But I had assimilated all that the personality of my master could give me, to the degree of being able to execute vigorous steps usually reserved for men, and it became evident to me that I now needed a woman's tuition. Madame Sokolova was no longer attached to the theatre school. She held a class of her own, to which Pavlova went daily. I now joined it. My decision proved a timely one, as this year, 1909, brought me highly responsible work. Immediately after my taking the lead in *The Swan Lake* I was given *Corsair*. This latter part was considered an incontestable success of mine ; I owed it greatly to Madame Sokolova. Most of the ballets of the old repertoire she had danced herself, and had the parts at her finger-tips. When she set herself to show me dances and mimed scenes, what worlds of tender graces she brought to life : and that in spite of the corpulence usually following on a dancer's retirement. The small room where we practised allowed no space for a piano. My mistress sang, rendering the *roulades* and *fiorituri* of the old music with admirable clearness. Knowing, besides her own part, those of all the others, she often acted for different persons so as to give me cues. Her vigilance went beyond the class-room ; she sat in the stalls every time I rehearsed on the stage, and, if prevented from doing so, she summoned me to come straight to her from the theatre. There, over a cup of coffee, I had to give minute account of every step, occasionally getting up and dancing round the table. Generally, we understood each other perfectly, humming the tune and playing tattoos on the table with our hands. The most complicated steps could be rendered thus. To a profane observer we must have looked absurd. At times she would telephone to me : " How did you do that ? . . ." singing from her end. " That was all right, but I could not quite get this little bit . . ." singing from my end. The telephone service, though recent in Petersburg, was very efficient : we went through five acts uninterrupted by any whims of the exchange.

She enjoyed a modest prosperity and lived in her own house on the other side of the river, far from the centre. From the street, the house was masked by another small wooden building, in which she let flats, reserving one for her school. She was lavish of her time and labour. Nominally we were entitled to a daily class, but she insisted on my coming to her in the evenings as well when there was coaching to be done. She would not allow any previous engagement to stand in the way of work ; no pleading appeased her. " Stage before all." The old lady lived her career all over again in her pupils. Herself happily married, the mother of grown-up children, to us she preached celibacy. Her mind apprehended many far-fetched evils falling to the lot of married ballerinas. The preaching of her social and artistic doctrines generally took place at supper in her house, where she insisted on my coming after work. During work, she did not allow digressions. The same foresight, as in respect of matrimony, made her forestall any possible complication on the stage. " Show me how you are going to tie your shoe-ribbons. . . . That's not the way. The knot must be on the outside of the ankle. Take care to moisten it with spit lest it should come undone." She wanted to see how I would take a call. A dancer must never walk on flat fleet, she impressed on me. " Tripping lightly, you come into the middle, curtsy to the right—Imperial box ; curtsy to the left—director ; two steps forward, semi-round curtsy to the parterre ; back now, raise your eyes, smile in curtsying to the gallery." I remember how, teaching me the part of *Giselle*, she was satisfied with everything but my fall in the death scene. On my mentioning that I had bruised myself in trying to get the fall right, she sent to the house for a mattress, over which I would fall backwards ever so many times with no worse consequences than a slight concussion in the head. In the end I got the fall perfect.

Our supper conversations were always shoppy ; my execution was discussed, anecdotes and triumphs of her own career related by my mistress, all the simplest acts of life passed through the mesh of a special code of dancers' ethics as laid down by Madame Sokolova. Drinking beer was anti-æsthetic for a ballerina. " Edouard Andreevitch, how many times have I told you that you should not tempt Tata with that coarse drink ? "

Before my appearance in *Corsair* she was evidently nervous. " How will you plan to spend to-morrow ? " she asked me on the eve of my performance. I said I might go for a little walk if it was fine. She was horrified. " You won't do such a thing. Why ! you should lie down and concentrate on your part. Feet up, and don't forget to put on light-coloured stockings ; it is more restful." From cautious little hints of my mistress, I knew she was trying to bring Svetloff round to " orthodoxy." He was a great personal friend of hers, and his severe criticism of me was a thorn in her heart. By now, though, his attitude was more benign, and even some scanty praise had begun to creep into his notices, usually with a rider appended. " We should recommend to the young dancer more care of her general appearance. In the ballet of *The Four Seasons* what seemed to us a long bit of white tape was hanging from underneath her skirts."

It may have been a stroke of strategy on her part in order to make Svetloff take interest in my work, when Madame Sokolova borrowed of him a volume of Byron for me to get inspiration for the part of Medora. The poem gave me no direct bearing on the plot, which was greatly modified for ballet purposes ;

but it helped me by bringing a concrete vision of Medora to my imagination.

An unmistakable sign of my rising in the hierarchy was the fact that my first performance of *Corsair* was given on a Sunday night. Young aspirants to the title of ballerina were relegated to Wednesdays, when the Marinsky was not half so smart. As a mark of my favour with the direction, special costumes had been designed for me. These concessions predisposed my mood; I arrived at the theatre that night in a proper frame of mind, my nervousness merely that of anticipation. Contrary to the precepts of my mistress, I tried not to dwell too much on my part; my experience showed that it was ruinous to my self-possession if I concentrated on it to the exclusion of other thoughts. My nerves would spend themselves before the moment of action. And now I let the old Alexandrushka, while she was laying out my dressing-table, spin her yarns. She had two great wishes—to cure her husband of drunken fits, and to marry off her plain daughter. Some indications of Tania being about to find a suitor Alexandrushka related to me with gusto; for the cure she trusted to the prayers of Brother Ivanushka, a monk who pledged drunkards and organised religious meetings. I'm afraid the husband's thirst proved more compelling than the Brother's orisons.

The success of the first apparition often predetermines the course of the whole evening. The first coming on of the ballerina in *Corsair* is very effective; traversing the stage in diagonal leaps, the dancer concludes her entrance with a series of difficult pirouettes. This first bit fetched loud applause; a link with the audience was established, the confidence of the public gained. Perhaps no other ballet offers such varied opportunities to the leading lady. The romantic quality of Medora's part is set off by a little episode of spontaneous gaiety; Conrad is sombre, and to distract his mind Medora, in boy's apparel, dances for him. She seems to say by her frolicsome dance : " Alas, I have no moustache, but my heart is as valiant as a man's own." A never-failing effect comes at the end; Medora, through a speaking trumpet, cries words of nautical command.

The short, pleated skirt, bolero and fez of the costume that Maria Serguievna Petipa herself wore had been replaced by the ample trousers and turban of a Turkish boy. Madame Sokolova disapproved of the flagrant breach of tradition. The costume led me astray. Precepts of coy grace were forgotten; the trousers wanted me to leap and romp. From there the logical conclusion was not to apologize for the want of moustache, but to pull fiercely at an imaginary one. Encores told me of the success of my spontaneous inspiration. Guerdt, my darling Conrad, in the passionate embrace of the concluding scene, in a ventriloquist whisper, conveyed : " Well done, god-daughter."

The choreographic climax of *Corsair* was reached in the third act, called *Jardin Animé*. The curtain falls on the Pasha's seraglio. A short action goes on in front of the curtain. It is raised within a minute. The stage by now is a garden, complete with flower-beds. The *corps de ballet* in white tarlatans, wearing wreaths of roses, lead a graceful saraband. The daring effect is reserved for the ballerina, who ends a dance with a long leap over the front flower-bed. Naturally an impeccable line had to be kept in the air, or the effect would have smacked of the circus.

The *Jardin Animé* practically terminated the responsibility of the leading part. The last act did not require any dancing or histrionic skill, but was ever such fun for me. The whole of the scene represents a choppy sea. Under painted canvas hired sailors run on all fours. A storm breaks, and the sailors run on two legs. At the back, the *Corsair's* caravel pitches and rolls over a trap-door. Birbanto, leading a mutiny, treacherously attacks Conrad, and is killed by a pistol-shot. Medora, still in tarlatans, now looks through a telescope, now prays on her knees.

What the stage directions were I never quite knew, but we took them to be *ad libitum*, and, in the heat of make-believe, rather over-acted this scene and played at shipwreck like excited children. Guerdt shouted orders through the megaphone; when the caravel split and sank in two tidy halves, my female attendants and I screamed. But screams, cannon, megaphone and orchestra were all drowned by the thunder and howling wind. The rebellious corsairs all perished with the ship, Guerdt and I, creeping low and making swimming movements, reached the wings. There I hastily put on a white chemise and let down my hair preparatory to appearing on a crag now jutting out of a quickly pacified sea. Up there, arms raised to thank Heaven for landing us on a desert rock, we struck the final group of the apotheosis.

My reception after the performance proved that I had had my hitherto greatest success. From this time on I was allowed to give up my secondary parts, and my position became that of prima ballerina in all but title and salary.

After the *Corsair* Svetloff wrote his first notice of undiluted praise about me, and this melted the ice between us. I no longer thought that a personal dislike prompted his notices, and time proved him my staunch friend. No longer could he reproach me with carelessness; he realised that I needed time to find my own self, and that my failings had been due to my inadequate strength in pursuit of an ideal set high. But even in later times, when he became my panegyrist, little skirmishes occurred. " Now listen," he would say. " Why on earth have you, in *Carnaval*, hooked on ringlets of a colour different to your hair ? " I would maintain that a lighter shade of ringlets could not have been noticed from the audience. " I beg your pardon. I did notice you were piebald." All such remarks he now could make privately; I became in time one of the intimate circle of his friends, who gathered round his table. He was genuinely hospitable, and the first invitation was a standing one. His suppers, at which the unobtrusive host paced up and down the room while we, not having dined, made the most of the excellent food, were a real relaxation after the strain of the evening. Svetloff had a collection of rare prints of dancers and some relics

—a shoe of Taglioni's, her contemporary bronze in *La Sylphide*, the Spanish comb of Fanny Elssler. . . . His reverence for the past, profound knowledge of ballet and love of tradition did not impair his broad-mindedness ; he admired Petipa and believed in Fokine. He sided with the modern movement, its firm apologist against attacks led by another faction of the critics.

PART III

EUROPE

CHAPTER XIX

Ballet in Paris—Oneguin—Diaghileff—First Performance of the Diaghileff Ballet—A Galaxy of Talent—" La Karsavina "—An Open-air Performance—Marinelli

THE summer of 1909 saw the invasion of Russian art into Europe, Western Europe I should have said to be correct. Any Russian, speaking spontaneously, would have said "Europe" to designate the countries to the west of our frontier, but instinctively we set ourselves apart. Little was known about us outside our domain. A few amiable specimens of the race were welcomed abroad. The whole of our vast country to the average occidental mind still remained a land of barbarians. Russia, crude and refined, primitive and sophisticated, the country of great learning and appalling ignorance ; Russia of immense scale, no wonder that Europe would not attempt to understand you, to your own children enigma. Perhaps the best manifestation of this complex and vital temperament (*la saveur âpre qui est l'âme slave*—to quote a sentence of origin forgotten), Russian art was hardly known outside its own country. A year before Diaghileff had organised in Paris the picture exhibition, *Mir Iʒkoustva*, and a few representations of *Boris Godounoff*. He was now forming a troupe of ballet and opera to venture a whole Russian season in Paris. Naturally, his intention was much discussed in our circles. There had been before a few instances of a small troupe headed by a star going to dance abroad. Those were economical little efforts in the nature of small commercial enterprises. Nothing so ambitious had ever been thought of ; and, though Theatre Street and the Marinsky hummed with excitement, no one as yet dreamed that we were soon to set our mark on European art.

189

Little did I think what changes it would bring into my life when, one afternoon, I sat waiting for Diaghileff in my small sitting-room. I had my own home by now. "The red plush of that suite—like a provincial hotel," I thought, looking at my furniture. A piece of Dresden china, my first acquisition in the bibelot line, seemed alone capable of bearing witness to my taste. I moved it from the *étagère* to the piano ; it looked better where it was before, though not so conspicuous. I moved it back again. Six o'clock ; he should have come at five. My agitation grew. It was not on account of an offer to be discussed ; there was an emotion of a different kind making me conscious of the red plush and apprehensive of what Diaghileff, the æsthete, might think of me.

I had first met Diaghileff three years before. We had found ourselves next each other at a big supper-party given in honour of Mathilda's benefit night at Cubat. In my own chronology the date of our first meeting went further back. I was fifteen and romantic. There was an interval in the rehearsal of *Casse-Noisette.* The majority of the artists were gone to the dressing-rooms to eat sandwiches ; the stalls, usually vibrating with subdued whispers, were practically empty ; a few of us pupils sat in a box. The imagination of a brilliant producer could not have managed an entry better than that of a young man who walked in during the suspense and sat in a middle row. A theatre in its unguarded moments, curtain up, stage abandoned, and lights lowered, has a strange poignancy. The faint ghostliness of it touches a vulnerable spot of incurable sentimentality, a professional disease of those bred in the artificial emotions of the footlights. I saw him scanning the stage warily. Disenchantment or boredom ? No apparent motive brought him in ; there was nothing going on. What made him get up suddenly ? He passed under our box. I looked close in the young and ageless face. The fresh colour of youth, an insolent little moustache, eyes oddly drooping at the corners, *une belle désinvolture* and a single grey lock cutting through the dark hair

—mark of Ahasuerus or mark of genius ?   At that time Diaghileff was attached in an official capacity to the director, Prince Volkonsky.

I did not then know even his name.   Yet in years to come every new manifestation of his remarkable personality related in my mind to that moment, as if, in those few seconds of dramatic intensity, I had felt enveloped in the aura of genius.

At that supper at Cubat when I first met him face to face, I told him of my childish infatuation.   I did not expect my " disenchanted hero " to be so pleased as he was with my post-dated tribute of admiration.

For several years I had lost sight of Diaghileff.   He was now coming to seal his offer by a ceremonial visit.   I was not then aware of his unpunctuality, amazing even from a Russian point of view.   I had almost given him up when I saw his coupé stop at my door.   Diaghileff never would drive in an open cab for fear of being infected with glanders.   Douniasha made me blush by her grotesque mispronunciation of my visitor's name when showing him in.   A meeting for discussing various artistic questions had kept him so late, Diaghileff explained.   I had a first glimpse of the feverish activities that he had called to life. Maquettes for scenery and costumes were painted, productions elaborated by conclaves of artists and musicians.   Diaghileff himself was then just back from Moscow, where he had engaged all the best and prettiest dancers as well as Chaliapin himself. He was telling me about it and answering my questions about Coralli.   Rumours of her beauty and precocious personality had reached us.   " It is certainly an unforgettable face, far, though, from perfection of features."   Coralli was to dance *Armida*.

" The high patronage of the Grand Duke Vladimir, and a subsidy is given to us," he told me, with satisfaction.   " By the by, I will send you your contract signed to-night; or is it Monday to-day—unlucky day, I will do it to-morrow," he said at parting.

The setting sun had by places illuminated the red plush to the brightness of pomegranate. I wore a copy of a Parisian model. My talk had been easy; *mondaine* I thought it. My real nervousness in the presence of a personality that fascinated and intimidated me did not show. Underneath this indulgent review of my bearing, a thought, like a small splinter, worried me. Only a secondary part is allotted me in Paris, and that mysterious forge where creative minds worked a new armour of art, will it ever open to me? That winter the *Pavillon d'Armide* had been produced by Fokine; Alexander Benois had painted the scenery, handling the plot with a penetration almost uncanny. A suavely potent philtre, his art left me athirst for more. At this time I went to all the exhibitions of the *Mir Izkoustva*, and a wonderful revelation they gave me. I did so long to penetrate into that holy of holies, where now they all worked together. Fokine would drop a word now and then relative to these artistic sittings at Diaghileff's flat. I stood wistfully outside the circle, nursing a feeling akin to that which I once had when, a very small child, I had watched the overnight preparations for a picnic. My last thought at night and first in the morning were of the picnic. All the grown-ups went; Lev was taken; I, for some good reason no doubt, was left at home. I made myself weary with crying in some hiding-place where Douniasha found me. " Come quick, Miloushka, Ivan Petrovitch has ridden back to fetch you."

The theatre of the Hermitage had been put at Diaghileff's disposal, and we began our rehearsing. Court flunkeys served tea and chocolate in the intervals. All of a sudden there was a break in our rehearsals. After a few days of anxious apprehensions and persistent rumours predicting ruin for the enterprise, we resumed our work, this time in the small " theatre of the crooked mirror " at the Ekaterinsky Canal. In the interval the *régisseur* of our troupe announced that Sergei Pavlovitch asked the artists to pass into the foyer to partake of refreshments. During this collation, Diaghileff made a brief speech. Though the high patronage had been withdrawn, he said, the enterprise would not suffer. He trusted to the good sense and loyalty of the troupe to carry on their work unaffected by malevolent rumours. The reason of Diaghileff's disgrace, as I heard from him afterwards, was his refusal to be dictated to in what concerned the choice of repertoire and distribution of parts. With full reason he wished questions of artistic purport to be his prerogative. The events could not remain a secret ; it was openly talked about as well as the intimate reasons which brought about this setback.

Few people knew how hard the blow fell on Diaghileff. Fewer still realised his fortitude and his undaunted spirit. The withdrawal of the subsidy left his enterprise without means. Men of lesser calibre would have shrunk from the risk of such an undertaking. In this crisis, support came from a group of Diaghileff's friends in Paris. Madame Edwards raised by subscription the funds necessary to pay the rent of the Châtelet Theatre.

I left before the others to fulfil my engagement at Prague. I was to join the troupe in Paris. I did not see the exodus, but I guess it must have been not without its picturesque side. I set off to Paris in an odd mood of expectancy and dismal forebodings. Paris to me was a city of eternal pleasure, dissipation and sin. So exaggerated had been my ideas of its inconceivable elegance that in my heart of hearts I expected the streets to be like ballroom floors and to be peopled exclusively with smart ladies, walking along with a frou-frou of silk petticoats. " You can tell a Parisienne in thousands from the way she gathers up her skirts, inimitable," I had heard people say. On my way from the station in the early hours of the morning I met chiefly workmen and good housewives, comfortable fat bodies in nondescript shawls and shoes worn down at the heels, their provision basket on their arm. Above all, I dreaded that I should be too provincial for Paris. I had tried to raise my own standard of smartness before coming over. In buying hats and dresses, I wanted an assurance that such were worn in Paris.

This assurance was never wanting, strengthened by loud protestations that this was the last word of Parisian fashion. Soon after my arrival, I happened to pass along some back street. A little crowd of urchins interrupted their game to follow me. " There it is," I thought. " They are laughing at me," and I turned round to see if there were any witnesses of my humiliation. The grimacing urchins now raised a chorus, " Elle est gentille parce-qu'elle est chic." It was balm to me : Parisian gamins must have good taste, I thought.

These two months in Paris are unforgettable. The fortnight preceding our performances, arduous, feverish, hysterical. The Châtelet, the home of Michael Strogoff, a retail shop of cheap emotions, the paradise of concierges, was well-nigh shaken to its foundations by the tornado of what was to be the first Russian season in Paris. The stage hands, gruff as they only can be in Paris, the administration pedantic and stagnant, regarded us all as lunatics. " Ces Russes, oh, là là, tous un peu maboule." At the back of the stage a party of workmen hammered and sawed, making a new trap-door for Armida's canopied couch. In the auditorium a larger gang out-hammered them. The five front rows of the stalls were being done away with to make room for the orchestra. " I don't like the pit, I will have boxes instead," decided Diaghileff. Hemmed between the rival gangs, we rehearsed. At times the din drowned the feeble tinkle of the piano. Fokine, in a white frenzy, would call out in the dark : " Sergei Pavlovitch, for mercy's sake, I cannot work with this blasted noise." A voice from the dark promised that all would be quiet, and entreated us to carry on. We carried on till a new interruption. At noon all noises stopped as by magic ; the workmen deserted the Châtelet. Noon is a sacred hour. Paris feeds from noon till two. After a few days it became evident that we must push on, and the intervals allowed for our meals had to be cancelled. Our troupe remained at the theatre the whole day long. Diaghileff gave orders—roast fowls, pâtés, salads speedily arrived from a restaurant. Empty packing-cases made quite good tables. Picnic feeling, excellent food, young appetite—in themselves a joy—where should there be room for the pathetic? Yet it was how it struck the old Oneguin. " Dirt, dust, yourself all bedraggled, eating off those dirty boards, poor child." A political emigrant, a stern and forbidding old man, Oneguin was a conspicuous figure. I had brought with me a letter of introduction to him from my relatives. In the turmoil of the first days I forgot all about the letter. The old man, warned of my coming, came to seek me at the Châtelet.

Nothing like the " dear old thing " I had pictured him to be. Rather embittered, ready with withering remarks—this was my first impression. From the first he established a claim on me. He would come daily to the Châtelet, from there followed me to my hotel and sat with me. " Your beau is here, Tata," Diaghileff used to tease me. I became used to him as to my shadow. A curious companionship ours became, with his snappy remarks and my cheeky retorts. Nothing I did was right; yet a grudging admiration lurked at the back of his sarcasms. An admiration, I suppose, for my simplicity of those days. " Hide away your darning; the maid is here with your chocolate." " What's wrong with my mending stockings? " " You are a star, and it's unworthy," and added gently, " What keeps you so unspoilt? "

Oneguin lived in a tiny flat on the ground-floor in the Rue de Marignan. " You are not allowed to touch anything," he met me at the door. He began showing me his Poushkiniana; portraits; a death mask; beautiful editions; a picture of Smirnova, to whom the poet had dedicated one of his loveliest sonnets. Glad to assert my knowledge, I rattled off the sonnet. The old man blandly nodded to the sonorous rhymes. " Clever. I never thought you would know it by heart." A pathetic figure, gruff, friendless, a miser in general opinion, he allowed himself a single meal a day. In all seasons, in all weathers he walked down to the Café de Paris to lunch, saved a few bits of sugar from his coffee, which he would distribute to carthorses. The rest of the time his bent form could be seen at his window. Day in, day out, he sat at his desk ready to show his museum of Poushkin relics to visitors. Few ever came.

Hectically, convulsively, in a cataclysm of squabbles between artists, musicians and producers, we approached the day of the dress rehearsal, virtually a first night in Paris. The pink of society, literary, artistic and critical there and then determined success or failure. The indescribable bedlam of those days, looked back at, becomes highly entertaining. Opera and ballet disputed the stage ; Diaghileff arbitrated. The vanquished side, gathering " props " resentfully vanished to the remote parts. Under the roof, in an atmosphere to breed salamanders in, we often rehearsed for long hours. The nearer the day approached, the more it seemed improbable that out of this chaos a co-ordinate spectacle should emerge. *Armida* presented the greatest difficulties. The supers could not be taught to walk in time to the music ; the trap-door jibbed ; the magic tapestry seemed determined to display its supernatural powers. Fokine grew thinner every day.

Whenever a hitch in the rehearsal occurred, I ran to the back of the stage to practise endless pirouettes with Nijinsky. The " General " stood by and approved. For we had come over with a suite. Svetloff was there, historian of the new phase of our ballet, faithful chronicler ; some bloods too, *balletomanes* of the parterre, in the background and the venerable General Bezobrazoff, arbiter of technique. Like a merchant's wedding, of which the glory would not be complete unless a General hired for the purpose gave away the bride, so had we a dignitary to countenance a moment of not lesser importance. Nominally an adviser on matters of classical ballet, virtually a figurehead, in Bezobrazoff's person Diaghileff paid a compliment to tradition.

In spite of constant collisions between the various elements, in spite of tempers lost, words bandied, the whole of the troupe, our own staff included, worked like one man. Outbursts of highly tried endurance were natural; soon nobody paid any attention to them—" only another squabble."

Unmistakable signs of success were in the air; interest was aroused. The papers told the expectant public about the prodigious endurance of Russian artists. Dethomas sketched Nijinsky in every attitude of his practice. Robert Brussel wrote of me in the Figaro : " Les hymnes orphiques l'auraient jadis célébrée entre le ' parfum des nuages ' qui est la myrrhe et le ' parfum d'Aphrodite ' qui n'a point de nom. . . ." " Elle semble ne fléchir que sous le poids des grâces ineffables." " Don't you believe it—French flattery," said Oneguin. Above all soared Diaghileff, moving in an areopagus of satellites.

On the first night we gave *Prince Igor, Pavillon d'Armide* and a suite of dances under the name *Festin*. Much has been written about our season in Paris and about the memorable first night. It would be futile for me to emulate the men of literature in trying to describe this epoch-making venture. They wrote of what they had seen; I could not see, as I was in the making of it. To me it was seen from a different perspective; it filtered through my own experience.

It seemed to me that the hitherto quietly admiring mood of the public burst into enthusiasm when a *pas de trois* with Nijinsky, his sister and myself was about halfway through. The first quiet movement of it, as if leading up to the climax of virtuosities, stirred a murmur of approbation; whispers ran. Then an unrehearsed effect took place. Leaving off a figure of the trio, Nijinsky should have walked off the stage to reappear in a solo. On that night he chose to leap off. He rose up, a few yards off the wings, described a parabola in the air, and disappeared from sight. No one of the audience could see him land; to all eyes he floated up and vanished. A storm of applause broke; the orchestra had to stop. Had his frolic been the origin of the intentional effect of the same kind, the famous leap through the window in the *Spectre de la Rose*, I wonder? Once all reserve thrown away, the evening worked up to a veritable frenzy of enthusiasm. Again the orchestra stopped after my solo. After the dances of *Prince Igor*, where Bolm scored an unprecedented success, the curtain rose I don't know how many times.

The next item on the programme was *Festin*. It was a series of separate dances. One of them was a *pas de deux* danced by Nijinsky and myself, and called by Diaghileff the *Fire Bird*, though it actually came from the *Sleeping Beauty*.

Fire Bird, the ballet, had come to me through a stroke of luck. In Petersburg I had wistfully considered that the best chances had been given to elder and more accomplshed dancers than I. *Fire Bird* had been intended for Mathilda, but she changed her mind and refused to come to Paris.

A vivid, if somewhat unrefined, account of what was happening in the audience when Nijinsky and I danced this *pas de deux* on the first night I will borrow from Michael, our courier. . . . " But when these two came on, good Lord ! I have never seen such a public. You would have thought their seats were on fire." I realised something unusual was happening to me and round me ; something to which I could give no name, so unexpected, so enormous as to frighten almost. My senses were all blurred on that night. The familiar barriers between the stage and the audience were broken. The side doors with their ingenious locks and stern notices—of no avail. In the interval the stage was so crowded with spectators that there was hardly room to move. To perform the usual rite of practising our steps and lifts before going on, Nijinsky and I had to dodge. Hundreds of eyes followed us about ; scraps of exclamations : " He is a prodigy " and " C'est elle ! " . . . And then a breathless wait in the wings, when my heart beat in odd places. Nijinsky paced up and down with that soft, feline step of his, stroking and unclasping his hands. Then Diaghileff appeared to say " God-speed " to us before we went on the stage. Then that phenomenon occurred in the audience that Michael described so graphically. And after, all was happy confusion ; crowds again, somebody exquisitely dressed stanched the blood trickling down my arm with a cobwebby handkerchief—I had cut myself against Nijinsky's jewelled tunic; Diaghileff picking his way through groups of people, calling, "Where is she?—I must embrace her." From that day he always called us his children. Somebody was asking Nijinsky if it was difficult to stay in the air as he did while jumping; he did not understand at first, and then very obligingly: "No! No! not difficult. You have just to go up and then pause a little up there."

Next morning rose hot and beautiful, as indeed the whole time we remained in Paris. I do not remember a cloud in the sky. June worked its gay witchcraft over Paris. The glitter of vermilion gold that tinted the whole atmosphere dwelt in one's heart. Even to the dark passages of the Châtelet it descended like a whiff of scent lodged in one's clothes.

Oneguin brought me the newspapers in the morning. He sat with me as I had my coffee, himself refusing to share in the meal. I wore the wrap of double usage, that of opera cloak and dressing-gown, and, as usual, darned stockings. Both items memorable through Oneguin's sneers. I learned amazing things about myself on this morning, and that I was " La Karsavina." There was quite an extemporaneous feeling of wonder in me as at suddenly perceiving my double. Some vanity there must have been in me; I always secretly wished to look fatal. Therefore, of all the clever and good things said, I treasured a trite madrigal:

> Ses yeux adamantins et son sourire d'une douceur cruelle.

My gruff friend would not accept it wholly. According to him, a smirk in a passably pretty " muzzle " was all there was of my *sourire cruel*. As to my adamantine eyes he agreed, and afterwards called me Adamant. He kept a diary, and one day let me see the entry: " Adamant came to see me, said she was hungry, made her a cup of chocolate."

The most strenuous time was over. Ballets played on

alternate nights with the opera. Chaliapin sang. Even in Petersburg he was a rare treat to us, his work being, for the most part, in Moscow. Naturally I was unwilling to miss a chance, and came often to hear him, now fortunate enough to get squeezed into the electrician's box, now standing in the wings. No matter how great the discomfort was, my admiration amounted to ecstasy before the divine artist.

Not in me alone there vibrated this unceasing enchantment. To me, of course, the life was new and full of savour; my happiness knew no bounds. The dreaded trial was over, and Paris loved, petted and flattered me. " We're all living in the witchery of Armida's groves. The very air round the Russian season is intoxicated," so Diaghileff characterised the moment. I was going through my morning practice on the empty stage; he passed across in one of his meteoric appearances—he seemed not to tarry anywhere in those days, appeared suddenly and vanished in the middle of a sentence. Mortal limitations alone frustrated his brave attempt at omnipresence. For it was Diaghileff's will that set in motion every cog and wheel of the unwieldy machine of his season. A truer definition of the atmosphere enveloping the Russian season and its audience could not have been found, a subtle, light, gay intoxication. Something akin to a miracle happened every night—the stage and audience trembled in a unison of emotion.

It was an essential feature of Benois that he not merely reconstituted an epoch, but invested it with weird, irresistible power over one's imagination. To see his production, to take a part in it, was like living again through forgotten experience. No wonder the simile of Armida had been chosen by Diaghileff to describe the state in which we all lived at this time. The phantasmagoria of the stage intruded on life, tinting it with a sense of magic. It was the authentic features of Russian art, so authentic that, for our part, we were hardly conscious of them, that appealed most strongly to the French, not the intuition of style; there were slight reservations in the praise of Armida as if the French reproached us for transgression into a culture so entirely their own. Paris was captivated by the barbaric splendour of frenzied movements, the nostalgia of infinite plains, the naïve spontaneity of Russia, the studied ornateness of the East. " The art of the dance has fallen into complete decadence in our country," wrote Marcel Prévost . . . " une sorte de convention de laisser aller s'est établie entre les artistes et le public. Des prêtresses sans foi accomplissent au petit bonheur des rites périmés devant des fidèles sceptiques et distraits."

The Russian season, like a gust of fresh wind, passed over the stale convention of the French stage. " La danse nous revient du nord," said another critic.

I wonder if Diaghileff, in his proud moments, ever praised himself for the galaxy of talents he brought together—Chaliapin himself; Benois (Le Maître); Bakst, whose name was on everybody's lips (*le bateau de la saison russe*), and whose sly dandified primness, imperturbable good nature stood in sharp contrast to the stormy chaos of our rehearsals. " Electricien, donnez-moi du bleu jambon." So often came his quiet reiterated demand that it became attached to him as a motto. Fokine shouted himself hoarse, tore his hair and produced marvels. Pavlova made but a fleeting appearance and left us after a couple of performances; a Muse of Parnassus, said Jean Louis Vaudoyer. The most virtuose of all contemporary ballerinas, Geltzer, was there too, admired academically. The sense of exotic found its supreme expression in Ida Rubinstein; her Cleopatra was unforgettable. Nomenclature may become tedious; yet I must add " Nijinsky "—volumes could not say more than his mere name. There was an amusing suavity in the way the French pronounced the names of Feodorova, Fokina, Schollar; the very inflexion of the voice seemed to express admiration.

Our season in Paris ended with an open-air fête given by Madame Maurice Ephrussy. I saw Diaghileff but once before leaving Paris. He gave no hint of his plans. No thought of our future, lasting and intimately bound work was then in my mind ; yet his first season had sealed our collaboration. Much later, when the pre-war years seemed those of the very distant past, we liked going back to little incidents of that time. The one he called a manifestation of Tata's " *vertu farouche* " Diaghileff told with mastery. In which restaurant it was I cannot remember that Diaghileff took me to dinner one night ; they all were to me fascinating to bewilderment. We were to meet an influential director, a man who furnished grotesque material for Parisian anecdotes, a clown, and yet a man of remarkable insight into stage matters. What he took me for I wonder till now. His talk to me through dinner would have been unbelievable were it not for a buffoonery that most of the time made me think his remarks were not personal. Diaghileff's witty repartees turned it into other channels. The incident happened when we got up for dinner. Diaghileff described the moment afterwards. " Can you imagine my consternation when, on being pinched by G——, Tata gasped and flopped down with a shriek. She refused to get up till finally I persuaded her to take my arm. What happened afterwards Nouvelle can tell. He had to drive her up and down the streets till the crisis subsided. He had driven many miles before he persuaded her that her virtue was not blemished."

Not unlike the girl of the Russian proverb particular in her choice of a husband, I was in a dilemma. Theatrical agents from everywhere now made their respective offers to me. To America I would not go ; the possible sickness barred it off the list. I was prejudiced against Australia by the loose phrasing of an alarmist geography book. London was near at hand, and attracted my fancy—I did so love Dickens at school. I signed a contract for London to follow on the Paris season, and with it a printed form too long to be read. In due course I realised that it would have been wiser to have gone through this appendix entitled " normal contract." With every difficulty of a practical sort I usually went to Baron Günsburg, who had known me from childhood. He was now in Paris taking an interest in the season and, I believe, doing his share of help. " That was rash of you," he said. " You might have sold yourself into slavery." Alarmed, I read paragraph after paragraph of the lengthy normal contract, while Günsburg explained them to me. It appeared that I had signed away my right to accept any other offers than those coming from my present impresario for a long number of years ahead. I went with Günsburg to see my impresario. Oneguin being about, we took him with us. In the waiting-room there were many applicants. The somewhat resigned and humble attitude of all these girls touched me; none made the slightest protest when I and my two supporters were shown in before all others.

I had been worked up by Günsburg, and now made a tempestuous protest against what I termed catching people into slavery. Marinelli, gallant little man, tore the offending document with a " N'en parlons plus, madame." We began to discuss my engagement. My impresario said he would himself take his star across.

CHAPTER XX

*My First Visit to London—First Impressions—The Coliseum—
Adeline Genée—A Bribe—First English Friends*

I KNEW not a soul in England and not a word of English.
Marinelli brought me to London on Sunday and lodged
me in an hotel in Leicester Square.

Who does not know that funny feeling, a small vacuum in
place of the heart and a perpetual inner tremble that one cannot locate ? " Draw a deep breath to relieve the pressure
of the solar plexus," a doctor told me one day. I had but
my own panacea in those early days : " King David, and the
meekness of his heart." After our two performances a week
in Petersburg, the rest of the time spent in careful and
loving preparation, the idea of two shows a day with one
short, perfunctory rehearsal on the first morning, fairly
terrified me.

Marinelli, spruce and neat, stood by me on the stage. The
rehearsal had not begun yet, the artists were unpacking their
cases at the back, taking out ingenious contraptions. The
stage hands were getting ready a conglomeration of ornate
objects of furniture, the pride of the Coliseum and known as
the " Lewis set." Marinelli praised the beauty and orna-
mentation of the auditorium ; another such house as the Coliseum
was not to be found. I was conscious of a strong draught ; my
attention fixed on the stage boards, wondering how I was
eventually to dodge all those brass plates with numbers ; I
listened but absent-mindedly. I fretted and fidgeted ; it
seemed as if nothing was happening, and I was forgotten. The
respective " numbers " began coming forward and strolled
about, hands in pockets, while the orchestra played. A pause ;

someone was evidently not on the spot. Ramases was called, and soon came running fast—a tiny man in a corduroy jacket. Our number didn't come till the very end, and something must have gone wrong; the musicians were rummaging amongst their music, the conductor sat tragically resigned. Marinelli explained to me that many parts were missing in my score. I had trusted Michael the courier to put my music in order while yet in Paris. Was the disorder of my music not so bad as appeared from the general confusion, or had the Coliseum employed fairy hands to copy the missing parts in time for the matinée, I do not know; I felt warm gratitude for Mr. Dove, who had pulled me through. As played at this first matinée, the music was even strangely reminiscent of Tchaikovsky, its composer.

Excellent linoleum has since been spread over the brass plates, but I was a pioneer of ballet at the Coliseum, where the stage was then all it ought not to be for dancing purposes. An extremely hard floor and the unavoidable brass bruised my toes and made them bleed. My first week was hardly over, and I dreaded the remaining three. Worse than my blistered toes was to me the feeling of not belonging anywhere in my present surroundings. I bore a grudge against the stained windows of the restaurant in my hotel, the noisy barrel-organ in the side street; it played in the morning, it played in the afternoon when I came to rest between performances. There may have been relays of barrel-organs in that street, or one single one of unique obduracy. There were some nocturnal goings and comings in my hotel. At times I thought I heard aggressive voices. That was all I knew of London this time, that and the Coliseum. There again I could not fit myself in properly. The tiled passages, the chintz-dressing-rooms seemed too clean, too sanitary. The familiar smell of dust and scenery, the rubbish of agglomerated properties, work-rooms, all the specific hus-bandry of the theatre, I sadly missed. Each week " numbers " departed; others, with their cases and contraptions, came and departed in their turn, leaving no imprint of their personality behind—just another hotel.

There was no lack of real kindness in my new surroundings, and any amount of good nature. Everybody wanted to be helpful. My dresser taught me some English after the Berlitz system, not the purest idiom perhaps, but very useful in my daily work—" Full aouse," " Quick chainge," " Next turn "—I knew what I was about within my small vocabulary.

The glamour and romance of the theatre was what I missed badly. Acclimatisation was painful. After my first week, Marinelli brought me an offer of prolongation. I could not fail to see the extreme fairness of the proposal; Sir Oswald (then Mr.) Stoll of his own accord wanted to double my salary. Still, a worse moment to talk of prolongation could not have been chosen. I was sitting over my lunch, swallowing tears, when Marinelli came with the offer. He met with an ungracious and lachrymose reception. Most of the time I was full of unshed tears in a state bordering on hysterics. Why the mid-day meal, and especially the little kickshaws denominated *friandises* always aggravated my misery I am at a loss to explain. At times I gave way to peevish fury, venting it on Marinelli. His original intention of returning to Paris in a day or two he delayed from day to day; negotiations on my behalf for the next year at the Coliseum must have kept him in London, but of this he did not dare to speak yet. His chief occupation in those days seemed to be pampering me. One morning he had called me to the drawing-room; half a dozen different puppies were displayed there for my choice. All were irresistible. I could not decide. A red King Charles came up, sniffed and licked me on the cheek; after this touching appeal I hesitated no more. " Prince Arthur " by his pedigree, I thought the name too long. The same night at supper, which my gallant little impresario invariably offered me, names were suggested and criticised till " Loulou " was thought of. Eventually Douniasha corrupted it into " Louloushka." Though he was

a crazy, insubordinate little beast, I became absurdly attached
to him, and he hysterically devoted to me. As I went up to
my dressing-room, coming off the stage, I could hear his agon-
ised howl. My neighbours, a family of acrobats, told me he
never left off crying during my absence. The little pet brought
a wonderful change into my life; my meal hours lost their
bitterness, the cunning manœuvres of Loulou made them
entertaining. He would lull my vigilance by keeping good
under the chair; when reassured as to his behaviour, I would
suddenly see him pop out like a jack-in-the box by the carving
table. I never belonged to the sensible class of dog-lovers:
why grudge the poor, short-lived little creatures their small joys?
The right instinct must have prompted Loulou to select a lady
in the far corner, who used to come daily, prim and fair. Thus
he ensured a never failing titbit for himself, and brought about
my acquaintance with Adeline Genée. She was the first to
speak to me and to say sweet and encouraging words which,
coming from her, I much treasured. She was dancing at the
Empire. Unaided, she was doing magnificent pioneer work
for the cause of ballet in England, which was far from being
established at the time. Adeline Genée was the first to fight
the strong remains of Victorian prejudice, not only by the
purity of her art, but by her high spiritual integrity. She won
not only admiration for herself and for the art she represented,
but genuine respect.

Marinelli's kind present proved sound policy as well; I had
been put in a good humour, I had become amenable. He could
now talk to me of engagements unrebuked by my angry tirades.
A few more days of a now meek peevishness and I signed the
prolongation. I am ashamed to think of all the accusations I
used to heap on Marinelli's head; their gist was that he acted
as a slave-driver, victimised me, harrowed me with too insistent
offers. I never half believed what I said. Because I knew he
was in the right, pursuing my success on a hot scent, because I
felt I would have to give in, I stormed the more.

A tiny man, with a dramatic cast of features, he was always immaculately dressed, and wore a large " *Gloire de France* " in his buttonhole. A former man-snake, Marinelli liked telling me of his stage success, laying great stress on the artistry of his work. A moonlit landscape, a palm-tree round which he twisted and contorted—" Ah, mais c'était très artistique "—in his vivid description gave me a little shudder. I don't know why he put me in mind of Monsieur Turlututu; he might almost have slept in a cradle like the dwarf of Heine's " Florentine Nights," but, unlike him, was kind and courteous; a bunch of carnations was brought to my room every morning even after he had left.

When it was time to leave London I was half reconciled to it. To say I had found friends would be taking credit for what I had not done; friends found me. A letter came one day; its author came on its heels. He was also the author-to-be of the first book in English on the Russian Ballet. As yet only one chapter of it, on the *Fire Bird*, had been written, and Arthur Applin came to read me a French translation of it. I had now a friend; Loulou got a smart collar with his name on it. Sundays became brighter; Applin and his wife took me for drives, and back to charming actors' suppers. I hardly knew any great names, and it was entirely on personal merit that I enjoyed meeting Fred Terry and his beautiful daughter. Arthur Applin dexterously shuffled half a dozen words in French sufficient to keep the conversation on a highly intellectual level. For I wanted to know from authorised sources whether in truth English poets were " seraphic," as Balmont had made me believe from his translations into Russian. A volume of Swinburne and an English grammar sent by Applin could have enlightened me had I been but able to read them. The gift in itself confirmed my faith in that active kindness of heart which is so thoroughly English. Indisposed as I was to see anything good in my surroundings, I made no mistake on that point. Nothing is left of my prejudice now. My love of exploring finds profitable employment in London. When I have finished this book, I shall pursue the interrupted thrill of discoveries. Pity, though, that nowhere there are Persian geraniums, no pots with balsams in the windows; the nasturtium is considered a vulgar flower, which I regret : still, London would have suited me thoroughly, were it but in walking distance of my own town and Theatre Street.

CHAPTER XXI

Diaghileff — Beginning of our Long Association — Thamar —
Stravinsky—Changes—The Ballet To-day

EVENTS of each year I remember by my own mile-stones.
I have never kept a diary. At school I started once:
" I begin this diary with a view to improving my character "—
I thought it must be the right beginning, I got it from a recently
read novel. My diary languished for a few days; the novel
could not furnish any more hints. My own system of recording
works quite efficiently, if in some ways crazily. Events of
importance have to be traced backwards to find themselves
exactly located. That is how my closer knowledge of Diaghileff
and of the laboratory of his creative thought seems to start from
the day when I got up to answer a telephone call, slightly
annoyed at the interruption of my work. I was then diligently
translating Noverre into Russian. The idea must have just
crystallized in the mind of Diaghileff when he spoke to me that
day. He had thought of a wonderful rôle for me, he said, as
if hurrying to impart some great news. In a few words, but
how graphic, he told me of the *Spectre de la Rose.* By a casual
remark Diaghileff could pull aside a curtain and open a lovely
vista to the imagination.

I believe in his early youth Diaghileff studied composition;
he wrote symphonies and submitted them to the judgment of
Rimsky Korsakoff. I was told he had also studied singing at
one time. No doubt superior education, breeding, refinement
of taste contributed to making Diaghileff what he became eventually; but these were minor factors. Some dabbling in art,
enlightened understanding—the incontestable qualities of our
gentry rarely served a greater purpose than forming so many

amiable dilettanti. By luck or by a dispensation of Providence, the personal ambitions of Diaghileff received no encouragement ; he was saved for a unique task. I can only speak of Diaghileff from the time I came into contact with him, that is speak empirically. My fond vision supplements the lack of positive knowledge as to the precocious growth of his intellect. I see him as an infant Hercules doing mighty deeds straight out of the cradle. The cradle of Diaghileff's career was the foundation of the *Mir Izkoustva*. A young man then, he already had that grasp of the absolute, an unmistakable attribute of genius. He distinguished between transient and eternal truth in art. When I knew him, he was unerring in his judgment ; artists believed implicity in his opinion. It pleased him to divine a seed of genius where a lesser intuition would see eccentricity only. " Mark him well," Diaghileff pointed to Stravinsky. " He is a man on the eve of celebrity." This remark was made on the stage of the Paris Opera while we were rehearsing *Fire Bird*. A few days later Stravinsky's fame blazed out. At home Stravinsky had been practically unknown. Diaghileff, after hearing his first opus at a concert, commissioned him to write the music of the *Fire Bird*. In the winter preceding our second season abroad, we spoke of Stravinsky as Sergei Pavlovitch's new discovery. Ida Rubinstein was numbered among his early ones. Diaghileff unhesitatingly defined the promise of her remarkable countenance. In the roll of celebrities his hand has written many names. Diaghileff's exploration for new talents did not exclude his respect for those fully recognised ; but he could not help seeing a potential gem. That search for any new manifestation of beauty accorded so well with his temperament ; for, hardly his task accomplished, the impetuous spirit shifted it off to press forward towards a new one.

A link had been formed between Diaghileff and me by our first collaboration. To suit his purposes he had need of a young, receptive personality, of a clay unhardened in a final shape. He had need of me, and I had implicit belief in him.

He enlarged the scope of my artistic emotions; he educated and formed me, not by ostentatious methods, not by preaching or philosophising. A few casual words fetched a lucid conception, an image to be, out of the dark. Often did I sadly ruminate as to what he could have done for me had he but tried systematically to educate my mind. Who knows, perhaps these peripatetic lessons were what I needed most. Reasoning, logical conclusions never helped me; the more I reasoned, the fainter grew the image I tried to focus. My imagination would set to work only by the action of some hidden spring. I had but a slender luggage of real experience. The emotions called forth in embodying the tragic of which my parts had a large share could not be but potential ones. By uncanny intuition Diaghileff could set in motion these hidden springs, of which I had no key as yet.

On his way from the stalls, where he had been watching the rehearsal, Diaghileff stopped to say a few words as to my interpretation of " Echo." " Don't trip lightly as a graceful nymph; I see rather a monumental figure, a tragic mask, Niobe." He scanned the last word and went his way. And in my vision the heavy metric structure of the tragic name became the mournful tread of sleepless Echo.

And *Thamar*, that I had almost given up in despair. My original misconception called for a special visit of the Master.

" Omission is the essence of art." That and " livid face— eyebrows in a single line." Nothing more, yet that was enough to touch the spring that made me see all Thamar in a flash.

I returned from London having signed an agreement with the Coliseum for the next spring. Great was the annoyance of Diaghileff when he learned this. His season in Paris began shortly after my engagement in London, and he could not spare me for any part of the time. Mutual recriminations began; he reproached me with not having kept myself free for him; I retorted that he should have warned me of his plans. The anguish was great on both sides. I would have willingly given up the material benefit of the London engagement not to miss anything of the Paris season ; but I was bound by my signature. In Diaghileff's agreement with the Opera my name had been stipulated ; even should he have wished it he could not give his season without me. In pursuance of the common cause we left off reproaches and started devising means how to get out of the difficulty. Frantic telegrams, many of them, I sent to Marinelli. The same answer came—there can be no question of shifting the Coliseum dates, engagement must be fulfilled. There was a great strain on me during this period. I bore a very considerable part of the Marinsky repertoire, rehearsed new parts for the spring, and was being literally tormented by Diaghileff. I dreaded the telephone, as it was not easy to resist Diaghileff's pressure. He would wear out his opponent, not by the logic of his arguments, but by sheer stress of his own will, by tenacity incredible. It seemed natural to him that everything should give way before his progress, and he hoped to persuade me to break off my previous engagement. His tentacles closed more and more around me—a perfect moral inquisition. Diaghileff constantly requested that I should come to him in the evening to see the work of the Artistic Committee and " talk things over." Much as I liked to breathe the atmosphere of the new season in the making I knew my visit would be an ordeal.

In Diaghileff's small flat beat the pulse of his formidable enterprise. Strategic moves and counter-moves of his ingenuity, planning, budgeting, music in one corner, discussion in another. A Chancery and a small Parnassus in the restricted space of two rooms. The lines of each production were discussed there first. Around the table sat wise men ; the Artistic Committee drinking weak tea and hatching daring ideas. Quite unrepeatable were those days, unimaginable the boyish exuberance of these pioneers of Russian art. However much experience was gained in latter years, nothing can bring back that early enthusiasm.

The artistic forces commanded by Diaghileff were of the highest mettle. Benois topped the Areopagus. In him inspiration was coupled with clear thought, wisdom with practical adaptability. He overflowed with benignity, and his erudition was unique. His mastery of blending fantastic with real was the more wonderful because he effected his magic by the simplest means. The symbolic horsemen of day and night gave much worry to the committee while discussing the *Fire Bird.* "Impossible to let horses stamp all over the stage, pull the scenery to pieces. The apparition will be grotesque—let us fake it." " No," said Benois, " let the rider pass slowly along the proscenium. The symbolism will be evident when not underlined." Eventually it was done after Benois' suggestion and stood for a moment of stirring beauty. Quite different assets were those of Bakst. He was exotic, fantastic—reaching from one pole to another. The spice and sombreness of the East, the serene aloofness of classical antiquity were his.

Roerich—all mystery; a prophet with impeded speech, he could do infinitely more than ever he promised. When Dobujinsky joined the work, an adorable element of prim mischief was introduced. A great master of the stage, great romantic, shy, naïve and simple.

While they sat in one room, in the next Stravinsky and Fokine worked over a score and appealed to Diaghileff in every collision over the tempi. I had seen a Japanese performer once, exhibiting feats of quadruple concentration. I failed to be impressed by him : I had seen Diaghileff at work. He brought quick, unhesitating decision to every doubt. He had the sense of the theatre to an uncanny degree. Engrossed as he was in his part he kept a vigilant eye on his collaborators : " Gentlemen, you are wandering off your point," came now and then from his corner. Diversions constantly occurred. Tradesmen burst in ; alarming news arrived : unless Anisfeld has more canvas at once, he won't be able to finish painting the scenery.

On the eve of my departure for London a more than usually

pressing " come to talk things over " brought me again to Diaghileff's flat. I think he wanted to re-exercise the almost hypnotic power he had over me before I could escape from his influence. There the air was tense, all nerves worn down, as usual nothing ready and time short. He took me to his room, the only uninvaded spot. I had promised to solicit leave from the Coliseum after my first fortnight, and Diaghileff reminded me of my promise. We both had outlived the strife, if there was one; mutual anxiety had brought us closer. Diaghileff spoke affectionately; we cried a little. I looked round. The image lamp was lit; Diaghileff looked weary, a mere human. The room was bare of adornment, I had expected it to be fastidious. I could not realise then that the glamour of his personality spent itself in creations of fancy. His gentle words had a touch of resignation. He knew that on his way one obstacle hardly removed another will arise. After all, he had got over worse difficulties in the past. Referring to this past, he told me an amusing story. His valet, as was indeed natural to Russian servants, would come unbidden constantly in and out of the rooms. Diaghileff and his friends were staggering under a recent blow, and there was much talk of intrigues and intriguers. When the situation crystallized in Vassily's mind, he suggested direct action. " Barin, shall we do away with the villainess ? " " What do you mean ? " The hand moved in dumb show, brushing something aside. " What can one do, Vassily ? " " Shall I, Barin. . . ." Another dumb show demonstrated the action. " Just a little powder." No common hireling, Vassily had towards his master an unquestioning devotion of an old retainer. When crossing to America, Diaghileff daily ordered Vassily to kneel down and pray for the safety of their voyage. And while the valet performed religious exercises his master paced up and down the deck in better spirits.

It would seem that one who by his birth and tradition was still linked with feudal Russia of the Serfs, one so picturesquely

Russian in intellect and habit as Diaghileff, might be lost when completely cut off from his natural surroundings; but this is not so with him. There is no- toxin of sentimentality in Diaghileff. Not only does he not regret yesterday, but all his mental attitude tends towards to-morrow. He does not treasure relics, he does not turn back to look at the past. In this may lie the explanation of his untiring creative power. And yet on the tablets of memory he carves his own marks. In 1920, during our season in Paris, in the maze of corridors of the Grand Opera, where I to this day am prone to get lost, I saw Diaghileff advancing from the other end, arms outstretched. "I have been looking for you everywhere; to-day is the tenth anniversary of the *Fire Bird*." He was sincere when, on the night we gave the revival of *Giselle* at the Opera, he came into my dressing-room to take me down. "Come now, let us create *Giselle*, and bless you." No less sincere is he now, when he shudders at the very suggestion of reviving this ballet.

There is no inconsistency in the whole stretch of his work. In the long chain of his amazingly contradictory methods, he has paid a pious homage to each item at the time, paid his tribute and passed on to the next. And all is consistent; each day had had its glory, because it was the " present."

Though I am no longer in his inner counsels in the making of his seasons, still I have progressed with him through the Romanticism in which I had been brought up to the Modernism of Satie's *Parade*. I found I could easily attune myself to this. Though it required at times a great detachment from my own personal sentiments, I could follow him with a clear conscience in a difficult task, perhaps even with more satisfaction than in works to which I am more naturally suited. But there I had to stop. And now I follow his latest phases fondly and with sympathy, though now my feeling is one of conflict between my unswerving belief in his genius, that makes even his failures magnificent, and my fears that ballet is departing from its first vital principles.

Each art is only powerful in its own domain, and once it seeks to embody the principles of other art it is doomed to failure. The Eclecticism of the later phases of the Ballet is its greatest danger.

CHAPTER XXII

Two Engagements at Once—Lopokova in Paris—Giselle—
Differences with Nijinsky—I am made Prima Ballerina—
Chaliapin—Complications and Tears—Nijinsky and the Empress
—His Dismissal

I COULD find no practical solution of my simultaneous engagements. Besides, I realised that I was in the wrong and could only ask for a favour from Mr. Stoll. And in my heart I was ashamed to ask for this favour. However, things righted themselves. Marinelli grunted and sighed ; against his own interest he took up my cause. M. Turlututu now stood before me in an aureole of noble unselfishness. He was singularly devoted to me and did not shrink from the unpleasant task of getting my proposed defection sanctioned by Stoll. He failed ; I made him go again, time after time, till nothing was left but a last forlorn hope. In the personal interview with Stoll, Marinelli prompting and helping me, I must have displayed genuine despair and so have gained my cause. Again, I could not but admire Stoll's fairness of mind.

I was to leave after a fortnight and return back within a month's time. In the meantime, from the other side of the Channel, Diaghileff pulled the strings. He dispatched envoys to convey that he was expecting me. In the whole course of our acquaintance I had but one short note from him. His letterphobia had always been a standing joke. But telegrams he would send in profusion. His anxiety must have been great. Oneguin was then in London with me, nominally to look up some manuscripts of Poushkin in the British Museum. He remained there for a couple of days after I had left and wrote to me in a quasi laconic and facetious style of his own.

" Napoleon wired. I replied : ' Find her in Paris.' God has turned on all the mains. . . . It rains, rains, rains. Have seen Hampton Court—marvel ! "

Grand Opera ! The name had a fragrancy to me. I had learned to spell it respectfully ; now I was going to dance on its stage ; how sweetly it titillated my vanity. The gigantic scale of the place impressed me too. I could never learn where all the numberless stairs and ramification of corridors led to. The place is full of most amusing reminiscences to me. On the first night of *Fire Bird* our *régisseur*, a splendid fellow, but indifferent linguist, mis-signalled. The effect was so startling that Diaghileff rushed from his stall to the back of the stage, entreating in a forcible whisper to cancel that accursed moon. Both luminaries indeed had appeared simultaneously.

Young Lopokova danced this season ; it was altogether her first journey abroad. As she was stepping out of the railway carriage, emotion overcame her. She fainted right away on the piles of luggage. It had been her dream to be in Paris, she told the alarmed Bakst who had rendered her first aid ; the lovely sight (of the Gare du Nord) was too much for her. A mere child, she reminded me again of the tiny earnest pupil when, in the demure costume of *Sylphides*, she ecstatically and swiftly ran on her toes. She won a place of her own in the hearts of the public, and there was a touch of tenderness in the eulogies, of which the papers were full. No one gave a better portrait of her than Jean Louis Vaudoyer in his " Variations on the Russian Ballet." Amalia Loulou, he declared, the heroine of a tiny masterpiece of P. J. Stahl, by a singular caprice of fate has been dancing on the opera stage this whole month under the name of Lopokova II—the Princesses of the Dance as well as Sovereigns have their numbers, he gravely remarked. Amalia Loulou and Lopokova couldn't count thirty years between them. " The virtuosity of Lopokova is ingenuous and tempered by the imperceptible awkwardness of youth."

" I will make a Lopokova out of this one," our general used

to say in after years, to the end of his life attached to the Russian ballet; but he was mistaken—there was not another Lopokova to be made out of the ample material of young dancers each year replenishing the ranks. A clever impresario snatched little Lopokova, and for some years she danced in America. When she same back, there was a mastery in her technique which fully qualified her as a star; in some marvellous way her spontaneity and the unique blend of eagerness and naïveté that had frustrated the poor general's efforts for a replica, had remained unimpaired.

So intent were Nijinsky and I on making masterpieces of our respective parts in *Giselle*, that our eagerness to impose on one another our individuality led to tempestuous scenes. *Giselle*, on our stage, was a holy ballet, not a step of it to be altered. I knew the part as taught me by Madame Sokolova, and loved every bit of it. I was sadly taken aback when I found that I danced, mimed, went off my head and died of broken heart without any response from Nijinsky. He stood pensive and bit his nails. " Now you have to come across towards me," I suggested. " I know myself what to do," he said moodily. After ineffectual efforts to go through the dialogue by myself, I wept. Nijinsky looked sheepish and unmoved. Diaghileff led me off to the wings, proffered a handkerchief and told me to be indulgent : " You don't know what volumes he has written on that part, what treatises on its interpretation."

From now on Diaghileff acted as a buffer between us. We were both inflammable, and the learning of *Giselle* was not without tears, and many. Eventually understanding came ; and we got well attuned together. *Giselle*, according to notices, proved a great personal success for the chief interpreters—no more. *Sheherezade* and *Fire Bird* had an astounding success. As it had been clearly shown by previous experience, the exotic trait of Russian Art appealed the most to our public.

In choosing Paris as his sphere of action Diaghileff primarily followed his inclination. He shared with people of his class that love for French culture, which is ingrained in our gentry, nurtured by their upbringing. Very likely there may have been as well an element of calculation in Diaghileff's choice of place for his beginning, for he had the chess master's capacity for planning ahead and foreseeing the effect of his moves.

He had rightly chosen Paris, the centre point of theatrical opportunities.

At the end of our season Diaghileff made me an offer of an engagement for two years. It alarmed me. In signing this contract I felt I was signing away something more important than my summer holidays. Indeed, I saw dangerous signs in the rapidly increasing volume of Diaghileff's ambitions. As, enlarging his enterprise, he wanted more and even more of my time, we became constantly engaged in unequal struggles. Exhortations from him, ineffectual arguments from me—he would win at the end. Neither could I sever myself from his work, I loved it, nor would he spare me. "What an odd creature you are !" he used to say. "Can't you realise that the present moment is the hey-day of the ballet, and incidentally yours? Of all the arts it has the greatest success, and you the one who has the greatest success in it. . . . A rest," contemptuously, "what for?" And, quoting, "Have you not all eternity to rest in?" He revelled in the life of constant activity; I faltered in the face of it.

Not only the spring and summer months I eventually worked abroad, but also a part of the winter. The absences during the Marinsky season were made possible in virtue of the exceptional position I held at the time. In 1910 I received the title of Prima Ballerina, and at the same time the management offered me a contract. This was unusual : contracts with permanent artists were never made. The meaning of this policy was explained to me. The number of years of my service did not entitle me yet to a high salary ; but a proviso existed in the budget, allowing larger salaries for artists engaged for a period of time. The management had an option to renew my engagement. Though in fact I remained permanently attached to the Marinsky I had the privileges of foreign guests as regards salary and the choice of time in which to fulfil the number of performances stipulated in the agreement. Leaves of absence were given to me liberally, but my work in Petersburg was intensified, compressed into a shorter period.

The productiveness of Diaghileff's Ballet or, properly speaking, that of Fokine down to 1914 was astonishing. Fokine was now an official Ballet Master of the Marinsky, but he managed to get through his work for the Imperial stage by the spring, when he began staging for Diaghileff.

The itinerary of the Russian Ballet was much the same every year. Though a young enterprise, it spread its roots deep and firm in Western Europe. The hazardous element of the first two seasons changed very soon in a permanent routine. We invariably began at Monte Carlo.

Our seasons at Monte Carlo often followed those of Chaliapin. By agreement with the Imperial Theatre he fulfilled a certain number of performances in Moscow and Petersburg in the height of the season, and for the rest of the time sang in the capitals of Europe and America. During his visits to Petersburg I rarely missed his performances, and we often met after the theatre at supper. No one, on hearing Chaliapin on the stage, would have said there was a trace of nervousness in him, but all who had seen him behind the scenes know how his nerves worked him up to a state beyond his control. He rapturously gave way to relaxation after the performance, talked delightful nonsense, would address the waiter in an expressive recitative, and sometimes would tell us of his past vicissitudes, of his life among the Volga boatmen and of the first steps on the stage. He had started in a small provincial theatre, playing mostly at country fairs. Though his part consisted of two lines only, on his first appearing before the public Chaliapin shook with stage fright and managed to say the lines wrong. " But that was nothing to compare with the shaking my impresario gave me after—bang on one ear, bang on the other ! "

Since his first success, which was a full revelation of his genius both as a singer and as an actor, Chaliapin had heard and read about himself only superlatives. Nevertheless he always asked for criticisms. One night I remember him sublime in *Boris Godounoff*; never, it seemed to me, had his performance been greater than in the death scene. I dabbed my eyes surreptitiously, and felt slightly annoyed at my guest in the box, who never took his eyes off the score. That same night we met at Cubat; Chaliapin seemed nervous as if watching for somebody. Michael Terestchenko — afterwards Kerensky's Minister for Foreign Affairs—came in and Chaliapin hailed him. " Tell me, Mischa, what about to-night ? Was it quite all right ? " When reassured by Terestchenko, reputed for his absolute pitch, Chaliapin revived; in the flow of his high spirits he began improvising verses to me :—

> " Egyptian maidens, almond-eyed,
> Tribute of nard and myrrh will bring . . ."

He couldn't fit the second line about himself singing my praise at the foot of the Pyramids. He still maintained the pose of comic courtship towards me as on our first meeting at the Hermitage, only I was no longer intimidated by his presence.

In the year 1911 Chaliapin remained at Monte Carlo long after his season was over. We met many times a day on that thoroughfare of Monte Carlo, the verandah of the Café de Paris, and usually made up a party after the theatre—himself, Diaghileff, Nijinsky and I. He was then in a state of great depression, and it eased him to talk on a subject that was a great sore to him at the time. Chaliapin's worshippers in Russia had become greatly incensed with him for what they deemed to be an apostasy from his Liberal opinions. The incident which brought about his temporary unpopularity had been so distorted that, though my sympathies were with Chaliapin, I was glad to hear his own explanation of it. It happened at the Marinsky on the benefit night of the chorus. The Emperor being present, a patriotic demonstration took place : the curtain was raised in the interval ; the whole company, Chaliapin at the head, sang the National Anthem. Suddenly Chaliapin fell on his knees, and the whole stage kneeled before His Majesty. The Emperor stood pale, visibly moved. In my own mind I thought the moment supremely beautiful. Liberal youth, at whose gatherings Chaliapin used to sing the hymns of freedom, had been vehement in accusing Chaliapin of hypocrisy. " I reasoned not ; I do not know how it happened," said Chaliapin, and his puzzled, worried look better than any apology exonerated him from any suspicion of insincerity, if such could have existed in the minds of his listeners. A great sensitive artist could not but spontaneously respond to the wave of sudden emotion.

After Monte Carlo, Paris and London followed without interruption ; part of the winters were spent in Germany and Vienna ; we frequently returned to Paris and London about Christmas time. This covered six months in the year, which I gave to Diaghileff, but soon it became insufficient : his demand really grew alarming. To refuse him was next to impossible : I asked for more and more leaves and was only refused on one occasion. The Imperial Theatre had been getting slightly annoyed : I was becoming a rare guest in Petersburg. The pretext which served Teliakovsky for establishing his nominal right on my services was a flimsy one ; but out of it ensued quite a dramatic episode. We were then performing in Berlin in the *Theater des Westens*. In those days that part of the town was vaguely provincial, redolent of frowsy cosiness. After the 1914 war it had so changed that, in the whirlpool of gaieties that it had become, I hardly recognised the place of my acute anxieties.

My leave was expiring ; with the winding-up of the Berlin season I was going back to Russia. The Russian Ballet had had a success, equal to that of Paris, and no less enthusiastically if more ponderously acclaimed. Oscar Bie added a chapter to his admirable book. The Royal Opera House of Dresden invited Diaghileff for several performances, to follow Berlin. Quite casually Diaghileff said, " You are not of course going to leave us, Tata ; they have made stipulations for your appearance." —" My leave will be over, Sergei Pavlovitch."—" Nonsense, it is carnival now, nobody in the Marinsky but moustacheless youth, send a telegram asking for prolongation of leave." Though it was only a matter of matinée performances for schools, my reiterated demands were refused. Through side channels Diaghileff addressed high circles in Petersburg. It was of no avail ; Teliakovsky remained adamant. There was nothing for me but to go. Luckily for my shattered fortitude, Svetloff took my side. He followed us pretty often, a faithful friend. No fortitude unsupported could have stood against what I had to stand during the last ten days in Berlin, miserable days spent chiefly in tears in the telephone cabin. Diaghileff called me up at short intervals ; every evening he got hold of me " to talk things over." I realised that he risked forfeiting his contract should I fail him. His arguments exhausted, he bowed to the inevitable, and it was heart-breaking to see his dejected face. On the last night he sat in my dressing-room. My eyelids were swollen with continuous crying, and looked like two little red sausages. Diaghileff sucked the knob of his stick, a sign of depression, and then very wearily, on the off-chance, he said, " Let us look up the A.B.C." He then calculated that starting on the night after the Dresden performance and travelling by the North Express I could arrive at Petersburg early in the morning on the day of my matinée. It seemed a Heaven-sent solution, but he did not take the elements into account. Accordingly I danced at Dresden, rushed off the stage immediately after the performance, threw a shawl over my ringlet wig, a coat over my Egyptian dress and arrived at the station just in time to catch the last train. I washed off my nut-brown complexion of an Egyptian maiden as best I could in my compartment. The express sped on till on the second day, when a large snowdrift caused a delay, the train was six hours late. From the station I hurried to the theatre. My understudy had been got ready, but there still remained ten minutes of interval. When, in the costume of Sugar Plum Fairy, I came on the stage, the overture had finished and the curtain was going up. Teliakovsky thought it sporting of me. Next day I went to see him and obtained permission to leave on the morrow. With rough good nature he said, " Have you not yet pocketed all the money there is abroad ? "

His brightest star, Nijinsky, Diaghileff had no need to dispute to the Imperial Stage ; he was no more a member of the Marinsky troupe. Monstrous as it will sound, he had been expelled. Here again, as in my small incident, the maintenance of discipline was the sole reason. I remember well that night of *Giselle* at the Marinsky. The Dowager Empress sat in the Imperial box. It seemed to me that Nijinsky on that night reached such heights of inspiration as never before. He had put on a costume designed by Benois, consisting of a trunk hose and a very short jerkin ; the regulation trunks he refused to wear. There had been an altercation about it with the official in charge of production ; the curtain went up a few minutes late on account of it. Whether Nijinsky's insubordination in itself determined the management to act as they did, or whether the rumours that the Empress disapproved of the costume were true, I do not known, but the next day Nijinsky was ordered to send in his resignation.

The same night brought me an honour. The Empress had sent for me. Giving me her hand to kiss, she said, " I am told you have had a great success in England." I saw at once that Lady Ripon had been instrumental in bringing about this favour and thanked her on our next meeting. " Oh yes," she said with her sweet smile, " I took down all your photos to Sandringham for the Empress to see."

CHAPTER XXIII

Lady Ripon, the Good Fairy—Sargent—South America—
Nijinsky's Wedding—" Maestro "

THAT was characteristic of Lady Ripon's attitude towards those she called her friends. A fond schemer, she arranged her good fairy jobs secretively, so as to give a pleasant surprise. " Dear little friend," she wrote on Queen Alexandra's Day, " will you wear this bunch of roses on your shoulder to-night, when you dance in *Spectre de la Rose* ; I feel it would please your audience. . . ." Apart from the wonderful delicacy of feeling which prompted this suggestion, the active and inspired patroness of Russian art in London, Lady Ripon, well knew that to put the success of our season on a firm basis could only be done by giving it social standing, and winning the love of the audience. My adopted country, you are generous and infinitely tolerant to a foreigner, but in your heart of hearts you are mildly surprised every time you see the foreigner using his knife and fork in the same way you do. You readily excuse kinks of alien mentality inexplicable to you, you even excuse unpunctuality to meal hours—but you don't take a foreigner seriously, unless a trustworthy sponsor introduces him to your heart and to your consideration. Introductions properly done, there is no country more loyal than England in her once accepted recognition. So it is in the matter of foreign art. There might have been a chance of the Russian Ballet achieving a success on the strength of its merits alone. Thousands of people would have seen it in a variety show ; they would have seen it comfortably, lulled into good humour by the fumes of a good cigar. They would have taken a vaguely pleasant emotion to the door of the theatre and, while waiting for their cars, expressed their views on the

Russian Ballet : " I say, that fellow with the teasing name *can* jump, can't he ; rather jolly ! "

Lady Ripon realised that the first appearance of the Russian Ballet must be in Covent Garden, and she had brought it about. The coronation performance started our first season brilliantly. To add further to its record, Lady Ripon had erected a beautiful little theatre in her ball-room at Coombe. The permanent setting of it had been done by Bakst in his favourite blue and green which he was first to intermarry on the stage. " *Bleu Bakst* " since has had unequalled vogue. In this theatre Nijinsky and myself danced for Queen Alexandra. We used the little theatre on another occasion, that of a fancy-dress ball given by Lady Ripon. Our little party, with Diaghileff at the head, came early ; the hostess was not down yet. A softly veiled dewy evening of a glorious July looked through the open door. The white balustrade of the verandah, French parterres down below, the drooping willows at the end of the alley and a bit of sky gathering dusk.

> Sur le monde assoupi les heures taciturnes
> Tordent leurs cheveux noirs, pleurant des larmes nocturnes.

A few brief minutes of hushed poise in the turbulent round of days and months ; all the scattered gifts of life's cornucopia gathered into one immense wealth.

It was no small gift to have known Lady Ripon, to have had her friendship. Around her all was serene ; the petty, the mean fled at her approach. In the meekness of her heart she made herself a servant of those protected by her. Not only did she serve the cause of the Russian Ballet, but found time and thought to look after our personal interests. There was not a good portrait of me in existence ; " Sargent will like to draw you," she often said, and one day took me to his studio. The drawing Sargent made of me in *Thamar* was to be a pendant to his head of Nijinsky in Lady Ripon's room at Coombe. Sargent used to make a drawing of me each year, till the war put a temporary stop to the Ballet coming to London. He generously gave me his drawings and, what in some odd way touched me even more, presented me with an enlargement of my photograph in *Carnaval*. His valet had done it; Sargent was very anxious that I should appreciate the merits of the work. As he drew he talked incessantly and liked me to talk. But there was little or no chance for me : so engrossed was he with the idea of adapting *Vathek* to the stage. Every time he brought the story to the point when that excellent lady, the Calif's mother, broke pots of scorpions over her festive table, that peculiar rattling ejaculation, so well known to Sargent's friends, so impossible to transcribe phonetically, except in Arabic perhaps, interrupted the narrative, and turned its tide back again. The whole story of *Vathek* I learned later when I had learned to read English.

My ignorance of the language caused me some inconvenience. I either arrived at wrong addresses or did not arrive at all when expected, not being able to give intelligibly the name of the street. Few amongst the many people I constantly met I knew by name ; life in London had now puzzling, now delightful surprises for me. And so many good things had been wasted on me. Sargent, who admired the work of de Glehn, introduced him to me and I sat for him. At one of the sittings Ruth Draper came in. As a generous compliment to the Russian Ballet in my person, she wanted to act before me. Not a word could I understand, but if ever her art had to stand a severe test and come out victorious, it was then ; for, not knowing what it was about, I could not help feeling I was seeing an actress of great power in front of me. Her face lighted and faded with each change of mood.

*   *   *   *   *

So, for five consecutive years, Diaghileff's enterprise, the Russian Ballet, followed its routine of seasons and the " Ritzonian " world, as Benson characterised it, partly or bodily was represented in each of the respective towns marked by vogue to be the right place for the time of the year. There were places, however, this world did not venture to visit in its smart peregrinations. We embarked for South America in the autumn of 1913. I well remember my reluctance to go there. By this time Diaghileff had accepted my little revolts and took them as an unavoidable drawback in an otherwise meek and amenable woman. The sea voyage and the alarming thought of going to the Antipodes were at the bottom of my unwillingness. I did not go so far as to share the patristic belief that I would have to walk like a fly on the ceiling, but a feeling of dizziness overtook me every time I looked at the Terrestrial Globe and thought of South America. Diaghileff induced me to accept this offer by saying that even he, hating sea voyages, would go there and that it would be as smooth as a pond. So it was during the whole of the eighteen days on board, but Diaghileff did not come; he had misgivings at the last moment and went to the Lido instead. His representative, Dmitri Günsburg, went with us.

I can record no artistic emotions of any special value from this tour. I came back by an English steamer. A bugle called us at 7 a.m.; at eight breakfast was over, no entreaties would procure a single biscuit after this hour. Salt beef at lunch, salt beef at dinner—no pampering, but the decks like a ballroom floor. It was an uneventful trip but for Nijinsky's wedding.

I longed to get back to Europe, and there was one place in it to which I particularly longed to return. Since that single visit to Rome in 1912 I had never re-visited it. Though it was Exhibition year at Rome, there were few parties; at least there was not so much claim on my time as in London or Paris. In consequence I could spend my time profitably. All through my tours abroad I worked regularly with Maestro Cecchetti. Often I had to shorten my daily lesson with him to be in time for a luncheon party; after late nights it was not easy to get up in the morning and Maestro would grumble. In Rome there were hardly any interruptions in my lessons with him. Here, in his own country, the Maestro's spirits rose high; he was in a frenzy of teaching, and an equal frenzy of learning possessed both Nijinsky and myself. However early we arrived the Maestro would be there waiting, cracking jokes with stage hands, making the wise black poodle of the doorkeeper perform his tricks. The dog loved money and knew the use of it. Given a soldo he sedately walked across the road to the pastrycook's, put his coin on the counter and came with a cream bun to eat at his leisure. But on certain mornings there would be no question of practising on the stage; even access to the theatre was difficult. The doorkeeper would be outside the entrance; as one approached the stage door his gesticulation, usually vivacious, took a highly dramatic tenour. In the corridors there would be more " hushers " and all round walked on tip toes—Toscanini was rehearsing.

Diaghileff often came round in the morning to fetch me on his way to Theatre Costanzi. " Maestro, you say ? The old man will wait; it is a sin to be indoors on such a morning," and he would take Nijinsky and myself for some enchanting drive, pointing out here and there an arch, a view, a monument. He would hand us over to the Maestro with a request not to scold the children for being a bit late. Maestro, with unusual blandness, would excuse his unpunctual pupils; he knew he could make up for the time lost, the stage, with rare exceptions, being always at our disposal. For the sake of discipline, though, Maestro would go through a show of disapproval; twirling his cane, thus giving time for escape, he would sling it at my feet; a well-timed skip cleared the missile.

Enrico Cecchetti was born in a dressing-room of the Tordinona Theatre at Rome; the theatre had been his nursery. When five years old he appeared on the stage. The same old gentleman sat every night in the same box adjoining the proscenium. Every night little Enrico watched for the appearance of a coin on the barrier of the box. Coming to take the call with his parents, the child reached his hand for the coin and blew a kiss. "Brava, my little girl," would say the old gentleman : tiny for his age, curly headed, little Enrico wore pink tarlatans and fairy wings. The family was performing at Genoa. The boy followed his parents in their strolling performances and was determined to become a dancer. All efforts to keep him at his books failed, and after Enrico hurled an inkpot at his master's head, his father abandoned the original idea of having him educated for law, and sent the boy to Florence to the dancing academy of Giovanni Lepri. At sixteen, an accomplished dancer, Enrico left the academy. The theatre became his home and his country only a stage in his peregrinations. At the time of his appearance in London the newspapers without exception acclaimed him. In the early 'eighties Cecchetti first came to Petersburg to dance in the Summer Theatre, Arcadia. He was a dancer of prodigious virtuosity. "Saltating demon, gifted with indiarubber limbs." The Imperial theatre engaged him, and for several years he seemed to have settled down in Russia, but before the termination of his agreement he quarrelled with the direction and left Petersburg for Warsaw. Periodical outbursts of his temper and still more the irresistible spirit of an artistic vagabond made it impossible for Cecchetti to remain long in the same place. He returned, however, and Madame Cecchetti, sweet and valiant woman, believed that her constantly frustrated hope of a permanent home would this time come true. Cecchetti opened his own school and eventually I became his pupil.

Cecchetti's reputation as a master was that of a wizard who could make dancers. In fact he was the only absolute teacher of the academic dance in our time, the keeper of the invaluable science of the great theorist, Carlo Blasis, whose pupil, Giovanni Lepri, had been Cecchetti's master. Before the advent of the celebrated Carlo Blasis, the teaching of our art based itself on an intuitive search. In all justice he should be called the first pedagogue of our art. The starting point of his theory being that the immutable laws of equilibrium applied to the human body necessitated the finding of a precise formula determining the perfect balance of a dancer. And if this system of Carlo Blasis may have seemed to be pertaining to geometry, his is the merit of having made a positive science out of the elusive elements of bodily virtuosity. To elucidate his formula to his pupils Carlo Blasis drew geometrical schemes, in which the correlation of the different parts of the body was expressed by planimetric terminology—curves and right angles. When a pupil had assimilated the lineal structure of the dance, Blasis passed on to rounding the positions, giving them a plastic perfection.

Maestro handed down to his pupils the great principle of his stage ancestor uncorrupted and pristine, if somewhat simplified in exposition. He balanced his cane across his finger and clearly demonstrated the horizontal position of the body, supported by the vertical line of one leg, as the basic principle of an arabesque. The same cane in his hands acted as a corrective, judiciously applied to insubordinate limbs, it became an instrument of wrath when in sudden and incontrollable fury Maestro hurled it at the pupil; the same cane blandly beat measure to a softly whistled tune—he used no other music at his lessons.

Some enterprising young *balletomanes* used to ride on top of an omnibus which passed outside Maestro's school in Petersburg; through the uncurtained windows of the second storey they could see the dancers at practice and this from a *balletomane's* point of view was worth several rides forwards and backwards. The uncurtained windows and summarily furnished flat spoke of nomadic life; quantities of photographs and other portable relics and the figure of Madame Cecchetti, who could be seen through the enfilade of rooms bent over her sewing, alone suggested the idea of stable if peripatetic domesticity.

Though herself a former dancer and now a mime of great ability, Madame Cecchetti was above all a sweet and dignified woman, and her simplicity and quietude contrasted sharply with the excitable manner and irascible tempers of her husband. In him the blood of a strolling player and the vivacity of the Italian temperament concurred to make a picturesque uncommon figure. The theatre was his birthright; on the stage and in life Cecchetti was an admirable, sincere, undiluted actor. When, with a finger pressed to his nose, assuming the guise of a simpleton, in a squeaky treble he cunningly asked, " Had your meal yesterday ? " and to the answer " yes," resumed " Aye, but have missed your lesson—bread and butter to you "—he was the personification of a mischievous masque of Italian comedy. The same strain of improvisation, priceless inheritance of the *Commedia del Arte*, governed him on the stage and at home alike— a great actor, so fond of his part as to create the consistent spectacle of a life begun in a dressing-room of the Tordinona terminated in the midst of a lesson.

Alexander Benois was at Rome our invariable guide. His knowledge of art and its history, his erudition might have been intimidating were it not for small lapses in his information; he contradicted himself as to the place where a speciality of iced zabaglioni was to be found. My brother, now married, was at Rome, too, studying patristics. I regarded him now in the light of a young sage; with affectionate mockery he called me his " famous and virtuous sister." Like in olden days we wandered together, not in search of penny volumes, but to see churches and forum, temples and catacombs.

Rumours circulated previous to our beginning this season. Italy, it was said, the country that prides itself on her ballet, the cradle of the amiable art, was bound to be hostile to us for going beyond classical tradition. On the first night the chief of the *claque* presented himself at my room : I left Günsburg to deal with him and went on the stage. There, too, apprehension was felt; Diaghileff told me to be prepared. . . . " Cabbala." With him stood the Russian Ambassador, who advised us to inspect the stage for nails and bits of broken glass.

When no hostile manifestation came I was slightly disappointed. I rather fancied myself holding head to the hooting
audience. Neither were there unfavourable criticisms. On the
contrary, they could not have been more enthusiastic. It is
true the latest sensational productions were not given at Rome.

CHAPTER XXIV

" L'après midi d'un Faune "—Dawn of Modernism—Rehearsals with Nijinsky—Debussy—Cocteau—J. L. Vaudoyer—" Spectre de la Rose "—Strange Beginning to a Friendship—Dethomas —Nijinsky's Tragedy—Our Last Meeting—Strauss—Massine —Felix—Da Falla—Picasso

NIJINSKY'S first production *L'Après midi d'un Faune* had been first given in Paris and raised a perfect riot of contending emotions. The audience clapped, yelled, hissed; across a barrier between two boxes a quarrel burst. Diaghileff's intervention restrained the frenzy of the public, and the performance was allowed to go to the end. I was not taking part in the ballet and sat in the stalls that night. I could not see what had offended the public so much.

Both *L'Après midi d'un Faune* and *Sacre du Printemps* of Nijinsky were of the same nature as the Pre-Raphaelite movement and revolutionary as well. Fokine had amplified the scope of plastic possibilities; he had broken through the unique formula hitherto enclosing the ballet; but his work was progressive, his standard of beauty essentially the same as that of his predecessors. Against the accepted harmony, softness, roundness of line, the vision of archaic Greece, as evoked by Nijinsky in *L'Après midi d'un Faune* and the *Sacre du Printemps*, interpreting with angular jerky movements, the stone age of prehistoric tribes, stood as a direct challenge. In these two works of his, Nijinsky declared his feud against Romanticism and bid adieu to the " beautiful." In his next ballet, *Jeux*, he made an attempt to find a synthesis of the twentieth century. " We will date it on the programmes 1930," said Diaghileff. This ballet had been given in 1913. Then was the noonday of futurism.

It is a pity that my puritan intolerance of those days made me tear in small pieces Marinetti's book. The gift was meant kindly. An exquisite dedication, a madrigal of superlative courtesy addressed me from the fly-leaf. The novel was preceded by the Manifesto of Marinetti and his disciples, an all-round anathema. Cursed were the moonlight and the canals of Venice, the nightingales as well ; cursed with a special vehemence the masterpieces of past generations and woman, on whom unsavoury epithets were lavishly poured—as lavish as the refined compliments of the author to the female recipient of his volume. The first chapter was " Le Viol des Négresses." It is a pity, after all, I haven't kept the book.

Nijinsky had no gift of precise thought, still less that of expressing his ideas in adequate words. Were he called upon to issue a manifesto of his new creed, for his dear life he could not have given a clearer statement than the one he had given to explain his wonderful capacity for soaring in the air. Certainly at the rehearsals of *Jeux* he was at a loss to explain what he wanted of me. And it was far from easy to learn the part by a mechanical process of imitating the postures as demonstrated by him. As I had to keep my head screwed on one side, both hands curled in as one maimed from birth, it would have helped me to know what it was for. In ignorance of my purpose I occasionally lapsed into my normal shape, and Nijinsky began to nourish a suspicion of my unwillingness to obey him. Best of friends on and off the stage, we often fought during the preparation of our parts. On this occasion our collisions were worse and more ludicrous than ever. Unaided by understanding, I had to learn by heart the sequence of movements and once asked, " What comes after. . . ."—" You should have known by now, I won't tell you." " Then I will give up my part." After two days' strike a big bunch of flowers was laid at my door and in the evening a complete reconciliation was brought about by Diaghileff.

On the first night of *Jeux* the same disagreement, only less noisy than that of *L'Après midi d'un Faune*, obviously divided the audience. What Debussy had thought of the interpretation of his music I don't know. He was reported to have said *pourquoi?* but it might have been evil tongues who reported it. To me he did not comment on the production. He often invited me to sit by his side. Madame Debussy and his little daughter usually came with him. He was so gently courteous, so devoid of pose and consciousness of his importance, so sincere in his admiration for the straightforward charm of the romantic ballets, for which he praised me, that in spite of his forbidding brow, in spite of his being an unfamiliar celebrity, I enjoyed our brief talks. But it was *oui Maître, vous avez raison, Maître. . . .* I was talking to an Olympian.

I never could get rid of that slight tremor of shyness on first meeting a celebrity, in spite of ample practice, for in Paris, which Diaghileff justly regarded as the climax of our season, not only was the Russian Ballet commercing daily with great people, but it also joined hands with the creative artists of Paris in comprehensive collaboration. During the first period of Russian Ballet, the pre-war one, only Paris had a share in its creative work. With the exception of Debussy, who never departed from a certain detachment of attitude, other eminent musicians and authors who came in contact with us delighted in closely following the various stages of production. There was nothing Olympian about Ravel; obligingly he would come to my help in the difficult rhythmic passages of his score.

There were many stumbling-blocks in the music of *Daphnis and Chloe*. In sonority suave, noble and clear as a crystal spring, it had some nasty pitfalls for the interpreter. There was a dance in it for me in which the bars followed a capricious cadence of ever-changing rhythm. Fokine was too maddened, working against time, to give me much attention; on the morning of the performance the last act was not yet brought to an end. Ravel and I at the back of the stage went thought—1 2 3—

1 2 3 4 5—1 2, till finally I could dismiss mathematics and follow the pattern of the music.

A permanent figure of the theatre was Jean Cocteau, the *enfant terrible* of rehearsals. Like a mischievous fox-terrier, he bounded about the stage, and had often to be called away: " Cocteau, come away, don't make them laugh." Nothing could stop his exuberant wit ; funny remarks spluttered from under his voluble tongue—Roman candles, vertiginous Catherine wheels of humour. That summer I sat to Jacques Blanche for my portrait. A quieter refuge from the feverish pulsation of Parisian life could not have been found than his large studio at Passy. The same restfulness emanated from the artist himself. There was before me yet another aspect of French mind. In his mouth the unavoidable personal remarks of artist to model had the flavour of dispassionate observation. His sense of the picturesque he said was curiously amused by the slender structure of my facial bones and the unexpected vigour of my neck. To bring out this peculiarity he had long studied me, finally deciding on the turn of the head, which seems to me gives something imperative to the pose of *Fire Bird* which he had chosen. The sudden appearance of Cocteau in the studio would bring a boisterous note. As if he had vowed never to locate himself anywhere, his voice now spoke from behind canvases, now called from the garden, unexpectedly addressed us from the top of the gallery. Standing there he forestalled our remarks and, pronouncing himself a preacher, a flow of extemporaneous speech immobilised him for a little while. Once only I saw him quiet : " Tell me the plot of the *Fire Bird*," he asked. While I was telling him the fairy-tale he sat attentive as a child. He had just begun work on the book of *Dieu Bleu*, for which Reynaldo Hahn had written the music. Of much the same verve and wit, sparkling but sly, was Reynaldo Hahn. He closely watched the making of his ballet. When the highly charged atmosphere of the rehearsal broke in storm he would wisely retire to the little café underneath the Châtelet. It was amusing on joining him there to see the incident we all took in earnest, show its real absurdity in Reynaldo Hahn's inimitable rendering.

The first author to bring his offering to the Russian Ballet had been Jean Louis Vaudoyer, who adapted for the stage *Le Spectre de la Rose*, the poem of Théophile Gauthier. It is close on twenty years since we first danced it at the Châtelet. It is now practically relegated to the lumber-room of souvenirs. "Ah ! this *Spectre de la Rose*," they sigh, who saw it ; and so complete had been its sway over the hearts, so subtly penetrating its fragrancy, that they sigh as well who had missed the *Spectre de la Rose*. To them it is a legend. The blessing of Terpsichore herself had been bestowed on this ballet ; it had been spared the infant ailments inseparable from others. Fokine had made it in one easy flight of his inspiration, in one blissful mood, finding no fault whatsoever with his interpreters. Unheralded by quarrels, demure as it should be, the *Spectre de la Rose* gently passed over the agony of the first night. That night there was no fuss on the stage—Diaghileff benign ; only Bakst moved about, helpless, agitated, carrying a canary cage. The cage was a feature of the scenery from his point of view, a nuisance from everybody else's. He had installed the canary over a window from where it had been banished ; Nijinsky had to appear through it, and the other window was to be free for Nijinsky's famous leap. "Levoushka, for God's sake, chuck the canary, the public is growing impatient. Oh, don't be ridiculous ; canaries don't stand on the chest of drawers."—"You don't understand, Serioja ; we must give the atmosphere." Bakst protracted the interval alarmingly, but he gave the atmosphere by finally hoisting the canary high up under a cornice. In further travel the cage, with its stuffed bird, was maliciously lost.

On one occasion at the Opera the whole ballet was encored on the insistent demand of the audience. Diaghileff sent me before the curtain, and I delivered my maiden speech to the effect that we would like to please our public by encoring, and that we entertained a hope that a charity collection about to begin would be generously supported. The performance had been given for the benefit of the victims of an earthquake.

My acquaintance with Jean Louis Vaudoyer began over the *Spectre de la Rose*. Making up the account of our long friendship, I will have to charge myself with a few blunders, but they belong to my youthful stage of social growth. Two young men, both tall and both in check trousers, had been to congratulate me after the morning rehearsal; one of them was the author—I only learned afterwards which was which. So I addressed my heartfelt thanks for giving me such opportunity as the part offered to the wrong young man, and for a long time I disapproved of the right one on account of a flicker of a *sourire moqueur*, which on closer knowledge proved to be the most enchanting touch of persiflage in an earnest and refined mind.

A total want of pose, remarkable for a time when the pursuance of originality not infrequently took an hysterical shape, characterised the literary circle to which Vaudoyer belonged. And another attractive feature of it was the elated friendship firmly binding its members, Serapion's brotherhood. On the strength of my interpreting this happy inspiration of Vaudoyer's, a place of honour had been given to me by all his friends. I enjoyed my rôle of a Muse on visit and enjoyed their company still more. It must have been in 1929, on one of my rare post-war visits to Paris, that Jean Louis reminded me that it was twenty years since our first season at the Châtelet. The statement alarmed me, but he said "How wonderful, is it not? that the present day finds us all in the same pursuit, still valiant." And he wore check trousers of the same pattern as when I first met him; and time and absence seemed to have made no ravages in the steady friendship. As before, the summons had been sent round and a handful of Serapions met at the same apartment of the Palais Royal; only . . . "Some are no more, others wander in distant lands," as Sadi wrote.

Dethomas is no more. I wonder what will become of the house in the Avenue des Thermes, so shaded as to make one feel at the bottom of a deep green pond. The myriads of Persian miniatures on walls never illumined by the direct ray of the sun, the dark canopy over the bed, with dragons and monsters and cyphers of the celestial empire were no mere accessories of a morbid taste. Dethomas's surroundings seemed to have captured him in an exquisitely sickly inextricable delirium; himself as homely as a housekeeper's purring cat, he strangely conveyed some tragic loneliness; with all his homeliness, he was as if out of life.

Some wander in distant lands, and some only come to Paris on short visits. Paris becomes too un-Parisian for Parisians of the pure mettle. The dinners of Comte Gilbert de Voisin, where all the friends of that circle met regularly, are now discontinued. There once I failed to pass the test in nimbleness of wit, at which they all were so brilliant. A book in which everyone was supposed to put his grievance against the host was offered to me. At a loss what to grieve at, I wrote down that there should be at least one King Charles in a house where souvenirs of Taglioni were piously kept in a glass cabinet. Gilbert de Voisin is her grandson. Shortly after I sent him an engraving of Taglioni with a King Charles in her lap. This was a poor return for a generous gift; Gilbert de Voisin had presented me with a fan of Taglioni's, which she had had during her stay in Russia and had used on the stage.

During that short stay in Paris over Christmas of 1928, Diaghileff proposed that we should visit Nijinsky, but on afterthought deemed it better to bring him to the theatre on the night I danced *Petroushka*. Since Nijinsky had left our troupe in 1913 to dance in America, I had not seen him; the news of his illness had reached me in Russia, and it was said that at first his mind became troubled and suspicious. He imagined himself surrounded with cunning hostility, and would not come on the stage without first having a man in his employ to look after the safety of the trap-doors and inspect the boards, so that no bits of broken glass should be maliciously put in his way. Soon he was no more haunted by fears : his memory became a blank ; he lost all sense of his own identity.   His own tragedy ceased ; the tragedy of those near to him must have been unspeakable when, striving to bring a spark of lucidity to his darkened brain, they told him over and over again who he was, and repeated his name to him.   But the sad incantation had no power over his spirit.   After a phase of delusions, painful to watch, but harmless, Nijinsky fell into a submissive apathy, and hardly ever spoke.

" He is in good spirits to-night," Diaghileff said, " and seems to like watching the ballet.   Wait for him on the stage."   It was the interval before *Petroushka*, the scene set, the company ready to go on.   For one moment I hoped that the familiar situation and myself in the costume in which he so often saw me dancing at his side might reclaim the lost thread of remembrance in the mind of Nijinsky.   The same hope must have suggested to Diaghileff our meeting on the stage.

Diaghileff spoke with a forced cheerfulness as he led Nijinsky on.   The crowd of artists fell back.   I saw vacant eyes and a passive shuffling gait, and stepped forward to kiss Nijinsky.   A shy smile lit up his face, and his eyes looked straight into mine. I thought he knew me, and I was afraid to speak lest it might interrupt a slow-forming thought.   He kept silent.   I then called him by his pet name, " Vatza ! "   He dropped his head and slowly turned it away.   Nijinsky meekly let himself be led to where the photographers had set their cameras.   I put my arm through his, and, requested to look straight into the camera, I could not see his movements.   I noticed that the photographers were hesitating, and, looking round, I saw that Nijinsky was leaning forward and looking into my face, but on meeting my eyes he again turned his head like a child that wants to hide tears. And that pathetic, shy, helpless movement went through my heart.

Nijinsky was taken back into his box, and Diaghileff came round afterwards to tell me more about him.   He spoke that night.   " Who is that ? " when Lifar came on the stage, and, when told it was the principal dancer, Nijinsky, after a pause, asked, " Can he jump ? "

*   *   *   *   *

To all who had followed its history abroad from its beginning to the present phase, it seemed that in the summer before the war the Russian Ballet reached the climax of its success. And, as if to make this summer of 1914 worth remembering, came other minor successes hand in hand. The gallery, at all times my staunch friend, now sent me a touching offering, a gold ballet shoe with the inscription, " To the Rose of Russia." A vogue of admiration made itself felt even in the humble circles of the Drury Lane staff. There was a little call-boy there who trotted at my heels most of the time. His admiration had many spontaneous outbursts ; when once I asked Teddy to fetch me some mineral water he gave a little cry of joy, stood on his head for a moment, pattered quickly on his hands to the door and, turning a double somersault, disappeared on his errand of love. Teddy was one of the stars of the Drury Lane pantomime and a familiar imp at my service. I came one morning to fetch something out of my dressing-room ; the key could not be found. On the previous night Chaliapin had had the room, and his Chinese valet would sometimes take the key in his pocket. As usual, I called Teddy, and, as usual, he didn't fail me. He climbed along the drainpipe of the outside wall, squeezed himself in through the tiny window of the back room and opened the door from the inside.

There was a sad gap in our midst, however ; Nijinsky was not any more one of us. But still there was Bolm at his best, and Fokine had achieved a masterpiece in staging the *Coq d'or*. For me there was perhaps the most wonderful part I ever had. This and the feeling that I was borne on the crest of a wave made for a plenitude of artistic sensations, the like of which I had not yet lived through. The stimulating power of success gave me a daring, unprecedented in my career. I had no fear, no hesitation in straining the diapason of my artistic means from the romantic to the tragic and sinister. And it pleased me to be in the same evening a *Chloe* and a *Salome*. When the plan of Diaghileff to have an interpreter of singular beauty for Potiphar's wife failed, I accepted the part without my usual doubts as to whether I was fit for it. Strauss himself came over to be present at the performances. At Drury Lane, where I had first to do this part, he watched my work closely. After every rehearsal I asked if the *Maître* was pleased. He was, but this and that might be improved. For the improvements he would come to my dressing-room, a huge barn of a room, and demonstrate what he wanted of me. " This run, look here." Singing the passage, Strauss would get to the far corner and run, trampling heavily across the room to the sofa representing the couch of the comely Joseph. I believe I got the run and the rest of the part to his satisfaction. Ever after, whenever *La Légende de Joseph* was to be given in Vienna, he sent me dictatorial telegrams to come and play the part. And to others in different parts of the world telegrams sped :—" Find Karsavina. Bring her here." But I was out of reach then, in Russia of terrible days.

*   *   *   *   *

After a lapse of five years I rejoined Diaghileff in London in 1919. I was strongly impressed by the amazing development of Massine. I had first seen him in 1913. I thought his Joseph, the only part he had then, quite remarkable. His very lack of virtuosity in those days lent pathos to the image he created, an image of youth and innocence. I found him now no more a timid youth. Our first collaboration in the *Three-Cornered Hat* showed him to be a very exacting master. He now possessed accomplished skill as a dancer, and his precocious ripeness and uncommon mastery of the stage singled him out, in my mind, as an exceptional ballet-master. It was his complete command of Spanish dancing that amazed me the most. On the Russian stage we had been used to a balletic stylisation of Spanish dancing, sugary at its best; but this was the very essence of Spanish folk dancing. During the Ballet's Spanish season Massine had been taking lessons from Felix, an expert performer of national dances. Felix had been brought over to London to continue these lessons, and Diaghileff, wishing to give me inspiration for my novel rôle, asked me to come and see Felix dancing at the Savoy. It was fairly late when, after supper, we went downstairs to the ballroom and Felix began. I followed him with open-mouthed admiration, breathless at his outward reserve when I could feel the impetuous, half-savage instincts within him. He needed no begging, and gave us dance after dance. In between, he sang the guttural songs of his country accompanying himself on the guitar. I was completely carried away, forgetful that I was sitting in an ornate hotel ballroom till I noticed a whispering group of waiters. It was late, very late. The performance must cease or they would be compelled to put the lights out. They went over to Felix too, but he took not the slightest notice. He was far away. The performance had given me something of the same feeling as listening to the gipsy singers of my own country—savagery and nostalgia. There, no hotel official would come to bring us brusquely back to earth again. To a Russian such a curfew is incomprehensible. A warning flicker and the lights went out. Felix continued like one possessed. The rhythm of his steps—now staccato, now languorous, now almost a whisper, and then again seeming to fill the large room with thunder—made this unseen performance all the more dramatic. We listened to the dancing enthralled.

The giving of the very best that is in them seems to be a Spanish national characteristic. Just as Felix had danced forgetful of everything, so two of the greatest figures in modern art forgot themselves completely in their collaboration to make the *Three-Cornered Hat* a success.

Da Falla, great musician, gentle and unassuming, reminiscent

of an El Greco portrait, did not think it derogatory to play at
our rehearsals.   A magnificent pianist, he had delighted Roucher,
director of the Paris Opera, with his rendering of the score of
the *Three-Cornered Hat*.   On another occasion he had played
for me alone the score of his ballet, *L'Amor Brujo*.

Although it was indeed presumptuous of me to sum up a
composer then at the height of his creative power, Da Falla
always seemed to me a happy genius nurtured from the vital
sources of his own country.   Though his work is of international
importance, he will remain a magnificent example of the intensely national artist.

Pablo Picasso in his daring search for new expression has never
lost sight of that consummate mastery of line, and while many
would laugh at his bolder experiments and say that they, too,
could make patchwork pictures, he alone possessed that precise,
strong and delicate inflection of line which seemed to be lost
with Ingres.   He also had an absolute sense of the stage and its
requirements, the abbreviated and strong formula of composition
and a neo-romanticism far away from the sentimental.   At the
time of the rehearsals he had completed all the costumes save
mine, and he would come and watch me dance.   The costume
he finally evolved was a supreme masterpiece of pink silk and
black lace of the simplest shape—a symbol more than an ethno-
graphic reproduction of a national costume.

On the first performance of the *Three-Cornered Hat* Diaghileff
welcomed me with a wreath that bore the inscription " In
celebration of the day on which you returned to your Father's
embrace."

*   *   *   *   *

On our reunion after the war, Diaghileff and I talked of our
respective experiences.   He told me of the difficult times he had
trying to carry on the enterprise.   I gave him the news of friends
that were still in Russia, and told him how a trifling request of
his had made me for months a wanderer in foreign lands at a

247

time when I longed to be in my own country. And this had been the trifling request.

Towards the end of our 1914 season I felt a vague uneasiness; I was no good at interpreting political events. All those round me were optimistic. All believed in mediation; so there was no definite apprehension in my mind, nothing but a sudden and acute longing to be home—such a longing as one has when overtaken by an impending storm. Were it not for that, I would have liked to have stayed a few more days in London. In the course of my frequent stays there, I had grown fond of it. I now had a partiality even for its winter fogs. The blaze of an open fire on these days of fog brought me a sense of comfort almost rapturous. But this time I intended to leave on the morrow of our closing performance. My luggage had been packed, and the facetious little ceremonial of each morning gone through; Céline, my French maid, after my telling her once that cream served with the morning was my " delight," never omitted, on ordering my breakfast, to repeat the same admonition :—" Surtout, garçon, n'oubliez pas les délices de Madame." On the same tray with my *délices* that morning there was a note from Diaghileff, asking me to stay till the next day; he had some matters to talk over with me. That one day was to cost me dear.

PART IV

WAR AND REVOLUTION

CHAPTER XXV

The Journey Home—The Theatre in War Time—The " Wandering Dog "—Diaghileff in War Time—Rasputin—Paléologue—Hugh Walpole—Learning English

GOING through Berlin I saw a maddened stampede of Russians towards home. The declaration of war caught us a few hours before arriving at the Russian frontier.

We were allowed to alight at the frontier, only to be pushed back into the carriages to be taken back to Berlin. Only a few hundred yards lay between the German side and ours, a narrow stream, a small foot-bridge alongside the railway line. In peace-time I used to speculate on the amusing contrast of our off-hand husbandry, scraggy chickens, an independent looking pig or two, and the thrifty brick houses and flocks of proud geese on the German side. In peace-time every porter of Virjbalovo would congratulate each Russian traveller with a " Safe homecoming," and look significantly at the tip ; the chief Customs officer, a *balletomane*, would open the state-room and order my luggage to be taken straight on the train. It seemed a cruel mockery, on reaching the Russian land, to be turned away within sight of it ; but there was no arguing with the German officer. It was dark and quiet on the opposite bank ; somebody said in a whisper that the first shots had been fired in the afternoon.

I walked from the station along the Unter den Linden, its pavements snowed under with crumpled proclamations. The maps of the future Germany were displayed in the shop windows. The infuriated mob, a seething mass worked up to a high pitch of hatred, made it difficult to move.

I paid a painful visit to the Russian Embassy. All shutters

down, it looked like a house of the dead. I vividly recalled its festive appearance when I had last been inside it. Only a few months before, a ball and a performance had been given there for the German Emperor. They were powerless to help me now; not a name could be added to the list of persons leaving that night with the Embassy train. The Ambassador gave me a note to his Spanish colleague, who gave me a pass for Holland. There I fretted between hope and disappointment, till at the end of three weeks I found a passage on a boat, which took me back to England. The spellbound circle had at last let me out; in another week, by means of varied locomotion, I arrived in Petersburg. Diaghileff's extra day had indeed cost me dear.

A dear friend met me at the station. On the way home she spoke in a low voice, and when we were indoors she continued telling me in the same hushed tone all that had happened for the last month in our capital. People speak like that when there is death in the house. She told me how sinister the late summer had been, breathless and still; low-creeping fires daily tightened their circle round the town, the peat marshes burned slowly; the sun was like the wrath of God. Strikes broke out, sullen and undemonstrative; a slow torpor was paralysing the land when the disaster of yet incalculable magnitude extinguished sedition. The war broke out, and the wave of forgotten patriotism heaved up. In the Russia of slow communications and uncontrollable delays, the mobilisation was achieved before the set time.

In the square of the Marinsky Theatre recruits now drilled; leading an attack they pierced with bayonets the hay-stuffed dummies. At dusk they returned to barracks; I could hear them pass under my windows singing patriotic songs as they marched. It would be on the stroke of six, I could tell it without looking at the clock—their passage marked the time. The mechanism of life in the town worked with the same regularity as before. As before, we set our watches by the noon cannon from the fortress. The signal for workmen to leave off for the midday meal, a remote symbol of fraternity. " The noon cannon " would say the capital in the same breath. Placid sensation in peace-time, the familiar sound now was a *memento mori*.

The theatres all through the war followed an unhalting course, not merely as a diversion for worried minds, but pursuing their own artistic aims ; and the usual plan of giving a number of new productions in each season remained unaltered, though, of course, economy suggested some devices. For mere revivals, costumes and scenery would be brought out of the thrifty past. In these sorrowful years the stage remained strangely serene. Fokine now worked exclusively for the Marinksy ; of all his productions the recent one, *Chota Aragonese*, was in his brightest mood. The drama reflected neither the war nor the dejection of actuality. Even more, the drama instinctively turned away from the present ; the great revival of the classics took place. That seeming aloofness of the theatre was in no way due to selfish unconcern ; the stage was fulfilling its mission in the war by protecting the eternal treasure, the high cult of beauty sheltered all through the world. And, of course, the very idea of unconcernedness of whomsoever at this time would be preposterous ; the war overshadowed everything.

The same queues formed outside the box-offices ; no empty seats disgraced the Marinsky ; but the physiognomy of the public was greatly altered—no more bright uniforms, no more lovely toilettes. Every night the public demanded the national anthems. As new allies gradually joined the cause, our intervals became longer. Now a full quarter of an hour would be required to go through the anthems. The frenzied enthusiasm which greeted them at the beginning gradually dwindled with the years as war weariness increased. The German origin of the British anthem roused some susceptibilities ; the theatres consulted with the British Embassy, and *Rule, Britannia*, took the place of *God Save the King*. In all the restaurants the bands played *Tipperary*.

In mistaken zeal for the eradication of the German flavour, Petersburg got rechristened; it became Petrograd.

Comparatively few among the artists had been sent to the Front. We still continued to meet at the *Wandering Dog*, an artistic club, distinctly Bohemian, as its name suggests. Artists of a permanent job and steady habits, relative Philistines of the caste, patronized but little the *Wandering Dog*. Actors hectically making a precarious living, musicians of prospective fame, poets and their muses, and a few æsthetes gathered there every night. And when I say " Muses," I would like to warn off any possible misconception towards this lovable species, some of unusual attire, but not failing to give expression to a distinct personality; there was no affectation and no tiresome *cliché* in the manner of the fair members of the club, whether of some social standing or none.

I had been brought there for the first time by a friend, a painter, in the year before the war. My reception on this occasion had a certain solemnity. I was hoisted up in my chair and, slightly embarrassed, acknowledged the cheers. This ritual was equivalent to bestowing on me the freedom of the cellar; and, though not qualified for a Bohemian, I felt the place congenial. It was a cellar of a big house, and originally used for storing firewood; Soudeikin had decorated it—Tartaglia and Pantaleone, Smeraldina and Brigella and Carlo Gozzi himself smiled and grimaced from the walls. For the most part the entertainments were unrehearsed ones. Acclaimed, an actor would come forward and give of what his mood suggested, if at all in a mood for doing so. The poets, always amenable, recited their new poems; and some nights nothing happened on the stage. Then the host would take a guitar and sing, and when he came to a favourite song all joined in the refrain : " Oh, Maria, oh, Maria, how sweet is this world."

I danced for them one night to the music of Couperin, the Cuckoos and Dominoes and the Chimes of Cytherea, not on the stage, but in the midst of them, within a small space encircled by garlands of fresh flowers. The choice had been mine; in those days I dearly loved all the sweet futility of hoops and patches and the sound of harpsichord like a glorified choir of insects. My friends responded by the "Bouquet," that day straight from the Press. In this almanack the poets had written their madrigals to me, and some fresh ones were made and recited at supper. "Quelle floraison vous faites éclore, Madame," summed up a man of the world; for in their zeal to make this evening select the *Wandering Dog* had invited some distinguished guests, amongst them a great friend of mine, whose British dislike of the demonstrative kept him looking at his watch, while my poets exerted themselves in recitations, and asking me how long I meant to stay with these microbes. The *Wandering Dog* lingered through the war, dragging its impecunious existence up to the second year of the Revolution.

Diaghileff sent me several requests to join him. For the most part he remained in Spain. An offer from New York came in time to help him out of his difficulties. Diaghileff wanted me for America, but I could not, and would not, leave the country. In the great sadness of those years I would not of my own accord have missed a day were I to live them through again. And who of us would have wished themselves away? There are sorrows whose sublime greatness one would not wantonly exchange against personal comfort.

Our retreat from Galicia was beginning. "The troops retreated in good order, effectively checking the advance of the enemy," one read in the official statement; and between the lines—unarmed soldiers faced the Austrian fire. The southern Front lacked ammunition, no more than a few paltry rifle shots could be discharged in a day; stoicism alone covered the orderly retreat. Abroad, the Russian Army never had been credited with the heroism of this unequal contest, though the quality of it was higher than the bravery of our brilliant beginning in the South. Europe had applauded the victories; history might yet right the injustice of the contempt under which Russia smarted at the time of the Galician defeat.

In Petersburg itself there was a feeling of impending tragedy. Incredible rumours circulated, sinister prophesies of Rasputin were repeated. I met him once out in the street by the spot which, like a grandiose piece of stage setting, stood on a small island between sleepy canals. I often came there to wonder at the incongruous majesty of the army magazines with their arch worthy of Piranesi. It was not the attire of the man coming towards me that arrested my attention—one had grown familiar with sheep-skin coats during the war—but the lank black hair and the eyes of strange lightness, set close, inconceivable with a peasant's face, the eyes of a maniac. I had heard before about the magnetic power of his eyes, and could not doubt for a second that it was Rasputin, this man I saw walking past me, a lady by his side. The gruesome story of Rasputin's murder has been told too often ; it has been mangled into innumerable plots of cheap novels of sickening vulgarity, and quite recently given as a statement of those concerned with it. In the morning of December 16th, the town knew what had happened the night before. It was difficult to say how the news percolated because the papers did not mention the fact till some days later, and then only covertly. Douniasha came into my room ; endeavouring to coax the growling Loulou, who always resented being fetched from my bed, she told me that Rasputin had been killed in the night ; the milkman had been her informer. He had heard it from the porter of the Yussoupoff Palace, which stood close to my house. The incredible story gained strength. There was an arduous visiting in Petersburg on the days following. I have heard many versions of the event from different people, and a very accurate account of it was given to me by Monsieur Paléologue, the French Ambassador.

The story, as told by him, over a cup of tea, had a quality of a chapter out of some masterly book. The sordidness of it was so magnificently dramatic, enhanced by the setting of a palatial house and the hour of night. And the description was implacably vivid, that of more than human resistance—the writhing form whom poison could not master and a bullet would not kill staggering to its feet as if possessed of charmed life. Those who, for the good of their country, trespassed the laws, human and divine, one dares not judge; and whether the unspeakable torture of facing the foul horror in itself would not atone for the deed is neither in one's right to decide. Paléologue did not tell me that, which in the mouth of the superstitious and sceptical alike sounded of ill omen—the alleged words of Rasputin, " The end of me will be the end of the dynasty." And perhaps the most uncanny story of all that surrounded the life and death of Rasputin was that whispered by few. The body had been thrown into the river, its hands bound by strong rope : found some days later, the right hand lay on the left shoulder, the last position of the sign of the cross.

Later statements show how correct had been the information of M. Paléologue. And my feeling " this is like a book " was due to his truly exceptional gift of eloquence and the uncommon imagination of an author. These qualities I particularly valued in him. Paléologue was a great lover of the theatre ; he said it afforded him well-deserved relaxation from politics to come and talk of the theatre with me. By no means a glib chat or an elegant gossip, these talks roamed far beyond technical discussions of a *balletomane*. He tried to find a definition of that degree of dancing virtuosity when the body seems to be delivered from bonds of subserviency to its own laws. He coined a phrase, *se faire un corps glorieux*, and offered it to me in a perfect structure of well-balanced sentences. Paléologue was a friend of Alexander Benois, and liked to join his Sunday afternoons where artists met to talk and draw from a model.

In these days, poor in delight for us, Paléologue brought some rays of sun. At his parties he offered not only the pleasures of the table and a congenial company, but also sought by some device to find always a new setting, turning into account the possibilities of the Embassy. One evening we dined in the ballroom to contemplate the beautiful tapestries; on another occasion dinner was fixed at an early-hour, and the table moved in front of the large window, to see the sunset over the Neva. This was a charming party; the sunset alone failed. Chaliapin had his concert on the previous night and would not sing; but, as usual, the interest of all present centred in him. In the rôle of a charmer he was also superlative. Paléologue was telling me what deep emotion Chaliapin's singing of the *Marseillaise* had produced last night.—" La patrie, la patrie chérie." . . . Tears had choked everybody.

It was good then for a Russian to feel the steady optimistic spirit of our Allies. In that respect I was more fortunate than most of my countrymen. Not only did I feel that spirit in my own home, but I had also the frequent companionship of an invariably cheerful and well-informed man in the person of Hugh Walpole. My acquaintance with Hughie, rapidly to grow into friendship, now began. He was working in Russia in the interests of British propaganda. We could not at first converse together: he had little Russian or French, and I absolutely no word of English. I felt at once a very real sympathy for him. He was interested in Russian life and character, not as a study in the exotic and freakish, but from a genuine love and under-standing of my country. He was sharing a flat with Constantin Somoff; and, at a time when life was so troubled and one was apt to grow morbid from the constant bad news and the signs of impending catastrophe, the calm atmosphere of this circle, where art still retained preponderance, was truly soothing. Hughie was an attractive, lovable figure, with his attempts to join in the conversation. With our Russian love of Dickens, we named him Pickwick, and the parallel was even closer through an episode I remember well. During a walk to Alexander Benois's flat, Hughie fell no less than fourteen times on the snow and thin ice, always continuing his talk without comment at the point reached before the fall. In later years he was the first to educate me in my new language.   He introduced me to English literature, and the very fact that I have been able to struggle through this book is due to him.   He gave me a list of books, and, just as I had begun my Russian reading with Poushkin, so now I began English with Lamb's Essays, Pepys, and the " Morte d'Arthur."   As a result my speech was a strange hash of archaicisms and blunders which vastly amused my new family. My husband always quotes an essay of mine on the Battle of Hastings.   " Harold was shot on the eye, and fell down his standard."   And there is another example that I am never allowed to forget.   In my enthusiasm for a new pig-skin bag, I exclaimed : " Look at my bag ; why, it is real pork."

Early in February I went to perform at Kieff.   No suite of *balletomanes* followed me, as it had a few years ago on a similar occasion.   Their ranks had thinned, their traditions slackened ; spirited escapades were now out of place.   My self-constituted knight and factotum, Vinogradoff, alone went to Kieff after me. Simple and illiterate man, his frantic devotion to the Ballet, and the fact that he had seen the glory of Virginia Zucchi alone qualified him as a leader of the gallery.   He was fervently attached to me.   Purple and apopleptic he used to rush from one end of the gallery to another shouting my name as a war-cry.   He continued his bustling activities in Kieff, standing at the queues to ascertain the degree of eagerness of my prospective public, bringing me daily cheerful reports of how the sale of tickets progressed.   It was from him I heard the first rumours of revolution in Petersburg.   For three days there had been no trains, no telegrams.   When communication was restored we learned of the abdication of the Emperor.

CHAPTER XXVI

*Episodes of War and Revolution—Kshessinskaya's Palace—
A President in Tarlatans—Douniasha's Tragic Death—The
Chancery Servant—I am Suspect—Lev and the Commissar*

I ARRIVED from Kieff in the middle of the night. Not a
cab anywhere, not a soul. The town was guarded by a new
militia. On my walk home several stopped me; asked politely
to see my documents. They were mostly students, odd blend
of civil clothes and a rifle across the shoulders.

In the morning a novel sight from my window. The prison
opposite, a building which I always liked for its beautiful proportions and the two kneeling angels over the gate, stood blistered
by fire, a mere skeleton building. Douniasha told me our
window-panes were red-hot from the blazing fire on the other
side.

Arsenal, prisons, law courts had been set on fire. Only a few
private houses had been damaged; those of the Minister of the
Court and Kshessinskaya looted. I next met Kshessinskaya at
Monte Carlo in 1922. She was now Princess Krassinskaya, the
wife of the Grand Duke Andrei Vladimirovitch. Although she
had lost practically all her wealth, she was as cheerful as ever,
without a single wrinkle or trace of worry. Fortunately for her,
she was absent when the Revolution broke out, on a holiday
in the Crimea, which must have saved her from an almost certain
death. She told me with what mixed feelings of fear and hope
she arrived at Cap d'Ail, uncertain as to whether her villa had
been left her. Her joy at finding a home was immense. She
told me of her wanderings. She made a joke of her many
privations and viewed her present situation with philosophy and
courage. She had continued to practise her dancing even without

ballet shoes, and was as delighted as a child when I offered her a pair of mine.

*   *   *   *   *

After first days of furious excesses, cannonades, blaze of fires, a calm set over Petersburg. Proclamations of the new Government enjoined the population to confidence. The militia paid domiciliary visits to reassure citizens. The Revolution had its brief spell of optimism.

In the theatre the artists went out of their way to bring " Comrade " into conversation. A new director had been nominated, a man of letters, an eminent professor. The artists having organised their own committees, I had been chosen a president of ours. The presidency and prima-ballerinaship over-taxed my strength. I tried hard to maintain my artistic work unimpaired, fitting my practice into early hours, leaving committee meetings for rehearsals, and rehearsals for a table piled with papers. Complaints poured in: the youngest dancers claimed a rise of salary and promotions on the ground of justice and equality. The committee sat from morning till late hours. Our mild new director, contrary to etiquette, would come across to see me, presiding in tarlatans. The school becoming subject to the committee's rule, Varvara Ivanovna, too, came as a petitioner. Such reversion of rôles was distasteful to me; I begged the older woman to send for me whenever needed. . . . Next time I went to her. I saw her rooms for the first time. So it had been from these pleasant and cosy rooms that the feared figure in black silks had come forth. I was sorry the formidable bugbear of my youth was now robbed of her terrible prestige. A meek, slightly bent old lady solicited my help against the proposed reforms of the school.

The Marinsky was shorn of eagles and Imperial arms; greasy jackets replaced the former livery of the attendants.

I remember one night of a charity performance. A small

group, grey-haired and worn looking, sat in the Imperial box. They were the old political convicts, a couple of months ago recalled from Siberia; and homage was being paid to their martyrdom. The second phase of Revolution came, and they were swept off by the new wave and held in derision. That phase had done with optimism. The Front was breaking; deserters fleeing home : disorganised soldiers filled the trains, rode on the roof, clutched to the buffers. From the hungry town crowds set forth daily in search of food. The Government made frantic efforts to carry on with the war. At every corner improvised meetings were held. Lenin arrived ; he harangued the people from the balcony of Kshessinskaya's house, where he had established his headquarters.

Every day rumours multiplied like microbes in a diseased body. Newspapers born overnight spread panicky informations and coined libels. How the big posters on the main street escaped my attention, I don't know. I walked home that day and did not notice my name on them. In the evening the telephone rang ; an old friend anxiously asked : " Are you safe ? " I could not believe my ears when he told me that the posters that day had my name in full and " German spy " underneath. I was going to sell programmes for a charity ball at Marinsky that same night ; he entreated me not to go, and thought I was not even safe that night in my flat. I decided to go, believing it a sound policy. All was as usual that night ; not a whit of suspicion or hostility towards me. An apology was published in a few days.

*   *   *   *   *

Douniasha's sight was failing rapidly. She went to a " very special " doctor, who told her to wait till her cataracts were ripe. Not until now had I realised how weak she had grown and how helpless. She would come into the room and, forgetting her purpose, stand motionless, her fingers working fast, playing a tattoo in the air. We cherished a plan to go to Log for the summer; food would be easier to get there, and I longed to revisit the place. She looked forward to it.

She came to me one afternoon, a little bundle under her arm, to ask me if she might go to the Russian bath. A few minutes elapsed, and there was a knock on the door. A servant from the next flat was there. " Your old woman has been knocked dead by a car; they have taken her to the Navy barracks." The barracks hospital was opposite my house. The sailor in charge of the mortuary was rude, but let me in all the same. I saw her body and cried. The sailor softened. " Was she your mother ? " I said she had been my foster-mother. He handed me a wooden snuff-box found in her pocket. She must have considered it a vice; nobody knew she took snuff. I buried her in the Finnish village that had been her home.

*   *   *   *   *

On the morning of the 8th of November I saw cadets marching down the Millionnaya towards the Winter Palace; the eldest of them might be eighteen. Sporadic shooting started in the afternoon. Loyal troops had barricaded the Winter Palace Square and the access from side streets. The chief fighting was round the telephone exchange. For several hours I sat holding the receiver to my ear; at intervals there would be an answer; now men's, now girls' voices asked " What number ? " I could follow the exchange changing hands many times. The information I could gather from various people was that the other side of the river was cut off, all the bridges up; a destroyer faced the Palace from the Neva; the fortress was in the hands of Bolsheviks; a battalion of cadets and women defended the Palace from inside, and a few loyal troops still held the positions outside. The wine cellars all through the town were being looted. . . . It was a ballet night. I started from home soon after five. In about an hour's time I arrived at the theatre, by many détours.

By eight o'clock there was about one-fifth of the company at the theatre; after a short deliberation we decided to raise the curtain. The few performers on the vast stage were like the beginning of a jig-saw puzzle, a few clustered pieces here and there—the pattern had to be imagined. Still fewer people in the audience. A cannonade was faintly heard from the stage, quite plainly from the dressing-rooms. After the end some friends waited for me outside; we were going to supper with Edward Cunard, whose flat was opposite mine, near the Winter Palace. The square of the Marinsky was free; we hesitated which way to go: the firing made such an echo in the square it was impossible to say where it came from.

Pickets barred our street. We met Havery, the Chancery servant of the British Embassy, arguing with the soldiers through the din. " I can't help your troubles; I have letters to post."

Some day a memoir should be written of this dauntless product of London. When he had letters to post, telegrams to send, a King's Messenger to see off, street battles left him cold. He got there somehow, once even in an armoured car—it took a Cockney to find a convenient armoured car and wangle a passage on it.

Cunard's flat was higher up the Millionnaya than mine, only a hundred yards from the Palace Square. Machine-guns rattled with renewed zest; I had an uncomfortable feeling that I might get hit on the shin-bone. At supper we could hardly hear ourselves speak—field-guns, machine-guns, rifle-fire were deafening.

Cunard brought out a pack of cards, and we played many games of " Cheating " round the supper-table. The candles burned down, began to gutter. A grey winter light stole through the chinks of the curtains. The fighting had died down—only an occasional boom of gun-fire. We broke up, the men escorting the ladies to their respective homes.

From my window I could see the barracks. A solitary figure in soldier's uniform crept from the shadow of the gate and started running towards Champ de Mars ; a shot and the figure fell in the snow. I drew the curtain. In the morning we had a new régime—Lenin was Prime Minister.

* * * * *

Candles were scarce. Darkness set in at three, and the time till six when electric light was given was especially hard to live through. The unhealthy quiet of the town, portentous silence of the empty streets magnified apprehension to an unbearable tensity. Hearing had grown to such acuteness as to catch from afar a faintly audible sound of footsteps on the thick snow. A rifle-shot, a burst of machine-gun fire—and all quiet again.

On some evenings lights moved to and fro in the dark court-yard down below, soldiers come for perquisition. I had been spared their visits. The searches were chiefly made on the instigation of the house committee. Though my new servant belonged to it, she always behaved decently to me.

* * * * *

On the first anniversary of the Revolution, manifestations were held in the town, processions moved about. One was safer indoors. The day before, I had had a dispute with our Commissar on behalf of the company. My husband said, " You'd better be careful." Hardly had he spoken when we heard a scuffle outside, sound of many feet running upstairs ; my door resounded with heavy blows. On the landing stood a group of soldiers ; my husband's warning seemed to have come true. My fear suddenly changing into irritation, I spoke angrily to them, and the soldiers, amazingly mild and even confused, explained that they were searching for the porter who might be hiding in my flat. He apparently had offended them by an ironical remark. On my assurance that I was not hiding him, the soldiers went off.

* * * * *

About Christmas I fell ill and sent in my resignation from the presidency. For two months I dragged myself from bed to sofa. At times I could not bear the darkness of the flat, and went out into the street, where there were still gas lamps. My fever came and went. Combined with a constant feeling of hunger, it gave me a strange obsession—to find again Pilot's Island. Father had taken me there once, a memory so distant that at times I was not sure the island ever existed. On one of these explorations I felt I could not walk any more, and hailed a cab—there were still a few of them about. Not far from my house the horse fell, a small crowd gathered pitying. Someone sternly said there was no room to cry for horses when every day people were dropping from hunger.

Towards the spring I was able to resume my work, and now and then went to dance in the provinces. These were foraging expeditions ; food was easier to get farther away from Petersburg. In Moscow the Commander-in-Chief came to my dressing-room. The high dignity ill-suited the young man, a mere boy. He blushingly asked might he offer me—not a bouquet—a sack of flour.

*   *   *   *   *

Under the new régime artists were treated with great consideration. Maybe from motives of policy—*Panis et circenses*. If bread was scarce shows were liberally given to the people ; we were constantly commanded to perform in suburban theatres for a public of soldiers and workmen. But I think there must have been another reason for the good treatment of artists, a genuine love for the theatre. When, after years of separation, I again met my brother, exiled from Russia, he told me of an incident that had happened during his prison days. In the night he was awakened and summoned before the Cheka. These nocturnal examinations were particularly ominous, and my brother had incurred their special wrath. The Commissar was stern ; he put before my brother one of the incriminating points : " You are in correspondence with abroad." " Who are your correspondents ? " " My sister." " What is her name ? " " Same as mine : Karsavina." " *You* are the brother of Karsavina ! " The Commissar veered round in his revolving chair. " *Giselle* is her best part, don't you think ? " " I can't agree with you," said my brother, " I consider the *Fire Bird* one of her finest achievements." " Oh, do you ? " The conversation wandered on to the principles and aims of the art ; the prosecution was forgotten. " Won't you write to your sister ? " asked the Commissar at parting. " Tell her to come back." " Tell her she will be received with honours." My brother's sentence was to be exiled with all his family, the Government paying all expenses.

* * * * *

The 15th of May was the last night of the season. This and the ballet *Bayadère*, a much-loved piece, excited the ovations to a degree high even for the Marinsky. I was then loved greatly by the public. Referring to this time, the leading critic said that my art " was robed in magnificent mastery." This was to be my last performance at the Marinsky. I did not know that, but felt unusually depressed ; it is why I accepted the offer of a girl I did not know to go by the back door to her flat opposite the theatre ; the people outside, she said, were waiting to carry me shoulder high. I felt too sad for a triumph. From her window I could see the square gradually empty itself. The night was clear as a sunless evening, a white night. When I came out I saw no one—only a big rat crept round the wall of the theatre.

* * * * *

Petersburg grew visibly depopulated. It had a new tragic beauty of desolation. Grass grew between the flags of its pavements, its long vistas lifeless, its arches like mausoleums. A pathetic majesty of desecrated pomp.

The British Embassy had left in February. I had to stay behind. In June, my husband returned to fetch me. Unexpected difficulties arose with our passports—it was the time of the British landing in the North. When we had almost despaired of ever getting out of Russia, my husband was called to the telephone. A woman's voice told him that a permit to leave would be sent round to him. She rang off quickly, and he never knew who his good fairy was.

CHAPTER XXVII

The Dangerous Journey

I SUMMONED a friend, Katiousha, to help me pack. When I moved to this flat, I brought only my most cherished belongings, but they were too many now. What to pack and what to leave? I tried to fit two old portraits into my trunk. A portrait of a lady in stiff green silk, paste flowers in the high coiffeur and a stiff rose in her hand and that of a child with a lap-dog had come to me from my grandmother—the only link with the old house beyond the Narva gate. A new building is now on its site. Distant as the time was since I have been in it, a very small child, my memory could still recall the carved emblems—quivers and cornucopias of the frieze and a tangled garden. The portraits would not fit into my luggage, neither would the carpet with the Mameluke in the centre find room in it. Katiousha advised me not to over-burden myself with useless things, but I clung to all that would remind me of the sad joys and blessed sorrows of the past few years. We re-arranged my trunks several times till both exhausted. She went to sleep, curled on the ottoman, and soon I abandoned my hopeless task of selection. I went to bed with an uneasy conscience: the key of the kidney table holding my letters being mislaid, I was leaving my correspondence behind, to anyone's indiscretion.

Someone was weeping close to me. I opened my eyes and saw a child kneeling by my bed; she had a little cross on a pink ribbon, which she now placed on my neck. I had never been sufficiently gentle with Mara; her waiting outside the stage door to dog my steps and other manifestations of her worship I had always taken for the exaltation of a hysterical child. She must have been up in the small hours to have come to me from the other end of the town before it struck seven. I forgot to ask how she knew I was leaving this morning; I was so lost in pity for the poor girl, whose devotion I doubted no more.

Katiousha and I rather protracted our farewell meal, morning coffee. My husband was getting uneasy. From the flat below, Prince Argoutinsky came up. It had been a comfort to me living in the same house with Vladimir Nikolaievitch. Many a long evening we had sat together by the light of a single candle; often warmed ourselves by the same fire, darkness all round where the fitful flickers could not reach; strained our ears to the silence outside. He was my ever-sympathetic listener and the best person in the world to be silent with. Begun under bright auspices, our friendship grew deeper as it passed through the crucible of the last relentless years. We did not refer to the grief of parting, nor did we speak of an uncertain meeting. He brought me an ikon to accompany me on the journey. I commended to his care the portraits, knowing the futility of my request. Liza, the cook, joined us in the room. In obedience to an immemorial custom all sat down, silent for a few instants, crossed ourselves and said " Good-bye." Liza kissed my hand, though, now a member of the house committee, her social standing was superior to mine. Argoutinsky and Katiousha came to see us to the boat. They stood on the pier, waving handkerchiefs till we lost sight of them.

Our route lay down the great waterway down the Neva, through Lakes Ladoga and Onega. Our plan had been to alight at Petrozavodsk and continue to Murmansk by train. Three days in our small, crowded steamer, and we came to Petrozavodsk. My husband went on shore to see what he could find out. I had got my baby son, Nikita, and my luggage ready, and stood waiting on the deck when I saw my husband coming back. From his dejected look I saw there was grave news. Indeed, the situation looked hopeless. The French liaison officer, the only foreign representative left in Petrozavodsk,

warned my husband to get back on board as quick as possible.
The British troops were advancing; some Bolshevik Commissars
had been shot in the fighting; only troop trains were going
north, and these no place for Englishmen. We must return to
Petersburg. Even there, things were worse than ever for the
British : Count Mirbach, the German Ambassador, had been
assassinated and the crime imputed to the British. There was
no choice but to follow the Frenchman's advice.

On the steamer was the young Count M. His destination
also was the English lines. His mission was a dangerous one.
A light-headed youth, at each stop he raced to the village and
returned panting, with milk and fresh eggs. I see him now,
running in seven-mile leaps, waving his booty to us on the deck.
M., on learning our dilemma, questioned the peasants on board,
and learnt that there was a disused, but still available, post-road
which through the forest of Olonetz led to the Gulf of the
White Sea ; from there a small craft might take us to the other
shore, where, according to his information, we should find the
British.

On the fifth day we got off the boat in a small village, Povenetz.
No sign of Red Guards. Peasants would willingly give us
horse-carts for the next relay. We bade farewell to M. Our
luggage being too bulky for the present mode of journey, I again
repacked my trunks, leaving the necessary only. The rest I
entrusted to the purser to deposit at the Embassy on his return
to Petersburg. A passively curious crowd of peasant women
gathered round me on the pier as I was busy with my trunks ;
I distributed the surplus of Nikita's wardrobe amongst them.

The peasants gathered to see us start. " God-speed " ; they
were friendly in this village. Our train consisted of no less than
five carts. We drove for a whole week through dense forests
by innumerable lakes with deep and dark water. No towns, the
villages far apart—the country cheerless, sinister. At sunset
dense swarms of mosquitoes obscured the air : in places their
dark, quivering cloud hung over a tree or rose from the ground

in pyramidal shape. The peasants we met working in the fields were wearing muslin veils over their heads.

For several days we met no impediment on the way, but the sense of lurking danger was with us the whole time. My tiny boy, who, in Petersburg, used to say " Paff " at the sound of shooting in the street, now, as if in apprehension of some terror, clutched my dress and cried and screamed day and night. He slept but occasionally; at times my knees grew numb under his weight, but the slightest movement of mine would set him screaming and clutching desperately at me. At night we stopped at some village; the peasants willingly gave us shelter, a samovar and the whole of the floor to sleep on. Curious as to the purpose of our travel, the peasants of this outlandish district seemed to have small or no concern in politics. Of the movements of the English they knew little, and their comments were placid. " Why, let him come; the Englishman is a good fellow, people say."

At every village where we put up, my husband tried to draw from the peasants what information he could with regard to the next place we were bound for. In some villages they had Commissars; " No Red troops have been seen round." We were playing for high stakes and playing blindfold.

About two-thirds of our way had been covered when we came, later than usual, to a prosperous-looking village. In the morning we had heard from our hostess that on the previous day a consignment of vodka had been brought in. The women folk apprehended trouble. Worse still, the moujiks in this village had a Soviet. While, in the yard, preparations were being made for our start, several peasants walked into the room. I saw they were drunk, aggressively drunk. Contrary to the deep-rooted custom of Russian peasants, their leader didn't doff his cap on coming in—" Bad sign," I thought. He started with the usual questions as to where we were going. I gave the name of the next relay. " Would not your honour fancy for a nice boat; these here lads "—he pointed to his silent reeling comrades—" are willing to row you across the lake." The day was windy, the water rough, and I refused to take any risk on account of my small child. A wicked look came across the moujik's face, the mask of politeness fell off, and the impudent words : " What matters if the little cur gets drowned ? " infuriated me. What words I then hurled at him I can't recall, but curiously enough he backed to the door, muttering apologies.

The same party came back, however, one degree more drunk ; in their wake came a mob of peasants. By now they were filling the yard where the horses stood ready. An altercation was going on ; I saw my husband desperately arguing, but still keeping his temper. To my knowledge of peasant crowds, this was a wrong policy. " Forged passports ! Lock the whole lot in a barn." Once a suspicion gets into a moujik's head, he is to be feared. I picked up Nikita and came out : the offensive alone could save the situation. My husband described my attitude as that of a tiger cat. Our passports certainly were dubious pieces of paper, but fortunately I remembered that there was another document in my husband's pocket, quite irrelevant now, a pass to Moscow dated some months ago and countersigned by Chicherin. With this in my hand, I bluffed, threatening to report them for disregarding the orders of their government, and called them a name or two. The signature of Chicherin produced an effect on the peasants. They stood hesitating. Till now meekly sympathetic, the chorus of women raised their voices—" Shame, let the young *Barinya* go, and her with a tiny mite too . . ." Maybe this intervention helped us ; the moujiks let us go. The man who had been offering a boat evidently held a leadership. His was the last word to the peasant he sent with us :—" Hand them to the Commissar at the other end."

The anxiety of this day's drive is even now painful to recall. It was sultry and leaden ; towards dusk we stopped by a lake ; on the opposite shore stood a village where we were to be handed over. The luggage was unpacked and loaded on a raft ; our unwelcome escort came with us. He took my husband to the Commissar; B. soon returned, saying the Commissar was coming shortly to see me. The wait seemed interminably long, though there was nothing to mark the time, only my anxiety and growing darkness outside. Around a small kerosene lamp on the wall there was a pool of feeble light, the rest of the room in semi-obscurity. Big shadows leapt across the ceiling if anyone moved.

A man in khaki entered, and I moved to meet him. I couldn't see his face well; his voice was that of an educated man. " I will give you a pass for twelve hours from midnight," he said. " But we still have 60 versts to the White Sea," I objected. He stood silent. I could now see prominent grey eyes and realised the strange intensity of his regard. He repeated, " For twelve hours "—each word came separately—bowed and was gone. I doubted not there must have been a meaning in his words. There was.

We were up and waiting in the yard before sunrise. There was a tiresome suspense; the peasants had, as always, led off their horses to graze in the forest after work. At last the horses were caught, and we started. On the way we crossed several reconnoitring parties; they would stop us and ask if we had seen any troops on the road. At the crossroads there was a small village; we debated whether to stop there to get some milk; B. said we must push on. Our destination was Sumskoy Pasad, a small town from where pilgrims used to cross to the Solovetsky Monastery.

Barricades were heaped up round the town, armed citizens guarded the gates. What were they—Reds? B. produced his reddest document, the Chicherin pass. The sentry examined it askance. B. produced a Foreign Office passport. The man beamed. The village was in the hands of the Whites. " British —Drive in quick." Inside the barricades the whole town was agog. A town of ancient churches on a hillside, a bridge swarming with excited crowd, people running, gesticulating—

it was like a well-staged scene in a theatre. Panic-stricken citizens rowed off—a whole flotilla was seen on the estuary. A small tug under full steam was about to push off. We called to them to take us, and answer came, " English ? Quick, throw your bundles in." It was the last boat in Sumskoy.

On the other side of the horseshoe formed by the Gulf of the White Sea at Soroka was a British cruiser. The Reds, shelled out of Soroka, were retreating by land towards Sumskoy, whose population was flying before their approach. Any moment they might be here, and woebetide any English they might catch. The town had sent across the Gulf a desperate plea to the cruiser for help. The reason for our welcome was clear. From the tug all passengers were transferred on board a collier. Next morning we landed on the other shore—British bluejackets were standing about, unconcerned as at Portsmouth in peace time. Now the cards of the involved game lay face upwards. I understood the full meaning of the Commissar's enigmatic words, and over and over again we blessed our luck for not having tarried at the crossroads. Five minutes later—and I dare not think what would have happened.

The record of the further journey may appear uneventful. The train took us to Murmansk. I have never seen more desolate country than the extreme north of Russia. Endless marshes and stones, a few tortured dwarfed trees, not a blade of grass anywhere—a God-forsaken land. At some place we all alighted and walked over the damaged track to the next formation of railway cars. A part of the way we rode with soldiers. Tommies immediately produced chocolates for Nikita. The child was really famished. During the whole of the last week I had never seen myself in a looking-glass, and was not conscious of my appearance till on the train, when an officer offered me a pot of cold cream. At Murmansk we found friends, Edward Cunard, Thornhill and others. We had been given quarters in one of the stationary railways cars, and lived there for several days. On the day of our leaving Murmansk, Thornhill was starting off on some gallant and secret expedition, and we saw him off. " Thornhill has taken the veil." B. joked at the mosquito net hanging over his cap.

A passage had been arranged for us on board a collier, but no liner would have seemed so luxurious as the accommodation on the *Wyvisbrook*. The captain gave up his suite to me, saloon, state and bathroom, though in the ship's books my husband was but a purser, myself only a stewardess. And if *Wyvisbrook* steamed only 8 knots, as she sailed through the fiords, we might have been a yachting party out for seeing lovely scenery. Unstinted food and, for the first time since we started on the journey, a feeling of comparative security. Only once there had been an unpleasant shock. We were moving in sight of the coast of Scotland in convoy. I found it quite an emotional sight to watch the small fleet moving in perfect formation, not a single ship dropping out. Admiral Kemp's secretary, Mr. Jenkinson, was on board ; he spent most of the time on the captain's bridge, and had seen what had happened. I was sitting in my saloon over a pleasant game of solitaire, when there was a loud explosion. The ship shuddered. The steward, kindest of souls, rushed in, seized Nikita and rushed up on deck, crying " torpedo ! " I scrambled after them, my limbs suddenly heavy and numb ; another explosion, and I shut my eyes. When I looked again, all was as before—*Wyvisbrook* whole and sound. " Depth charges," said the steward. I did not know the meaning of the word, but understood that we were not going to sink and saw Nikita blissfully unmoved, pulling at the steward's woolly hair. From Mr. Jenkinson's account, a torpedo had missed our bows by a few yards.

That night we arrived at Middlesbrough. Blast furnaces lit up the sky—the Marinsky and Theatre Street left behind for ever, these were the footlights of a new world.

PART V

DIAGHILEFF

CHAPTER XXVIII

Diaghileff's sway over the Minds of his Collaborators—His Exhibition of Historic Portraits in the Taurida Palace—Seen through the Eyes of a Common Friend—His Meekness over my First " Scene "—A Ripple on the Surface of our Friendship—His Indifference to Box Office Success—His mind and Background

*C*ASSE-NOISETTE was being rehearsed for the Christmas season of 1900. Abroad, where only the last act of it is given, no idea can be had of its pervading and subtle enchantment. The spirit of Christmas, the bustle and preparation at home graced by the mystic sense of the approaching feast, children's expectations of everything bountiful in a world that suddenly becomes beatific and mysterious. That spirit, seen through the prism of Hoffmann's weird and tender romanticism, finds its perfect expression in *Casse-Noisette*.

It was during the interval at the rehearsal of *Casse-Noisette* that I, still enraptured by the performance, first saw Diaghileff. He walked into the almost deserted auditorium and soon left. A casual act, seemingly unconnected with anything that was going on, but to me strangely appropriate, like another trick of magic by Dr. Drosselmayer.

Diaghileff's apparition left an indelible impression on me, and if I come back here to an incident already told it is because it is illustrative of an essential quality of Diaghileff's—that personal magnetism which played such a major part in all his great achievements, especially the Russian Ballet.

The first glimpse of him only gave me a premonition of his spell. Its full power I was yet to learn. The true criterion of his sway over the mind and will of all those within the sphere of his activities lay in his dominance over the council of his brilliant collaborators. Even Benois, that unique blend of erudition, of magnificent mastery, of judgment both sober and penetrating, often gave way before the now suave, now impetuous arguments of Diaghileff. And that in spite of his own superior culture and his sounder artistic education.

Dostoieffsky determined one specific trait of the Russian mind as the capacity for grasping the whole from its obscured and often scattered features. Russian to the core in spite of his cosmopolitan cloak, Diaghileff possessed this quality in a supreme degree. Perhaps even his artistic education, rather selective than systematic, did not just browse where wayward fancy led, but was guided by his genius along the paths of intuition. Maybe that he feared instinctively that his delicate sense of augury might be smothered by too heavy a weight of documental knowledge.

But, if less yielding to analysis than the ascendancy over his circle, that irresistible charm, captivating all alike at the first sight of him, was both a remarkable feature of his personality and one of the sources of his success.

Up to the time when I came into direct contact with Diaghileff, I knew but vaguely of his antecedents. It was therefore with an uninformed mind that I saw the marvel of the exhibition of historic Russian portraits organised by Diaghileff. He obtained the use of the Taurida Palace, never before used for such a purpose. He arranged that, contrary to Russian custom, the exhibition should remain open in the evenings. The vast halls of the Taurida Palace, in their repose but splendid mausoleums of a fabulous past, became uncannily alive in the light of the crystal chandeliers. The portraits looking from the walls hauntingly inhabited the rooms, dwarfing the onlooker into insignificance. They were the present and we the spectres of the future in their vision. Whatever rites had performed this conjury, the fact remained that the public, habitually loquacious at exhibitions, here was hushed as if spellbound.

This exhibition, the first and last of its kind, was a landmark in the historical evaluation of portrait painting in Russia. It made possible a reliable attribution of unsigned works of the past two centuries. It revealed some remarkable artists hitherto unknown.

Only much later did I learn of Diaghileff's superhuman efforts in collecting the portraits for the exhibition. The detail of the undertaking that appealed to me most was that Diaghileff not only personally went through the length and breadth of the country to find his exhibits, but that some masterpieces he, so to speak, rootled out. Often he forced his way to attics, lumber-rooms, servants' quarters, his key the irresistible charm of address and never-let-go grip. He may have known the casual way in which works of art were at that time treated in Russia. Three portraits of considerable importance to the history of the theatre in Russia were used in my father's old home as lids for water buckets. Eventually I rescued them from their ignominious use and placed them in a private museum.

But if my untutored mind had not then grasped the full significance of this exhibition, its influence on me was twofold. It strengthened my faith in Diaghileff; it gave me a criterion of the genuine, and cured me for ever of becoming a dupe of *pastiche*.

It was not so much the lack of opportunity that prevented my better knowledge of Diaghileff's personality at that time. I was secretly afraid to learn too much. The bulk of public opinion pronounced him " bad, mad and dangerous." I wanted to shelter my timid enthusiasm. But a feeling deeper than interest urged me all the same to seek the knowledge of the man behind his amazing work. And so, long before my relations with Diaghileff became established on a footing of mutual affection, the only keys to the understanding of him which I allowed myself to use were the friends we had in common.

One of them was Botkin. I have seldom met with so much tolerance nor with such perennial felicity of mind as in that middle-aged man. A doctor by profession and still more by vocation, Botkin was also an eminent collector, a friend too of the *Mir Izkoustva* group. Botkin's affectionate joke "Serioja uses my place as a half-way house" showed the degree of intimacy between them. Whenever he happened to be in the neighbourhood, Diaghileff would drop in and, after kissing Madame Botkin's hand, would ask her, "May I go and strum the piano?" He often remained for hours in the library picking out a score.

Later on, this instance helped me to understand that, indolent to all appearances, Diaghileff possessed unbelievable capacity for work. It is my belief that his mind never loitered, even when, a convivial host, he shared in round-the-table talk irrelevant to art. His deeper thought must have run parallel to the light *causerie*. His very unpunctuality was deliberate. That much he himself confessed on coming a day too late for an appointment with me. "The urgency of the immediate problem is my time-table; often I find it more profitable to pursue a matter in hand to its conclusion than to loosen my grip on it for the sake of an appointment elsewhere." I found his explanation convincing, the manner of its delivery candid and disarming.

My initiation into Diaghileff's true self was due to Botkin. It was he who laid the ghost disquieting to my, possibly too smug, rectitude. For at that time of my life I was a bit of a prig. Referring to the aspect of Diaghileff's life that was generally blamed, he said, "It is a cruel misjudgment to give an ugly name to what is, after all, but a freak of nature." My friend substantiated his opinion from his vast experience of mankind. His interest was not limited to the clinical aspect of illness; his compassion extended to all the aberrations and dark inhibitions of the human soul. He said to me once, in answer to a question, "As you say, watching by a death-bed is a tragic aspect of my calling, but there is in it a redeeming side —the thought that my hand may lend support through the dark passage."

I cannot dissociate that talk from its setting. It took place at Versailles. We had strolled into the *Bosquet d'Apollon*. The sun, merciless in the clipped walks of the formal avenues, here only dappled the marble of the fountain through the thick foliage. There was a tremor of light and shade on Apollo's face, a subdued plash of water, wise, enlightening words. That day, snatched from the tempestuous ambiance of rehearsals, was like a cooling compress on a fevered brow. It soothed my doubts and cleared my vision. Botkin made me see that it was the quality of love that makes it beautiful, no matter who the object. The quality of Diaghileff's affections was single-hearted, true and deep, bury them as he would beneath his blasé mask.

On the night of the fête which Madame Maurice Ephrussy gave at her house and which so prettily ended our first Paris season, I looked in vain for Diaghileff amongst the guests. Only when the prelude to *Sylphides* started and we, the performers, under the cover of pergolas, moved towards the top of the stage did I see him. A small baroque fountain in the centre had a backing of mirrors. The unrehearsed effect of white-clad figures elongated, dimmed by the greenish glass, was fantastically beautiful. But he did not see it. He was standing all alone at the far end of the trellis, the wings of our open-air theatre. He stood there with unseeing eyes, not belonging, as it seemed, to time and place; not aware of what he should have considered as his triumph. He looked anxious and weary. Just before my entrance, I saw him leave abruptly. Nijinsky was not dancing that night; he had been taken suddenly ill.

During the few days that elapsed between the end of the performance and the final winding up of the season, the company did not see Diaghileff. The artists must have felt disappointed and somewhat deflated by his withdrawal. For, from the stars to the humbler ranks, we all looked up for his approval or his criticism. We felt important when he occasionally harangued us either on some aspect of the production in hand or in moments of crisis. He did not do it often, but when he did, it was well staged and delivered with great *savoir faire*. Metaphorically, he wore a halo. His presence keyed up both artists and staff.

I knew from Botkin that Diaghileff was at the time very anxious about Nijinsky's serious illness. Nevertheless, when, before leaving Paris for London, I went to see him at the Hôtel de la Hollande, he was kind in an absent-minded way and readily granted me permission to help myself to such orchestral parts out of his library as I needed for my Coliseum season. He made no comment then on my independent engagement, but I got it with a vengeance later on, when my second engagement at the Coliseum clashed with his plans. I forgave him the vehemence of speech when he qualified my appearance " at a music-hall " as a " prostitution of art." I forgave even more readily the unmistakable signs of possessive jealousy as our association went on. Diaghileff would vituperate against my occasional longing for a temporary escape into private life. He would say, half in joke and half in earnest, " I hate your family. It takes you away from me. Why on earth could you not have married Fokine ? You would have both belonged to me." He resented the fact of my still clinging to the Marinsky Theatre. " I can't see what is the lure of St. Petersburg to you. Is it Teliakovsky's waxed moustache, or the hysterical ovations of the greenhorns in the gallery ? Or maybe you just like to show yourself off in your new carriage and pair ? "

But if Diaghileff could give it, he could take it as well. The incident in which I turned the tables on him is not typical of our relations. I was docile as a rule. But it is an instance of his good nature which more than compensated for his high-handed ways. It happened in the summer of 1910 when, entirely through Diaghileff's fault, I found myself with two simultaneous engagments and tried to obtain my release from the Coliseum. Diaghileff's attitude was nevertheless that of a person injured and betrayed. Not a shred of sympathy for my difficulties. Now, through the perspective of the years, I admire his indomitable will. I could not but feel a victim then. His emissaries badgered me. Telegrams were served to me with every meal. Others met me at the theatre. Their dreaded yellow envelopes wickedly popped at me from the corners of my looking-glass; they jaundiced my very make-up. But when finally I succeeded in getting leave from Stoll and joined Diaghileff in Brussels, his joy was touching. His embrace was that of a fond father, the banquet offered worthy of the return of the prodigal son.

I am ashamed to say that it was over the fatted calf that I made my first scene. He had asked me very apologetically not to mind if, for that night only, one of my parts was danced by Madame Geltzer. " She helped me out in your absence, and I simply could not take the part from her," he very reasonably explained. But I raged and stormed for form's sake, meaning all the while to meet his wishes. We had no more arguments that day, but he frequently came into rehearsal just to give me a look and a smile. On that evening, as I was making up, my mirror showed him behind me. He may have stood there for some time—he never knocked on doors. By that time I was no longer angry, but thought my dignity required me to look daggers. He said, " Here I am again. You have wiped the floor with me. You have boxed my ears. I've come for more." That night at supper we both laughed over the incident, I the louder of the two.

As I have said, I never resented Diaghileff's possessiveness. My allegiance had been given freely from the first. Moreover, even then I dimly felt that his occasional petulant taunts were not to be ascribed to selfishness alone. Now I fully realise that his harsher traits, his disregard of others, his ruthlessness in brushing away his once cherished collaborators when no longer fitting into his pattern were but the faults of his virtues. His devotion to art was his virtue, one of absolute integrity, a sacerdotal flame. He sacrificed others to the claims of art if and when those claims made it imperative in his estimation. But he also sacrificed his own worldly advantages. Had he preferred to commercialise his successes, he could have established his enterprise on a sound, even lucrative, basis. He chose a precarious existence in order to further his explorations of art and its future.

A full discrimination between the permanent and the transitory values of Diaghileff's work could not have been made at the time of its progress. I am not attempting it now. I am only giving evidence on the turning-points in his career as I followed them.

It was with much bewilderment and some dismay that I listened to Diaghileff talking of his future plans after the end of our second Paris season. He regarded the choreography of Fokine as belonging to the past. The future of the ballet had to be entrusted to a producer alive to modern influences. The bulk of our present repertoire was, in his estimation, just ballast to be got rid of. " What are you going to do with Fokine's ballets, Sergei Pavlovitch ? " He waved his hand impatiently. " Oh, I don't know. I may sell it all, lock, stock and barrel." In revealing his plans to me, it was Diaghileff's intention to find out whether I would follow him in his new orientation. I do not remember whether he mentioned Nijinsky as the future choreographer. I assured him of my adherence, but did not hide my distress. This talk shattered me. I could not dismiss my faith and my enthusiasm lightly. Diaghileff's words seemed an apostasy. I was not yet familiar with his avatars. I did not know how quickly the future rushed upon him, making the present seem stale and out of date. I am not aware what influences made Diaghileff subsequently modify his policy. But I am sure that, by retaining Fokine's collaboration till 1914, he avoided a schism in his company.

I have some hesitation in recording the traits of Diaghileff which do not fit his great mental stature. But I find that I can do so without being untrue to my entire and wholehearted devotion to his memory. For every shadow in his character there was an abundant light of ultimate sense of right. Moreover, there was something rather touching in his occasional finessing. It sat so clumsily on him, like borrowed clothes. And, if caught out, he could so prettily say "*mea culpa.*" This transparent finessing occasionally ruffled the surface of our friendship. Our relations were not all made up of endearing words. There were tiffs and rifts, inevitably ending in typical Russian reconciliations. Tears and sobs, embraces, celebrations.

It was after the production of the *Fire Bird* that I gradually became aware of Diaghileff's stratagems. This ballet, an unqualified success, had a heaven-sent part for me. Next season, my part in a new production, *Le Dieu Bleu*, was reduced to secondary importance. The real lead was Nijinsky's. This in itself gave me no alarm. When, however, in addition to this, the repertoire was so manipulated as to leave out many ballets containing my best parts, I felt anxious and humiliated. Finally, the situation became unbearable and things came to a head. One afternoon, during our winter season in Munich, Diaghileff swept into my room, a letter in his hand. He threw the letter on the table with an imperious " Read ! " and started pacing up and down the room. Now and then he hurled at me bitter accusations. I was a " snake in the grass." I was " an ungrateful child." I was " trying to cause trouble between him and his friends." The letter was from Lady Ripon. I could hardly read it through my tears, but the gist of it was this : she had espoused my cause in asking Diaghileff to retract his policy and give me my proper place in his productions. " N'exaspérez pas Karsavina," she wrote. I freely admitted that I had confided in Lady Ripon, but that I had done so only after having pleaded with Diaghileff himself. He was too angry to listen to my arguments, and left unreconciled. Luckily there was no performance that evening ; a look in the mirror told me that I was not fit to be seen in public. I ordered a meal to be served in my room. Shortly after it had been brought up, Diaghileff reappeared, this time calm. Somewhat constrainedly he asked me to join his party at supper. I demurred, but, seeing his eyes red and swollen, had the satisfaction of knowing that he too had had a good cry. I accepted his offer in lieu of an *amende honorable*. We made it up at supper.

What is more, Diaghileff made a reparation. He commissioned *Salome*, a ballet entirely for me. After that I had no cause to complain : marvellous parts simply poured into my lap.

Even when my strife with Diaghileff was at its tensest, there was never any question of rivalry between Nijinsky and myself. But while I could not then find an excuse for Diaghileff, I am able to do so now. Having a dancer of such magnitude as Nijinsky, Diaghileff naturally wanted to enlarge the scope of the male dancer, hitherto subordinate to that of the ballerina, and this needed no excuse. His tendency to levelling down women's supremacy may have had to do with his vision of the future of the ballet, the essence of which could, in his opinion, find better expression through the incisive, virile element than through that of feminine grace.

If, at times of tension between us, Diaghileff seemed to me unjust, there was solace, frivolous, I admit, in the thought that he reserved entirely to himself the prerogative of misusing me now and then, and punished severely every attempt on the prerogative due to his leading lady. A trivial incident revealed him as my champion. However petty it may seem, we on the stage attach a great importance to the proper billing of our names. It is in the tradition of the theatre. It is a microbe in our blood. So, when on one (and only one) occasion my name appeared beneath that of a minor member of the company, I drew Diaghileff's attention to it. He was sitting in an armchair in my dressing-room. Without a word to me, he called my dresser and sent her to fetch the man responsible for billing, incidentally the minor lady's husband. When the poor little culprit appeared, Diaghileff rose up. Showing him the bill, he said in a strangled voice, "If that ever happens again . . ." seized the man by the collar, shook him savagely and with all his might hurled the poor wretch against the wall. The man staggered out. I sat petrified. Diaghileff, with an "Excuse me, Tata," left the room.

This was the only occasion on which I saw him in an uncontrolled rage. Often have I seen him under provocation, but never, except that time, did I see him lose his self-control. And his presence of mind was admirable. His voice, rising over the riot of hostile demonstration at the Paris *première* of *L'Après-midi d'un Faune*, "Let the performance proceed," quelled the charivari. Anyone else in the circumstances would have rung the curtain down. Once in Paris, when a sharp altercation between the musicians threatened a break in a rehearsal, Diaghileff walked down from the back of the auditorium, looking more unconcerned than ever, his gait even more than usual that of a performing seal. He said very quietly, "This is not a propitious moment, gentlemen. You can settle your differences after the rehearsal." Discipline was restored.

To the spots in my sun that I have just been pointing out, I may add another little weakness, a very amiable one. It made, in my opinion, a bridge that linked the rarefied strata of his intellect with the temperate regions where anyone could follow. This weakness, if it was one, was his concern with public opinion, no matter how unworthy of notice. But this only applied to himself. Once a scurrilous paragraph appeared in one of the less-respectable organs of the St. Petersburg Press. I promptly wrote a letter to the Editor, a letter more indignant than coherent. The letter was printed. Diaghileff's gratitude was greater than the incident deserved. He was also extremely amusing in formulating his thanks. Without expatiating on the merits of my logic, he said, "I simply adore your attitude. What it amounts to is this :—'I love Diaghileff, and you are all dirty dogs.'"

On the other hand, where theatre was concerned, his indifference to box-office success was complete. He said once,

" The success of a production is unpredictable : all I care for is its merit."

I was by no means the only one to " love " Diaghileff.   There was a real devotion, an unquestioned deference to his wishes, amongst his staff.   He overworked them, he set them tasks as we only read of in fairy tales ; but he also knew how to warm the cockles of their hearts, when to give a word of praise, when to let his thunders rumble.   One of his fantastic commands, on the occasion of Chaliapin's being dissatisfied with his costume of Holofernes, was to order the wardrobe mistress, who was no costumier, to produce another within a few hours. How this tiny shred of a woman set to her task became graphic in Diaghileff's description.   " Her mouth full of pins, her bun of hair on one side, she buzzed round Chaliapin like a gnat round a Colossus.   Now on her knees arranging the hem, now on a chair to reach his shoulders, she managed to swaddle him in spite of his gesticulations in front of the mirror."   He was rehearsing his part, but occasionally let her know in recitative if a pin pricked him.   " Mind you, the whole heavy length of it only held on pins—not that I think it would have outraged her modesty if it had come down."   Chaliapin had his costume on that very night.

Diaghileff valued highly our wardrobe mistress.   The word " efficient " as applied to her would have been an understatement.   She had a talent for her job.   Surrounding himself with highly efficient persons was Diaghileff's speciality.   I cannot think of a single instance of miscasting.   There were real artists amongst his staff.   Waltz, the chief machinist, transformed the antiquated stage of the Paris opera into one equipped for any amount of *coups de théâtre*.   The modest, stuttering coiffeur was the author of Chaliapin's magnificent make-ups. The courier, Michael, ubiquitous and a great psychologist.   He used to ward off many a discontent among the stage hands of the Paris opera.   He did it without bothering Diaghileff, dealing with problems on his own and solving them supremely well. I knew it all from Michael himself. He was my great friend, and did me many a good turn. "There was a pile of albums brought, Tamara Platonovna. I autographed them all. You don't want to be bothered."

The ingenuity of Diaghileff in putting to right use moral qualities over and above technical abilities cannot be better illustrated than in the instance of his cousin, Pavel Georgievitch Koribut Koubitovitch. A more sweet-tempered, more placid benevolent and universally loved man than Pavka, as he was affectionately called by friends, I don't think could exist. He might have served as a model for Cardinal Newman's essay on gentlemen. His well-trimmed, rosy countenance, his slightly guttural voice with something of a cooing sound in it opened all hearts. Diaghileff could not let so much gentleness and charm lie fallow. He assigned to Pavka the part of "mothers' comfort." There was at one time need for someone to soothe maternal jealousy and bickering. Later on, mothers gradually dropped out of the train of the Russian Ballet, but at one time they threatened to become a nuisance. Possibly the shade of Madame Cardinal haunting the couloirs had set them on the warpath. The Paris Opera is said to possess a phantom or two. And so it often happened that Pavka excused himself from joining Diaghileff's party at lunch because he had to take two mothers to the Bois de Boulogne. Or else Diaghileff would say casually, "Pavka is not going to join us. He is going to give tea to Madame X who has fallen out with Madame Y, and later on he is going to try and bring them together."

No doubt it was not his faculty alone for utilising human material that made Diaghileff's association with his cousin close and permanent. Divergent traits constituted Diaghileff's mental make-up. Each one he neatly assigned to its pigeon-hole, raking them out at the prompting of either heart or reason, never or seldom letting them conflict. He had real tenderness, deep affection as well as shrewdness and implacable will. He loved goodness of heart and simplicity. He was genuinely fond of those with whom he surrounded himself. It occurs to me from some of his casual remarks that in his self-imposed expatriation Pavka supplied for him that bit of home atmosphere which made a link with his original background.

Reticent as Diaghileff was about himself, afraid of appearing sentimental in giving vent to reminiscences, I had enough opportunities and enough fondness to enable me to see that under the mask of detachment he cherished his memories of the past. Once, seeing me home after an evening party at Rome, he said, as if to himself, " What a beautiful night ! it reminds me of those evenings at home . . . those visits to my cousins . . . music the whole evening . . . we sang duets . . . the rides home . . . the moonlight." I think he had forgotten I was there—he spoke so low.

Few words of unadorned simplicity, but evocative of his former setting, significant of his entirety. A picture formed in my imagination—a capacious, maybe rambling country house where the present, woven into the past, wore the fresh complexion of actuality without destroying the faded fabric. The organic, the traditional features of a Russian country home grouped of themselves in my mind round the young man with fresh rosy cheeks and oddly drooping eyes, his Russian tunic immaculate. I am quite positive of the tunic. It was as much a feature of a Russian country home as tweeds of an English one. . . . At the end of a winding path, through not too trim a garden, there most likely stood a summer house, once a *temple d'amitié* or Cupid's bower. Its allegorical meaning forgotten, it would be a cool remote place to resort to in summer, the bench of ornate rusticity ample enough to recline on with a book. Of a deep verandah I have no doubt. There, meals were served, protracted by discussions on books, art and politics. Life must have moved smoothly on wheels oiled by the willing hands of servants and retainers. The framework of unhurried existence set no limits to the exercise of Diaghileff's passion for music. Whether assiduous or sporadic in his pursuits at that time, I do not conjecture : but that music saturated his whole being of that I feel quite sure. A more propitious atmosphere to encourage his early love of music could not have been imagined. The influence of his aunt, Kartseva Panaeva, one of the greatest concert singers of her time, must have played a part in his musical education. His ardent enthusiasm, his undying, unflagging passion for art had been first awakened by music. Later, it found outlet through various channels. If his rapidly changing orientations seemed a complete break with the past, it was not so in reality. There was a consistency in his revolution of taste. He worshipped at many shrines but always the same deity. It was his own instinct that led him. Fashion may have influenced him at times, but only superficially. I suppose the opinion of the French musical world, unfavourable to Tchaikovsky, may have had something to do with Diaghileff's long exclusion of that composer from his Paris seasons. But I remember and treasure his words, said not long before his death : " Tchaikovsky is a genius not yet fully understood in Europe."

I do not think my unrestrained imaginings have led me astray when unhesitatingly I put an *ikonnaya* into the background of Diaghileff's home. A small room, out of the way of comings and goings, was so called in our country homes. There, behind the glazed doors of mahogany corner cupboards, were placed the ikons of the family, ikons specially venerated, ikons given as blessings to newly married couples, the wedding candles with their white favours laid beneath them. Only the hands of trusted old retainers might trim the oil lamps of coloured cut-glass.

The opportunity of adding the *ikonnaya* to my setting of Diaghileff presented itself to my mind in the course of a two days' journey we made together. I had a powerful attraction in my compartment—an ornamental bucket of caviare, brought, together with chocolates, flowers and a small ikon, as a farewell gift. As the express, without undue hurry, progressed from

Petersburg to Monte Carlo, we ate caviare and talked. " Do you say your morning prayers, Sergei Pavlovitch ? " I asked rather timidly. " Yes . . . I do," he said after a slight hesitation. " I do kneel down and think of all I love and all who love me." Some silence and more caviare, and then again, with a somewhat bolder show of proselytism, " Do you ever search your conscience, Sergei Pavlovitch, for hurts you may have inflicted ? " " I do "—emphatically and warmly. " So often I reproach myself for lack of consideration. I think of how at times I went out in a hurry without saying good night to Nanny, forgetting to kiss her hand."

I ask you, reader, to bear in mind that at the time of this conversation I was barely out of my 'teens ; and that, Russians both, our souls furnished us with a subject of talk as naturally as the weather does to you.

Somewhat of a self-constituted recording angel, I added then and there piety of heart and lovingness to my list of Diaghileff's virtues. And later on I wrote " resignation " on the same tablets. That was when he told me of his precarious carrying on of the enterprise during the war, of ruin and disaster staring him in the face. For he meekly accepted defeat in the unequal contest. Awaiting a fatal blow, he said a daily farewell to his surroundings, without bitterness but with tenderness to life such as it had been to him. " Every morning I made my bed with my own hands. . . ." He patted it lovingly, he told me, thinking that that night he might not own it.

Oddly mixed with the essential sanity of Diaghileff's intellect was his superstition. Besides discrimination between the " bad " and " good " days of the week, Diaghileff feared omens. During one of his ever rarer visits to Petersburg—it may have been about 1912—I went to see him at the Hotel Astoria. I gathered from his talk that a possibility, though vague, of establishing his seasons in Russia was in his mind. I pointed laughingly, perhaps tactlessly, at the print in his room—Napoleon at Waterloo. He became visibly perturbed. " How is it that

I did not notice it before ? " In the course of our talk he returned to the subject of the print, asking me if I thought it a bad omen.

I will not go so far as to surmise that this incident was responsible for his abandoning his scheme. There were, there must have been, weightier reasons. But, dauntless as he was when faced with tangible obstacles, strong of will to the point of moulding circumstances to his own ends, his will and reason could be swayed by superstition. He was too much of a Russian not to be affected by fear of some undefinable forces conspiring against reasonable chances of success. After all, Poushkin, the sanest of men, had been known to turn his horse's head and ride back home if a hare crossed his path.

The last picture of Diaghileff in my mind is that of a friend faithful at heart in spite of our having parted our ways. He was then mortally ill. I was appearing at Covent Garden for a few performances of his season. I ran to meet him as he walked slowly behind the backcloth, leaning on the cane that he used to whirl round in such a debonair way. Arm-in-arm we came to my dressing-room. He leant back in an armchair, huddled and heavy. Gone was all the buoyancy, the peculiar lazy grace. He said, " I left my bed to come and see you. Judge of my love." But his face was not worried : he talked of Venice and some young composers in whose future he believed.

I like to finish my cumulative portrait of Diaghileff on this episode. His ruthlessness belonged to Art ; his faithful heart was his own.

INDEX

A

ALEXANDRINSKY THEATRE, 62; mob breaks into, 154

Amelia, my masterpiece in doll-making, 15

Applin (Arthur), one of my first London friends, 208

Après-midi d'un Faune, 236

Argoutinsky (Prince Vladimir Niko-laievitch, 270

B

BABOUSHKA (Grandmother), 30–3

Bakst, 138, 139

Bax (Arnold), 163

Benois (Alexander Nikolaievitch), 139; his unique erudition, 214; our guide at Rome, 234

Beretta (Signora), I study with her, 143–6

Berners (Lord), 163

Black Marias, 46

Blasis (Carlo), first pedagogue of the art of ballet, 232–3

Bliss (Arthur), 163

Bolm, in *Prince Igor*, 198, 244

Brussel (Robert), 197

C

CECCHETTI, 68, 111, 146, 230; his history, 231–4

Cerito, 98

Chaliapin, makes fun of me, 148; engaged by Diaghileff for Paris, 1909, 191; my ecstasy at his singing, 200; tells his reminiscences, 222–4

Châtelet (theatre), 193; rehearsals, 194; whole of first season described, 194–203

Christmas at home, 32–5

Cleopatra, 201

Cocteau (Jean), 239

Cohen (Harriet), 164

Coliseum, 204–9

Coppini, 128, 130

Coq d'Or, 244

Coralli, engaged by Diaghileff to dance *Armide* at the Châtelet, 191

Corsair, I play *Medora*, 150, 182–4

Cubat, a famous restaurant in Petersburg, 133; I sit next Diaghileff at supper, 191

D

DA FALLA, 246–7

Damis, The Trial of, I get my first opportunity of acting, 137

Daphnis and Chloe, 238

Debussy, I enjoy his company, 238

Dellera, 37

Dethomas, sketches Nijinsky, 197, 241–2

Diaghileff (Sergei Pavlovitch), forms the *Mir Izkoustva*, 139; gets together a troupe for a Russian season in Paris, 1909, 189; he engages me for the Paris season, 189–92; my first meeting, 190; in Paris, 194–202; his personality and help to me, 210–12; his "Artistic Committee," 213; a talk with me, and some reflections of mine, 214–16; his ever-growing ambition, 220–21; our reunion after the war, 247, 248; wants me for America, 255; dedication and portrait "in the mirror of my affection," 277–95

Dieu Bleu, 239

Doboujinsky, 139

Douniasha, taken back as my Nannie, 8; general history, 20–2; disapproves of dancing for me, 28; tells Mother of my religious fears, 39; in sore affliction, accompanies me to school, 52; led out sobbing at my début, 117

Dove (Mr.), conductor at Coliseum, 205

Draper (Ruth), 229

Duma, created by the Ukaz of Oct. 17, 1905, 164.

Duncan (Isadora) and Duncanism, 170–2.

E

EDWARDS (Madame), 193

Egorova, 139

Elssler (Fanny), 61, 185

F

FATHER, tells me tales of childhood, paints his little pictures and mimics me, 3; general description, 10–11; his farewell night at the Marinsky, 23–5; starts a library for Lev, 29; withdraws his mild objection to a dancing career for me and starts teaching me himself, 36; makes a toy theatre for Lev and me, 37; loses his place at the school, 67; lets his birds loose, 84, 85; begins to lose private lessons and catches a permanent cold, 96, finds work in a private summer theatre, 105

Felix, teaches Spanish dancing, 246

Ferraris, gets criticism in return for beer, 146

Festin, a *divertissement* danced on the first night at the Châtelet, 197

Fille mal gardée, 94

Fire Bird, 198

Flora, The Awakening of, ballet in which I got my first leading part, 135

Florence (Madame), polishes my halting French, 175

Fokine, 113, 114; begins his career as ballet-master; produces *Eunice* for the Marinsky, 172; a logical consequence of Petipa, 172; his choreographic principles, 172–4; at rehearsals in Paris, 194; works with Stravinsky, 214, 238; *Le Coq d'Or*, 244; works during the war only for the Marinsky, 253

Fraser (Grace and Lovat), 162–4

Freischütz, a parody in Pensionner-skaya, 99

G

GAPON, the priest who led the workmen to the Winter Palace in 1905, 155

Geltzer, 112

Genée (Adeline), my friendship begins, 207

Giselle, 94, 139

Glehn de, 229

Golovin, 108

Goossens (Eugene), 163

Gorsky, lectures on notation of dance movement, 71, 109

Grantzova, 37

Graziella, one of my early ballets with ample field for acting, 137.

Guerdt (Andrei), the poor lunatic brother of Pavel, 47–50

Guerdt (Pavel), 47; chooses me to become eventually his pupil, 69; teaches mime, 93–5; his method of teaching, 98, 111, 114; at my début, 117

Günsburg (Baron), 202

H

HAHN (Reynaldo), 239

Hamburg tea makes me sick, 132

Havery, Chancery servant at the British Embassy, 264

Hermitage, Court performance at, 147

Holst, 163

Homiakoff, my maternal great uncle, a leader of the Panslav movement, 90

I

Igor (*Prince*), one of the ballets danced at the first night of the Châtelet, 197

Istomina, 71, 102

Ivanov, one of our ballet masters, 80

J

Javotte, I dance *pas de deux* at my début (see also under Marinsky), 117

Jeux, 236–8

Johannsen (Christian Petrovitch), comes to see me dance and gives advice to Father, 103–4; I do not understand him, 131, 132; throws his fiddlestick at me, 132; is succeeded by Sokolova, 150

Joukova, gives me my first lessons, 27

Jouleva, 62

Journal of Orders, official gazette of the Marinsky, 123; Lydia Kyasht and I appear in it, fined a month's salary, 139

K

KAFFI, chief costumier, 93

Kamenny Ostrov, 100

Katiousha, a friend who helped me pack on my last night in Russia, 269

Korovin, 108

Kosloff (Theodore), 102, 104–5

Kshessinskaya (Mathilda), one of the idols of the school, 47, 113, 139; her mode of life and kindness to me, 140–2; gives up her part in *Eunice* to Pavlova, 172; refuses to come to Paris, 198; I meet her at Monte Carlo, 260

Kyasht (Lydia), 46, 55, 57; comes with us to Log, 85–8, 91; I push her head into soapy water, 100, 102; a go-between, 104–5; gets diphtheria, 109–10; makes me cut my finger-nails, 117; we are butterflies, 130; her brother takes us on a provincial tour, 155–7

L

LANSERET, painter of *Mir Izkoustva* group, 139

Lebedeff, chief property man, 129

Legat (Nicolas), 131, 150; I leave his class to join Sokolova's in 1909, 179

Legat (Sergei), mimics me, 131; coaches me separately, 132; "adorably funny as a jealous lover," 137; at the Hermitage supper, 148; cuts his throat, 162

Légende de Joseph, ballet by Richard Strauss, 245
Legnani (Pierrina), 68
Lepri, Cecchetti's master, 232
Lev, my brother, 5 ; Mother decides he must have a superior education, 25 ; shapes as a serious scholar, 90 ; plies me with learned reading, 106 ; brings fellow-students to study at our home, 116–17 ; his trial after the 1917 Revolution, 267
Lifar (Serguei), 243
Life for the Tsar, 124
Log, our summer holiday at, 85–90
Lopokova, 102 ; arrival in Paris, 219 ; mastery in technique, 220

M
" MAMMA," Nadejda Alexeievna's mother, 128
Marinelli, my first impresario, 203–9, 218
Marinsky Theatre, my début of May 1, 1902, 117 ; Part II, 123–85 ; offers me a contract (most unusual), 221 ; shorn of eagles, 261
Massine, 245
Medora, my part in *Corsair*, and a milestone in my career, 150
Michael, known as " Misha," courier of the Diaghileff troupe, 198
Middlesbrough, " footlights of a new world," 276
Minna, of the Jewish market, Petersburg, and her husband Abraham, 115
Mir I\khoustva group of painters formed by Diaghileff and seceding from the academic group, 139
Monte Carlo, 222–3

Moscow, I go to take part in the gala performance for the Tzar's coronation, May, 1896, 64
Mother, a cold compress, 4 ; her drastic education, 6–7 ; her economies, 14–15 ; thinks me odd for losing interest in toys, 30 ; a bad heart attack, 88 ; misjudges my undemonstrative ways, 95 ; wants me to stay another year at school, 107 ; makes my trousseau, 110 ; takes me dress-hunting in the markets, 115 ; I give her my monthly £6, 123 ; opposes my taking part in ballet revolt of 1905, but gives in to Lev, 158–9

N
NADEJDA ALEXEIEVNA, an elder dancer who gives me good advice, 124–5, 127–8 ; her parties, 128 ; teases me, 133
Nash (Paul), 163
Nicolini (Romeo), I get dancing shoes from him in Milan, 145
Nijinsky, 24 ; the Eighth Wonder of the World, 150 ; I see him for the first time, 151 ; recognition by Diaghileff, 151 ; rehearsals and performances at the Châtelet, 196–9 ; we disagree over *Giselle*, 220 ; story of his expulsion from the Marinsky, 226 ; his first productions, 236 ; differences over *Jeux,* 237 ; his illness and our meeting on the Paris Opera stage, 242–4

O
OBLAKOFF, school secretary, 110
Obouchoff, Nijinsky's master, 151

ERRATUM

The photo captions on pages 65 and 68 have been transposed and should read as follows:

Page 65 top

Corporal Garland Cain of the US Army, one of the many military test jumpers who pushed back the free fall frontiers during the 1920s, takes to the air.

Page 65 bottom

Floyd Smith, inventor of the first manually operated parachute.

Page 68

Leslie Irvin, whose demonstration of free fall and of Floyd Smith's manually operated parachute at McCook Field in 1919 was a milestone in parachute design and usage.

Oneguin, description of, in Paris, 195; sneers at me good-naturedly, 199

P

PALÉOLOGUE (Monsieur), French Ambassador in Petersburg, 256, 257

Paquita, 60, 156

Pavillon d'Armide, one of the ballets at the first night at the Châtelet, 197

Pavlova, 70, 118, 124, 139, 143, 158, 172, 179

Pensionnerskaya, a select set, 95; my last night at, 118.

Peterhof, State performance at, 82

Petipa (Marie Serguievna), 37

Petipa (Marius), 10, 80, 129, 130, 132, 168, 172

Pharaoh's Daughter, Father's farewell ballet, 23

Picasso, 247

Prague, my season at, 175

Preobrajenskaya, 47, 113, 129, 139, 146, 152, 153

Prévost (Marcel), 201

Q

Quixote, Don, ballet revived, 108; I am given charming little part, 109

R

RAVEL helps me through his music of *Daphnis et Chloe*, 238

Revolt of ballet in 1905 with Fokine, Pavlova and myself among the delegates, 158–62

Rimsky Korsakoff, 108

Ripon (Marchioness of), 226; a good fairy to the ballet and to me, 227, 228

Roerich, 214

Roncegno, I go there for my malaria, 143

Roxana, my first *pas de deux* with Nijinsky, 151

Rubinstein (Ida), 201

Rutherston (Albert), 163

S

Sacre du Printemps, 236

Sargent (John), draws me as *Thamar*, 228

Savina (Marie Gavrilovna), the leading actress of her time, 62

Schmoranz, Director of Prague National Theatre, 175–7

Schollar, 201

School (Imperial Ballet), my first visit: I am among the ten accepted, 41–3; I become a board pupil, 51–2; story of " lunatic Anne," 55; my last night, 118

Sergueieff, stage manager at school, 167

Siedova, 113, 124, 139

Skalkovsky, a leading critic of the ballet, 136

Slavina, 61, 99

Sokolova succeeds Johannsen as teacher, 150; I join her class, 179–82

Somoff, 139

Soudeikin, 139

Source, La, 128–30

South America, the ballet's tour in, 230

Spectre de la Rose, 240, 241

Stoll (Mr.), 206

Strauss (Richard), 245

Stravinsky, commissioned to write *Fire Bird*, 211, 214

Svetloff, the most important ballet critic, 147; critical of me, 181; writes first wholly laudatory article, 184; I become of his intimate circle, 184; believes in Fokine, 185; takes my side, 225

T

TABOUROT (Abbé), inventor of notation signs for dancing, 71

Taglioni, 29, 70, 185

Teliakovsky succeeds Prince Volkonsky as Director, 108; encourages national art, 138–9; takes care of me, 149; chides the participants in the ballet revolt, 164

Tereschenko, 223

Terry (Fred), 208

Three-cornered Hat, 245

V

VARVARA IVANOVNA, Directress of Imperial Ballet School: first look at me with her cold, grey eyes, 41; no frills on my hair, 52; sends for me, 61; 82, 91, 105; discusses with Mother my staying another year at school, 107; thinks *Faust* no book for me, 114; our tender farewells, all skirmishes forgotten, 118; subconsciously, I hear the swish of her skirts, 128; comes to me in the 1917 Revolution in the guise of a petitioner, 261

Vassily (Father), chaplain of the School, 73, 118

Vassily (Diaghileff's valet), 215

Vathek, 229

Vaudoyer (Jean Louis), adapts *Spectre de la Rose* for the stage, 240, 241

Vine, The, Fokine's first ballet with Pavlova and me in the leading rôles, 169

Vinogradoff, 259

Virshault (Mademoiselle), French Governess at the school, 45; discovers my tonic wine, 78

Vladimir (Grand Duke), admires my handwriting, 81; has supper with the artists at the Hermitage performance, 148

Voisin (Comte Gilbert de), Taglioni's grandson, 242

Volkonsky (Prince Sergei Mihailovitch), Director of Imperial Theatres, 1898, 92; resigns, 140

Vsevolojsky, predecessor of Prince Volkonsky, 92

W

WALPOLE (Hugh), 258, 259

Wandering Dog, a bohemian club in Petersburg, 254

Wilful Wife, The, an old ballet danced by Zucchi, 103

Wyvisbrook, S.S., the collier that brought my husband, Nik and me, to England in 1918, 276

Y

YEGOROUSHKA, Lydia's brother: takes her and me on a provincial tour, 155–7

YURKOVSKI, a producer of the dramatic stage, our neighbour at Log, 89

Z

ZUCCHI, 103, 114

14-300